Joss Whedon Versus
the Corporation

## WORLDS OF WHEDON SERIES

*Joss Whedon Versus the Corporation:
Big Business Critiqued in the Films and Television Programs.*
Erin Giannini. 2017

*Joss Whedon's Big Damn Movie: Essays on* Serenity.
Edited by Frederick Blichert. 2018

*The Whedonverse Catalog: A Complete Guide
to Works in All Media.* Don Macnaughtan. 2018

# Joss Whedon Versus the Corporation

*Big Business Critiqued in the Films and Television Programs*

ERIN GIANNINI

WORLDS OF WHEDON
*Series Editor* Sherry Ginn

McFarland & Company, Inc., Publishers
*Jefferson, North Carolina*

LIBRARY OF CONGRESS CATALOGUING-IN-PUBLICATION DATA

Names: Giannini, Erin, 1974– author.
Title: Joss Whedon versus the corporation : big business critiqued in the films and television programs / Erin Giannini.
Description: Jefferson, North Carolina : McFarland & Company, Inc., Publishers, 2017. | Series: Worlds of Whedon | Includes bibliographical references and index.
Identifiers: LCCN 2017043169 | ISBN 9781476667768 (softcover : acid free paper) ∞
Subjects: LCSH: Whedon, Joss, 1964– —Criticism and interpretation. | Corporate culture on television. | Corporate culture in motion pictures.
Classification: LCC PN1992.4.W49 G53 2017 | DDC 791.4302/33092—dc23
LC record available at https://lccn.loc.gov/2017043169

BRITISH LIBRARY CATALOGUING DATA ARE AVAILABLE

**ISBN (print) 978-1-4766-6776-8**
**ISBN (ebook) 978-1-4766-3109-7**

© 2017 Erin Giannini. All rights reserved

*No part of this book may be reproduced or transmitted in any form or by any means, electronic or mechanical, including photocopying or recording, or by any information storage and retrieval system, without permission in writing from the publisher.*

Front cover images © 2017 iStock

Printed in the United States of America

*McFarland & Company, Inc., Publishers*
 *Box 611, Jefferson, North Carolina 28640*
 *www.mcfarlandpub.com*

To Carol Giannini and Joseph Sheehan,
for their constant encouragement.

# Table of Contents

| | |
|---|---|
| Preface | 1 |
| Introduction. The Scariest Monsters of All: Corporate Culture in the Works of Joss Whedon | 5 |

**Part I. Antagonists, Complicity and Insidious Movements: An Overview of Corporate Culture in the Works of Joss Whedon**

| | |
|---|---|
| One. "Evil white folks really do have a mecca": The Corporate Antagonist in *Angel* and *Firefly* | 22 |
| Two. A Stranger Comes to a (Small) Town: *Buffy*, *Roseanne* and the Long Reach of Corporate Culture | 45 |
| Three. Who Owns the Show? *The Avengers*, *Agents of S.H.I.E.L.D.* and Marvel vs. Mutant Enemy | 61 |
| Four. In the Belly of the Beast: *Dollhouse*, *The Cabin in the Woods* and *Dr. Horrible's Sing-Along Blog* | 80 |

**Part II. Subverting Tropes, Corporations and Media: A *Dollhouse* Case Study**

| | |
|---|---|
| Five. "That is their business, but that is not their purpose": *Dollhouse* as a Subversive Text | 96 |
| Six. Curiosity or Arrogance? *Dollhouse* and the Troubled Relationship with Corporate-Sponsored Technology | 110 |
| Seven. "We're pimps and killers, but in a philanthropic way": Interrogating Corporate and Governmental Politics | 127 |

Eight. "Call us what you want, just not family": Undermining
  Whedon Tropes in the Dollhouse  157

*Conclusion. Whedon as Corporate Critique, or Can TV
  Change the World?*  176
*Chapter Notes*  183
*Bibliography*  187
*Television and Filmography*  200
*Index*  209

# *Preface*

With the recent celebration of the 20th anniversary of Joss Whedon's first series, *Buffy the Vampire Slayer*, the corpus of academic work around both *Buffy* and the entirety of Whedon's growing body of television and film work continues to develop unabated. The peer-reviewed *Slayage: The Journal of Whedon Studies* has entered its 16th year of publication; in 2005, it also added the undergraduate journal *Watcher Junior*, and it has held a biannual conference since 2004. Joss Whedon's work offers a great deal to study, from gender to race to his influence on his contemporaries.

*Buffy* was my entry into the often-paired worlds of fandom and academia. I would amuse myself during my lunch hour at work by reading academic analyses of the series (a needed break from medical editing), and I even wrote a few episode reviews for some like-minded online friends long before it occurred to me that this was something I could do professionally. The Whedonverse, I could argue, likely influenced my choice of graduate school; I received my PhD in 2012 from the university that held the first Whedon studies conference in 2002—the University of East Anglia in Norwich, England—which might not have come immediately to my attention without the *Buffy* connection.

Surprisingly, the subject of my research was not *Buffy* or *Angel* or *Firefly*, all of which had aired and were gone by the time I started my graduate program; instead, my focus was the effect of new technology and shifting television paradigms on the rise of product placement in niche television (such as *Gilmore Girls* and *Heroes*). Aside from a few mentions on *Angel* of Blackberry smart phones, and some recognizable cars on *Buffy*, the Whedon series were not a good fit for that topic—although I did get to touch on *Firefly*'s fake product placement of Blue Sun.

Once the dissertation was finished, I found my interests shifting to the ubiquity and (sometimes) nefarious behavior of corporations. Perhaps it was all that time spent reading advertising trade journals that precipitated my turn to examining the portrayals and effects of corporate culture. One can read only so many columns about the importance of eliciting the "nag factor" from children through advertising before losing all hope for humanity. The Enron and WorldCom scandals at the start of the 21st century were one thing; going through the courts to explicitly "personify" a corporation was something else entirely. Corporations across the spectrum, from the Koch brothers' hugely diversified interests and political meddling, to companies such as Nestle buying up water rights in drought-afflicted areas, were just a few of the "business as usual" actions of corporations knowing and flexing their political and social power. As I discuss below, film and television had their own way of commenting on this, with a steep rise in series that featured corporate antagonists.

It seems inevitable that my Whedon watching and my analyses of corporate culture would come together. Thanks to DVD and streaming, I was able to revisit (more than once) the Whedon series I had first seen on broadcast. Not having to wait a week (or a summer) for the next episode made it easier to see certain narrative concerns that cut across Joss Whedon's work. What struck me, especially in the fifth season of *Angel*, the fake product placement of Blue Sun in *Firefly*, and basically all of *Dollhouse*, was the increased presence and power of the corporation as antagonist. This being Whedon, however, it was rarely as simple as "corporations are bad"; even Rossum, the most nefarious of Whedon's corporate actors, was staffed with people that we may not be able to identify or sympathize with, but could recognize as in some ways closer to our individual realities of compromises and blind spots, both personal and professional. While excellent individual work has been done on Whedon series' corporations, such as Eve Bennett's analysis of *Dollhouse* and its implicit commentary on the entertainment industry (Bennett 2011), Jeannine Harrison's work around gender and corporate culture on *Angel* (Harrison 117–131), James South's early work on *Buffy* and the technological society through the lens of Marxism (93–102), David Lavery's comprehensive portrait of Joss Whedon through both his life and his work (Lavery 2014), and Stacey Abbott's many works around the series *Angel*, among others, my goal is to add to this existing scholarship by examining the bulk of Whedon's work primarily through the lens of corporate culture. By stretching back to Whedon's start on *Roseanne* up to his relationship with Marvel, I hope to shed some light on the ways in which corporatism in general has had a role to play in a majority of his oeuvre, as well as the interesting nuances that his series bring to the portrayal of corporations on the big and the small screen.

I would like to take this opportunity to thank Megan Sullivan Wills, as the first person with whom I watched and geeked out over *Buffy*, and Eve Bennett, for both encouragement and a conversation at the 2014 Slayage conference that led to this book. The Whedon area at the Southwest Popular/American Culture conference was kind enough to let me debut some of the research that eventually made its way into this work, and the Whedon Studies Association offered insight, info, and occasionally articles. Stacey Abbott and James South provided material I did not have access to and I am extremely grateful. Finally, my family and friends gave me the space and encouragement I needed. This book is dedicated to all of you.

# Introduction
## The Scariest Monsters of All: Corporate Culture in the Works of Joss Whedon

Five companies control the entire U.S. media landscape ("Democracy on Deadline"). It sounds like the start of a dystopian novel, but it has actually been the reality even before the passage of the Telecommunications Act of 1996 (Hilmes 388–398). "Our media ... far from being on the sidelines of the capitalist system, are among its greatest beneficiaries" (McChesney 21). Robert McChesney argues that media is "central to macroeconomic growth in the overall economy," which puts the media in a challenging position, as it, in theory, is also supposed to "grease the wheels of democratic self-governance" (McChesney 22), but in reality is seemingly more focused on its bottom line. This is a fear that Michele Hilmes, in her analysis of the various fears engendered by the post–Act merger madness, including "reduced diversity of voices" and "decline in creativity and originality in programming" (393); however, Hilmes argues that has not yet come to pass (398). Hilmes' assertion gains heft when one factors in the rise of streaming services such as Netflix, Amazon, and Hulu, which have offered opportunities to tell stories that may not have found purchase on terrestrial television, due to either language or content.

In other words, the media—whether radio, film, or television—is a corporation. One could even argue it is *the* corporation of the 21st century, manifested perhaps most clearly in a reality television star's successful bid for the presidency. Donald Trump, a man who must brand everything he touches, could be viewed as the apotheosis (or nadir) of the concentration of power in the hands of the few, selling a bellicose brand of fascism to his viewers abetted by constant coverage by the media. A study of the 2016 election coverage pinpointed the "false equivalency" between Trump's scandals (including the Access Hollywood tapes) and Clinton's (the use of a private e-mail server) as both a significant factor in Trump's victory and an example of the ways in which media outlets "allowed Trump ... to step in and provide the frame of reference for Hillary Clinton" (Wemple 2016); in other words, letting the one opposed to her set the context for her behavior. In an endless cycle, then, the media provided approximately $2 billion worth of free coverage for candidate Trump by March 2016 (Confessore and Yourish 2016), which lead to higher ratings and advertising rates for the networks, which lead to more coverage (Flint and Ballhaus 2015). In this respect, said coverage provides an excellent example of the type of governmental/corporate "puppet theater" decried in Joss Whedon's film *Serenity*. If the bottom line triumphs over content, how does any media creator, showrunner, or writer work within such a context?

While the above question is not quite the focus of this work, it needs to be asked. Because, concomitant with this rise in consolidating the fourth estate under a corporate banner, is an ever-increasing number of television series and films in which the corporation is the antagonist. Merriam-Webster defines corporatism as "the organization of a society into industrial and professional corporations serving as organs of political representation and exercising control over persons and activities within their jurisdiction" ("Corporatism," *Merriam-Webster*). The blandness of this definition does not do justice, in many respects, to what it means to live within a society in which a non-human entity is the "organ of political representation" that "exercis[es] control" over its citizens, shifting a supposed democratic society into a slick corporatocracy, that is, "a society or system that is governed or controlled by corporations" ("Corporatocracy," *Oxford Living Dictionaries*). Thus, the creation and consumption of particular works of art, whether it be novels, films, media, or other visual mediums, often provides a capsule of what fears or concerns cut across multiple segments of society (Giannini 2017).

In contemporary media, it seems as if the response by showrunners, creators, and writers is to position the corporation, already legally personified by 2010's Citizens United decision (Kennedy 2010), as a featured antagonist. Even limiting an overview of corporate antagonists to the past decade of U.S. television offers E Corp (*Mr. Robot*), Richard Roman Enterprises (*Supernatural*), Veridian Dynamics (*Better Off Ted*), LexCorp (*Smallville*), Max Rager/Fillmore Graves (*iZombie*), MMR (*Orange Is the New Black*), Massive Dynamic (*Fringe*), Kane Industries (*Veronica Mars*), and Tusk Industries (*House of Cards*), which range from private prisons (MMR) and military contractors (Fillmore Graves), to software development (Kane Industries). Further, these portrayals cut across genres: horror, science fiction/fantasy, drama, neo-noir, and comedy, offering a compelling argument that the contemporary evil empire across fiction of all stripes is the corporation, just as Russia/fear of communism infected and inflected upon popular media in the late 1940s/1950s (see King 1991 for an overview). Indeed, in *Supernatural, iZombie,* and *Doctor Who,* corporate machinations threatened to bring about the end of the world through turning the world into a giant abattoir ("Survival of the Fittest" 7.23), turning everyone into mindless zombies ("Salvation Army" 2.19), and upgrading human brains into emotionally inhibited metal shells branded with the corporation (Cybus Industries) logo ("Rise of the Cybermen"/ "The Age of Steel" 28.5/28.6, respectively). (The fact that one of these programs is British—rather quintessentially so—could be read as an indication that such concerns are not merely American in origin.)

The three aforementioned examples share one particular quality: all of these corporate antagonists are literally dehumanizing the population. Whether humans become food, zombies, or robots, they have no purpose other than that inflicted upon them by the sponsoring corporation. As I have written about previously, on the series *Supernatural,* the merger of the post–Fordist, technologically-based Richard Roman Enterprises, run by a demonic creature known as a Leviathan, with the high-fructose corn syrup manufacturer Sucrocorp ("There Will Be Blood" 7.21), allowed Roman (James Patrick Stuart) and the Leviathan unparalleled access to the world population, using much the same rhetoric/clichés seen in the real-world corporate environment (Giannini 2014). (Given that Roman is also revealed as the author of a book ["When in Rome"] about how to succeed in business ["How to Win Friends and Influence Monsters" 7.9], akin to *The Art of the Deal,* it is not difficult to make a parallel to the current political situation in the United States.) That the Leviathan's plan to devour humans will eventually lead to a complete depletion of what is a finite resource never seems to occur to them; a handy parallel to the use of the equally finite fossil fuels in contemporary society (Singh 2015). The series *iZombie* portrays Max Rager, an energy drink company owned by a narcissistic man-child, Vaughn du Clark (Steven Weber), whose product is creating literal zombies. Not only does du Clark not care, but actually hires people to eliminate the "zombie problem" ("Grumpy Old Liv" 2.1), as it might eat into his bottom line and scuttle the eventual sale of his company to a private military contractor, amusingly named Fillmore Graves. He views his only responsibility for the outbreak is to preserve his corporation and create profit for his shareholders (and himself).

The excesses of corporate America, brought starkly into the public consciousness by the 2008 economic crash, and the efforts of movements such as Occupy Wall Street, have thus proven to be a fertile ground for television; as Sera Gamble, showrunner for *Supernatural*, asserted in the commentary for the finale of season seven of the series (the season which featured the leviathans), the corporate environment was chosen specifically because "corporations are scarier than the government" and represented a "perfect fit for these ultimate monsters" ("Survival of the Fittest" commentary 7.23). Indeed, as I explicated in the aforementioned article, the denizens of neither heaven nor hell wreaked as much damage on the series' working class protagonists as the powerful Roman corporation (Giannini 2014); Sam (Jared Padalecki) and Dean (Jensen Ackles) lose their home, their father figure, and even their own identities (literally; they have to work to stay off the grid) to the corporate actors targeting them. The implication is that the truest American nightmare resides within the corporate setting.

One question that needs to be asked, although it is difficult to formulate an answer to, is why these anti-corporate narratives actually air on the very corporate media they are railing against? Why does, as per example, the NBC/Universal-owned USA Network air a series, *Mr. Robot*, in which the protagonists are extralegal hackers, and the bad guys corporate shills? How does a network whose popular series *24*, in which torturing terrorists is seen as a necessary part of the realpolitik, also air a series, *Dollhouse*, in which the protagonist proudly proclaims herself to be a "terrorist" ("Getting Closer" 2.11)? As Robert McChesney argues, it falls into what he calls the "half-truth" of the commercial media "giving people what they want" (McChesney 198). His contention is that that particular canard is, when "taken out of context ... serves as an ideological fig leaf to protect naked commercial interests" (McChesney 199) because, as he explains, "concentration and conglomeration ... raise significant barriers to an effectively operating free market" (199). The "narrow range" of television offerings (at least at the time when McChesney was writing) means that consumers must, in essence, pick the best of an extremely limited amount of options. That is hardly the recipe for offering "what they want"; "The people want 18 minutes of ads per hour on radio? Right" (McChesney 199). In this instance, media is basically a dollar democracy, and those with more dollars get more votes (McChesney 200), something the Citizens United decision, as mentioned earlier, codified into law. In this respect, the comparatively small audience shares of a cable series such as *Mr. Robot* could indicate that creator Sam Esmail's take on corporatism appeals to a smaller audience slice than watching Keifer Sutherland torture terrorists, and therefore may not be representative of the broader population.

While McChesney's arguments regarding the "narrow range" are applicable to the earlier network era, Michael Curtin and Jane Shattuc, among many others, argue that advertisers and networks are currently more focused on segments rather than broad appeal (Curtin and Shattuc 42–45). Even before the rise of streaming services with original programming, such as Netflix, Amazon, and Hulu, netlets such as the WB and UPN, and cable and satellites channels, had been eating into the so-called "Big Three" (ABC, CBS, NBC) dominance over programming for decades. With it went the reliance on what was known as "least offensive programming," that was one of the guiding lights of networks in the 1950s and 1960s; that is, programming with supposed broad-based appeal and minimal controversy (Bedell 1981). These multiple programming outlets, some of which are divorced from the usual process of program selection (known as the Upfronts, in which advertisers are presented with the upcoming fall slate of programming and pilots of new series [see Lotz 549–567 for an analysis of the Upfront process], could serve as a venue for stories and voices underrepresented on broadcast and cable networks. In that respect, there is space on the spectrum for any number of viewpoints; whether or not that real estate is truly representative or diverse is, at best, a work in progress (Hilmes 433–443).

What it does, however, is leave space for the growing presence of anti-corporate sentiments within corporate media. I am unable to answer the question of whether the presence of these narratives within the corporate media structure merely acts as sop to viewers who may hold similar ideas about the prevalence of corporate malfeasance—defusing resistance while confirming its necessity—or whether such narratives can educate and inspire said viewers. Phillip Lapote, in an article for the *New York Times* in 2000, decried the inability of anti-corporate films, such as *Erin Brockovich* or *A Civil Action*, to create corporate villains with any real nuance, settling for a parade of CEOs that represent "another empty suit." Lapote suggests that this difficulty is partly due to the question asked above—is it possibly to be subversive about corporations within corporate media—and concludes than none of the films he examined move beyond being only "seemingly subversive," with corporate villains, viewed from the outside, displaying a "fairy-tale thinness" of depth and characterization (Lapote 2000).

This characterization, Michael Pepe contends, does not include the more recent, post–Great Recession films such as *Margin Call* and *The Wolf of Wall Street*; these films are committed, for better or worse, to examining the corporate structure from the inside, perhaps to better illuminate where precisely things went wrong (Pepe 2016). Pepe divides these "insider" films into four categories: "capitalism as a patriarchal tradition, capitalism as a perceived deterministic given, capitalism as a moral transgression," and "capitalism ... as a cynical acceptance of and model for avarice that is nearly indistinguishable from a criminal enterprise" (Pepe 2016). These divisions provide an excellent frame with which to view the ways in which corporate culture is enacted and critiqued within the works of Joss Whedon.

While Joss Whedon's history has been examined by numerous scholars, including David Lavery's thorough *Joss Whedon: A Creative Portrait*, and the peer-reviewed journal *Slayage*, it is worth offering a capsule-sized version of his work within film and television. A third generation television writer, in the late 1980s, Whedon worked on the series *Parenthood* (1990) and *Roseanne*, as well as script-doctoring films such as *Speed* and *Waterworld* and working on the script for the film *Buffy the Vampire Slayer*. When *Buffy* was finally produced and released in 1992, however, it had been plagued by the challenges of a relative novice director (Fran Kuzai) and a difficult actor (Donald Sutherland), as well as producer interference; rather than the mix of comedy and drama that characterized Whedon's later work, Kuzai focused primarily on the comedy, particularly around the concept of a shallow cheerleader who fights the forces of darkness. This clearly was not what Whedon had envisioned (Lavery 68–73). Through the efforts of Gail Berman and Fran Kuzai (as Lavery notes, there is some debate over who had the greater impact in transitioning the film into a television show [226]), *Buffy* was repackaged as a series and (eventually) sold to then-new network the WB, debuting as a mid-season replacement in 1997. The character of Angel (David Boreanaz)—a 240-year-old vampire and Buffy's (sometimes) lover—was spun off into his own series in 1999; initially, the two series aired back-to-back on the WB, with at least two crossover events (the episode "Pangs" *Buffy* 4.8 with "I Will Remember You" *Angel* 1.8 and "Who Are You" *Buffy* 4.16 with "Sanctuary" *Angel* 1.19) during the first season in support of the fledgling show.

The short-lived *Firefly* followed in 2002 (airing on Fox, who also produced *Buffy* and *Angel*), eventually continued in film form, shifting studios from Fox to Universal (*Serenity* [2005]). Between the release of *Serenity* and the last primarily (Joss) Whedon-helmed series *Dollhouse*, he collaborated with his brothers and sister-in-law to create the web musical *Dr.*

*Horrible's Sing-Along Blog*. Since *Dollhouse*'s cancellation in 2010, Whedon has gone full-circle, working in the film industry on projects large (Marvel's *The Avengers/Avengers: Age of Ultron*) and small (*Much Ado About Nothing/In Your Eyes*).

It is his work, from his time as story editor on *Roseanne* to his partnership with Marvel/Disney and development of his own microproduction company, which will be the focus of this analysis. It is not just the narrative focus on corporatism that makes Whedon an excellent choice for this kind of analysis, but the large corpus of work that he has produced. With the exception of production companies such as MTM in the 1970s (*The Mary Tyler Moore Show*, *The Bob Newhart Show*, among several others), as well as perhaps contemporaries such as David E. Kelley (*Ally McBeal*, *Boston Public*) or Shonda Rhimes (*Grey's Anatomy*, *How to Get Away with Murder*), few writers/showrunners have created the amount of series and films that could both sustain such an examination, or allow the "reader" to see these narrative patterns emerge. Stacey Abbott, in her analysis of the series *Angel*, makes a compelling argument for the ways in which Whedon's series are part of a collaborative vision: "a television series is an ever-changing entity and as such the vision evolves along with its writing team" (Abbott 12); however, the presence and prominence of corporate antagonists across his body of work suggests that it is a particular concern of his, and one with a continued societal relevance. By way of introduction, the following is brief examination of the way many of Whedon's works fit fairly comfortably into Pepe's aforementioned categories of corporate portrayals.

## *Capitalism as Patriarchal Tradition*

Currently, Joss Whedon (along with brothers Jed [*Dollhouse*, *Agents of S.H.I.E.L.D.*, *Spartacus: Blood and Sand*] and Zack [*Deadwood*, *Fringe*, *Halt and Catch Fire*]) is one of the only third-generation television writers. Whedon's grandfather John wrote for early television classic such as *The Donna Reed Show* and *The Dick Van Dyke Show*; his father, Tom, was a writer with *The Electric Company*, *Alice*, and *The Golden Girls*. David Lavery, in *Joss Whedon: A Creative Portrait*, quotes Whedon as claiming he wanted nothing to do with television, but following graduation from college, an increase in television watching (his mother, a teacher, favored PBS), and his father's encouragement and connections, Whedon began to write spec scripts (Lavery 81). Whedon also credits his father's work for introducing him (somewhat accidentally) to the Marvel comics that would dominate the second half of his career.

Yet his influences were not limited to the men in his family. Two women, Lee Stearns (Whedon's mother), and Jeanine Basinger, his film studies professor at Wesleyan, also had an equally profound effect on Whedon's oeuvre. As Lavery elucidates, it was Stearns' position as both teacher and feminist that informed Whedon's academic and social education (35), and Basinger's approach to focusing on films' texts over the theory (50–52) around them that is evident in much of Whedon's work.

It is well-documented that the genesis of Whedon's first series *Buffy the Vampire Slayer* was born of the desire to upend the Hollywood formula of "the little blonde girl who goes into a dark alley and gets killed in every horror movie" (Billson 24–25). Originally a film that leaned heavily on the comedic, WB president Gail Berman offered Whedon the chance to create a series based on the character that would be the blend of horror, comedy, and drama Whedon originally sought (Lavery 92–93). Even in 1997, putting a young woman at the center of her own series (as the hero, no less) and surrounding her with a blend of friends, allies, and enemies of various genders and ages, with whom she saves the world, has conversations with other women that revolve around other things than the opposite sex, and who even can be viewed as, at times, unlikeable, was still uncommon. Robert Moore traces the women who proceeded Buffy (Sarah Michelle Gellar), including Lynda Carter's Wonder Woman and Barbara Eden's Jeannie, who were too often portrayed as needing to subordinate their power to the men in their lives, and those who came after. He cites Dana Scully (Gillian Anderson) of *The X Files*, and Xena (Lucy Lawless) of *Xena: Warrior Princess* as Buffy's direct progenitors, with the exception that Buffy was an ordinary young woman who had "her destiny thrust upon her" (Moore 145), as opposed to Scully's role as a FBI agent and Xena's as a semi-deity. In this respect, Moore argues, Buffy could better serve both as a role model and the first in a long line of rounded female heroes (Moore 141–145).

While Buffy struggles with the patriarchal forces around her throughout the series, Michael Durand argues that the concluding season of the series brings to surface how entrenched is this patriarchal order under which Buffy labors, combining the obvious evil and blatantly misogynistic character of Caleb (Nathan Fillion), a defrocked priest in service of what is known as "The First Evil" ("Dirty Girls" 7.18), with the Watcher's Council, the group who was designed to guide and instruct the Slayer as a "weapon" in their fight against evil. The revelation that the Council itself originated from what were known as The Shadow Men, who chained a young woman to the earth and violated her with a demonic essence to fight their battles ("Get It Done" 7.15), indicates that their dismissive and condescending attitude toward their Slayers ("she is an instrument" ["Checkpoint" 5.12]) is not a bug but the very feature the Council was built upon. "They are all part of a patriarchal power that is fundamentally corrupt at its core" (Durand 28), that is, viewing Buffy and other Slayers as either instruments or impediments rather than human beings. It is even more significant that the weapon that allows Buffy to break this patriarchal hold was forged by a group of women known as the Guardians, offering an alternate, and more female-oriented lineage for the Slayers ("End of Days" 7.21).

While I cannot claim that *Buffy*, as a series, directly engages with the patriarchal nature of capitalism per se,[1] the use of metaphor that the series constantly engages in—the biggest being, for the first three seasons, literalizing the idea that "high school is hell" by positioning Sunnydale High (where Buffy and her friends matriculate) over a hellmouth—it would be difficult to create a series in which a young woman is invested with power and not address the ways in which, as Holly Chandler terms it, the "literal structure of the town," Sunnydale, "supports the evil plan of the patriarchal figure who runs it" (Chandler 2003, para 6); in this case, the fatherly, family-values spouting mayor Richard Wilkins (Harry Groener), but also a police force and school administration willfully blind to the evil around them.

Yet the fact that it is later revealed that the a group of men (who in time became the Watcher's Council) had, in essence, weaponized a young woman to fight their battles, with little regard, even in contemporary times, for the empowered Slayer—her life is constantly on the line, and she receives no remuneration for her work ("Flooded" 6.4); other contemporary Slayers are shown to be taken away from family and trained as children ("What My Line, Part 2" 2.10) or live in poverty and abusive situations ("Revelations" 3.7)—not only underscores the ways in which women's labor is frequently unpaid and otherwise devalued, but by investing power in a single, and to them interchangeable, young woman, theoretically makes this "weapon" easier for the largely male council to control. As Quentin Travers (Harris Yulin) tells Buffy: "The Council fights evil. The Slayer is the instrument by which we fight. The Council remains, the Slayers change" ("Checkpoint" 5.12). The final episode of the series, however, eliminates this structure in favor of one in which the power is shared among thousands of young women ("Chosen" 7.22). While it cannot be called defiantly anti-capitalist, such a conclusion certainly calls into question the value of patriarchal dominance on a more general level. In this respect, both Buffy, and Whedon's earlier work on Roseanne Barr's eponymous series, offer some level of disruption of the patriarchal structures of present society.

## *Capitalism as a Perceived Deterministic Given*

As I've written about previously (Giannini 2015), there are numerous examples of films in the science-fiction genre that, despite their distance from contemporary times, show no significant shift in the capitalist structure that undergirds Western society. The continued presence of McDonald's in 23rd century Western society goes unremarked and unquestioned in *The Fifth Element*; the 22nd century of *Demolition Man* goes so far as to feature a future in which Taco Bell is the only fast food restaurant that has survived into a new century. The *Star Trek* film and television franchise seems to be one of the few science-fiction series that has imagined a post-capitalist future that is not simultaneously dystopian (Preker 2016).

Whedon's series *Firefly*, set 500 years in the future, is by no means post-capitalist; in fact, it features a corporate capitalist structure that is seemingly undiminished over time and literal space. Like the earlier series *Angel*, and later series *Dollhouse*, the corporate capitalist structure represents a large part of the narrative, primarily in the antagonist position. While *Firefly* was only 14 episodes long (only 11 of which aired on U.S. television) and therefore cannot represent a sustained critique, it was clear from the narrative that not only was there at least one megacorporation within the *Firefly* universe—Blue Sun, which produced everything from food to medical equipment—but that their power and control superseded that of the government under which they operated (known as the Alliance, a combination of U.S. and Chinese parliamentary rule). The episode "Ariel" (1.8) revolved around the pursuit, by agents of Blue Sun, of River Tam (Summer Glau), one of the passengers on the ship Serenity on which much of the series' action occurred; these same agents terminate several government employees without consequence. River, it is revealed, attended a corporate-sponsored school that performed experiments on her that both fractured her mind and increased her fighting and mental skills; her escape from that school triggered a massive (if secretive) search.[2] The Blue Sun logo appears on a neurological scanner in a hospital ("Ariel" 1.8), a t-shirt worn by one of the characters ("Ariel"), storage pods ("Serenity"

1.1), and nearly all the food products seen in both the series and the associated film *Serenity*.

While the series takes place in another galaxy (Earth's resources having been used up, according to the opening narration in both the broadcast episodes and in the subsequent film) and numerous planets, there is clearly a centralized government and corporate authority that mirrors contemporary society; the so-called central planets are wealthy and (mostly) urban, while the "border planets" have limited resources, smaller populations, rural environments, and frequently, environmental or social issues the government (or the corporation) chooses to ignore or repress. The first aired episode ("The Train Job" 1.1) highlights a planet, Paradiso, whose economy is supported by a mining operation that causes everyone who lives there to develop a chronic, degenerative disease. That the planet itself does not materially benefit from the mining operation is obvious from the poverty-level existence in which we see its residents live, setting up a "core and periphery" relationship between resource-rich but economically poor border planets such as Paradiso or Canton's Moon ("Jaynestown" 1.7), and the "central" planets such as Ariel or Bellaphron, where those who own said resources not only are wealthy, but have access to medical care and other amenities not available to others (Kahm 156–158). That those residing in the border planets are less important to The Alliance is clear when even the government-provided medicine for Paradiso is subjected to theft that the government merely winks at: "Tag it received and bounce it back. Locals can deal with it."

Howard Kahm agrees that Whedon created a world in which "the rise of an interplanetary Alliance predicated on the core-periphery relationships and attendant dependency of the outer planets on the Alliance core embodies an implicit critique of American capitalism and Chinese expansionism," particularly in the areas of labor and resource exhaustion (Kahm 156). The series' protagonists, both those who represent the crew of the spaceship Serenity, and its passengers, have chosen to absent themselves from both. The captain of Serenity, Malcolm Reynolds (Nathan Fillion), and his first mate Zoe Washburne (Gina Torres), specifically chose to exit from terrestrial life after the civil war between The Alliance and a group (mostly from the border planets) who referred to themselves as the Independents (or Browncoats). From the little the viewer sees of the battle, the Alliance clearly had far more advanced technology and weapons; much of the firearms of the Independents (and later, the crews) would be familiar to a 21st century viewer: shotguns and rifles. (Jayne even decries the more sophisticated Alliance weapons as essentially useless: "high-tech Alliance crap" ["Ariel" 1.9]). This defeat, it is established in the episode "Serenity" (1.1), robbed Mal of his will to fight and belief in something larger then himself; Mal, Zoe, and the crew attempt to stay in the outer reaches of space and survive through make-work (both legal and illegal) rather than attempting to take on the capitalist power structure of the Allied Planets. For them, at least, there is indeed a deterministic quality to the economic structure that cannot be easily underdone.

## Capitalism as Moral Transgression/Capitalism as Criminal Enterprise

The final two categories are, in Whedon's work, nearly indistinguishable. Wolfram and Hart, the law firm featured in *Angel*, and Rossum and The Facility, the corporations featured in *Dollhouse* and *The Cabin in the Woods*, respectively, function as both moral transgressors and criminal enterprises, despite ostensibly working within the boundaries of the law. As with many of the corporations/corporate actors within the Whedonverse, Wolfram and Hart manipulates current laws and regulations for their own benefit, viewing their employees as puppets and everyone else as unimportant collateral damage. Their evil is not signaled merely by the types of human clients they represent (including polluters, traffickers, and murderers) but, given the genre of *Angel* (neo-noir/horror [Abbott 27–43]) they also represent the actual underworld, that is, demons. As Sharon Sutherland and Sarah Swan argue, Wolfram and Hart takes "the contemporary idea of the evils of global corporations ... to the extreme: Wolfram and Hart is not only global, but interdimensional, and the law firm's power to shelter demons from the normal workings of justice sets up the firm's responsibility for evil greater than any single client could perform" (Sutherland and Swan 137). In this respect, Wolfram and Hart, as a capitalist entity, both facilitates and enacts numerous moral transgressions, and functions as a criminal enterprise despite its positioning as an avatar of law.

Rossum, as will be addressed in greater depth throughout this book, funds its well-regarded and legitimate research into illnesses such as Alzheimer's disease through human trafficking. (Although, it should be noted, they are accused of withholding their findings on things such as Alzheimer's research ["Instinct" 2.2]; while the reasons are not specified, the suggestion is that it is a monetary and/or proprietary issue, paralleling with the recent price hikes on treatments such as Epi-Pens by pharmaceutical companies to increase already fat bottom lines [Schuppe 2016], a point I'll examine in greater depth in Chapter Six.) From the start of the series, it is made clear that the Dollhouses, in which nominal volunteers have their personalities removed and replaced by those requested by well-heeled clients, are illegal, other elements revealed throughout the series, including accessing private medical records ("The Hollow Men" 2.12) and animal testing ("Echoes" 1.7) are within the letter, if not the spirit, of contemporary regulatory law. For their extralegal activities (not limited to the Dollhouse), Rossum works within the boundaries of the existing laws to change that inconvenient issue, putting, as will be examined in depth later in this work, an unwitting corporate puppet in a position to rewrite laws and regulations on their behalf. In this respect, they fall squarely into the category Pepe outlines, of a corporation that operates as a "cynical acceptance of, and model for avarice that is nearly indistinguishable from a criminal enterprise" (Pepe 2016). That their actions lead to a technologically driven apocalypse seems par for the course ("Epitaph One" 1.13, "Epitaph 2: Return" 2.13).

The Facility in *The Cabin in the Woods* offers all the features of a corporate office—numerous levels of employees, talk of bonuses and outcomes, and state-of-the-art technology at their disposal—whose main purpose is to enact a literal ritual sacrifice on unwitting young adults. As a stand-alone film, *Cabin* does not offer the same level of narrative depth into the corporation itself as both *Angel* and *Dollhouse* were able to do over multiple episodes; however, it fits easily into Pepe's description of a criminal enterprise that is nonetheless allowed to enact its yearly sacrifice undeterred by legal or governmental interference. Indeed, because of the consequences of not completing their corporate objective means that the world will literally end (if at least four people aren't sacrificed, the unseen "Old Ones" will rise and destroy the planet), it is likely that The Facility is allowed to work with relative impunity, both in the United States (where the main action occurs) and worldwide. That most of the employees seem to enjoy their work—going so far as to gleefully place bets on which evil creature will kill the victims—and show no sign of plausible deniability about what that work is a chilling indictment of the ways in which the "psychopathic" corporate person, in Joel Bakan's analysis (Bakan 2004) can affect those who work within in.

While within this introduction, I've focused primarily on Whedon's first four series—*Buffy the Vampire Slayer*, *Angel*, *Firefly*, and *Dollhouse*—and his films *Serenity* and *The Cabin in the Woods*, I will be addressing throughout the first part of this book both these four programs and two films, as well as Whedon's Internet musical *Dr. Horrible's Sing-Along Blog*, his early work on *Roseanne*, and his collaboration with Marvel studios for films *The Avengers* and *The Avengers: Age of Ultron*, as well as the ABC series *Marvel's Agents of S.H.I.E.L.D.*. Given either their short duration (*Dr. Horrible* was comprised of three 15-minute episodes), Whedon's limited association (*Roseanne*), or the collaborative nature of their association (Marvel films/series), they do not fit as easily into aforementioned categories. As per example, the portrayal of Stark Industries in the Avengers films, whose fortune was made through weapon manufacturing, clearly fits into the idea of capitalism as a patriarchal tradition (passed down from father to son; Tony Stark's [Robert Downey, Jr.] paternalistic insistence on creating a "suit of armor for the world" in *Age of Ultron*), and capitalism as predetermined; while Stark's personal decisions with regard to his actions are called into question (*Age of Ultron*), there is no sense that Stark Industries' work more generally should be curtailed or stopped, particularly since it is a main source of funding for the Avengers Initiative itself. One can also see the paternalism in the treatment of fast food and factory workers throughout most of *Roseanne*'s nine-season run, and the ways in which the working class are used and abused by the system without any recourse to changing that particular fact.

In examining how corporatism is portrayed and critiqued within Whedon's work, I shall be discussing a broad swathe of his work, from the early 1990s into the 21st century.[3] Chapter One will focus on the corporate antagonists in the series *Angel* (1999–2004) and *Firefly* (2002). From its first episode, the enemy in *Angel* was the corporate law firm of Wolfram and Hart; over five seasons, the law firm attempted to both antagonize and recruit Angel, a 240-year-old vampire with a soul destined to play an uncertain role in the apocalypse, over to their admittedly (and proudly) dark side. In *Firefly*, like the later series *Dollhouse*, the corporate entity of Blue Sun has a power that supersedes social and governmental control; its incursions into the body and mind of the character of River Tam are persistent and personal and unbound to any conventional law. In both *Angel* and *Firefly*, the corporate antagonist represents a prime driver for the series' narratives.

Chapter Two will explore how, even in the limited space they are afforded in their respective narrative, the corporation still affects the lives (and livelihoods) of the central protagonists in both *Roseanne* and in *Buffy the Vampire Slayer*. Focusing primarily on a single episode from each series, both Roseanne (Roseanne Barr) and Buffy find that fighting the corporate entity of fast food is difficult at best; there is no grand plan or visible enemy, only a slow wearing down of individuality mirrored in the machine-like processing of both employees and food within that setting. Regardless of the battles both have won, *Roseanne*'s "Chicken Hearts" and *Buffy*'s "Doublemeat Palace" offer no rousing victory; only an acceptance of economic and social circumstance brought on by lost opportunities and economic hardship.

Moving from a focus on narrative to that of the relationship between studio and writer/director, Chapter Three examines Whedon's own relationship with Marvel studios to create the two *Avengers* films and the series *Agents of S.H.I.E.L.D.* While I will examine the ways in which corporations are portrayed in both the films and the series, I will also widen the perspective to examine how Marvel Studios shares similarities with the corporations that Whedon's other properties vilify, particular the subordination of the director and narrative brands to that of the overarching Marvel brand, hollowing out the individual director/creator to create a brand ambassador for the studio.

Closing out the first part of this book is a look at *Dr. Horrible's Sing-Along Blog* as Whedon's response to the 2008 writers' strike, that is, a critique of the corporate media structure that is nonetheless responsible for Whedon's prominence within it, as well as the film *The Cabin in the Woods*, and the series *Dollhouse* from the perspective of its protagonists as descending into the heart of the corporate structure. In these texts, the corporate structure, both in and outside of the narrative, plays the strongest and most insidious role. Starting with *Dr. Horrible* as a response to corporate media (an extra-diagetic force, rather than directly engaged in the narrative), I'll move on to a deeper examination of both *Cabin* and *Dollhouse*, both of which also engage with deconstructing/subverting the corporate media structure within their separate narrative worlds, represented by their antagonists: The Facility and Rossum Corporation, respectively. These texts represent the apotheosis of the anti-corporate thread within Whedon's work.

The second half of this book will focus exclusively on what I consider Whedon's most subversive and anti-corporate text: *Dollhouse*. In this section, I'll explore four main aspects of the series. First, I'll offer an introduction into the various ways in which *Dollhouse* operates as a subversive text on both a narrative and a production level, from its initial running time to its reclamation of loaded terms to describe the nominal protagonist. Building on that, I'll then move into an analysis of the ways in the series interacts with corporate-created technology, viewing it both through the lens of real-world corporations such as the pharmaceutical industry (of which Rossum, *Dollhouse*'s corporate antagonist, is closely aligned) and the effect of the technology and the corporation on the character Topher Brink (Fran Kranz). The ways in which *Dollhouse* interrogates the intersection between corporate culture and governmental regulation (or lack thereof), particularly the post–Citizens United campaign finance structure, the power wielded by lobbyists, and the embrace of deregulation and Milton Friedman–type "shock" economics that allow said corporate entities to operate with near-impunity to increase their bottom lines at the expense of others is the focus of Chapter Seven.

Finally, I examine the ways in which *Dollhouse* even subverts the established tropes of Whedon's previous work. Certain elements have long been associated with Whedon's shows, included strong female characters, quip-filled and quotable dialogue, the reuse of certain actors, and the notion of family as a choice (that is, one creates their family by those they choose to associate with). Yet *Dollhouse* played with and inverted many of these particular tropes, particularly the importance of a created family, to create surprising twists and a different narrative arc than seen within the rest of his canon. I argue these subversions of his tropes spotlight the ways in which these tropes can be used in the service of corporate structure.

In this way, it can become clear the numerous ways, both in and outside the narratives of Whedon's series, he addresses, critiques, and illuminates the vital issues of 21st century corporate culture.

# Part One

# Antagonists, Complicity and Insidious Movements

*An Overview of the Corporate Culture in the Works of Joss Whedon*

CHAPTER ONE

# "Evil white folks really do have a mecca"
## The Corporate Antagonist in *Angel* and *Firefly*

HOLLAND: You don't kill humans.
ANGEL: You don't qualify. You set things in motion, play your little games up here in your glass and chrome tower, and people die. Innocent people.
HOLLAND: And yet I just can't seem to care ["Reunion" 2.10].

Positioned in the early to mid-position of Whedon's career, both *Buffy* spin-off *Angel* and the short-lived series *Firefly* (and its accompanying film follow-up *Serenity*), represent the first time that corporate antagonists are front and center within the narrative: Wolfram and Hart in *Angel* and Blue Sun in *Firefly*. While both series share this aspect, the interaction between protagonist Angel (David Boreanaz) and law firm Wolfram and Hart, and the passengers and crew of Serenity and the Blue Sun Corporation, are significantly different. While Wolfram and Hart considers Angel to be a "special project," devoting an untold amount of billable hours and resources on (hopefully) corrupting him, the Blue Sun Corporation only wishes to retrieve what they consider their asset: Serenity passenger River Tam (Summer Glau). Both focus particularly on a single individual; it is the degree of, for lack of a better term, personal attention that is paid to Angel that sets that series apart from the usual depersonalization that such corporations inflict upon Whedon's protagonists. In the case of *Dollhouse*, as will be examined in greater depth later in this work, that depersonalization is literalized.

Yet both *Angel* and *Firefly* are worth examining together, as the presence of this antagonist is the primary engine that drives both narratives.

In *Angel*, the basic premise of the series is a 240-year-old vampire with a soul who is working with the mysterious Powers-That-Be to atone for his evil past. By the end of the first season ("To Shanshu in LA" 1.22), a prophesy reveals that Angel is supposed to play a pivotal role in the apocalypse, although whether on the side of good or of evil is deliberately left unclear, underscoring the series' focus on the importance of free will and choice ("Epiphany" 2.16). Wolfram and Hart's goal is to ensure that Angel will be on the side of "Senior Partners," the evil counterparts to the aforementioned "Powers That Be." Their resurrection of his sire, Darla (Julie Benz) as a potential corrupting influence in "To Shanshu in LA" is the first large step in the chess match between Angel and the law firm; this game continues for the rest of the series, with an ending that leaves the fate of Angel and his companions deliberately unclear ("Not Fade Away" 5.22).

For *Firefly*, set in the 25th century, the main narrative thrust of the series is the conflict between individuals who want to live outside of the ruling system, and the ways in which that system continues to impinge upon various aspects of their lives following an interplanetary civil war. The conflict is evident in the first episode, "Serenity" (1.1), when the ship Serenity, whose crew supports itself mainly by extra- or illegal activity, takes on passengers: Shepherd Darriel Book (Ron Glass), siblings Simon (Sean Maher) and River Tam, and Lawrence Dobson (Carlos Jacott). Two of those passengers, unbeknownst to the crew, are fugitives—Simon and River—with Dobson as a government agent tasked with retrieving them. (After his near-fatal shooting of mechanic Kaylee and taking River hostage, Mal shoots Dobson and dumps him off the ship at the end of the episode.) While the first episode (as well as the follow-up film *Serenity*) seems to support the idea that it is primarily the government that is after them, that conclusion is complicated several times within the narrative. It is clear that the Blue Sun Corporation has a vested interest, and the apparent means, to retrieve River Tam, whom they consider to be vital to their interests.

The Blue Sun Corporation spans planets and is in clear collusion with the ruling government ("Serenity" 1.1; "Ariel" 1.9); there is also no evidence of any other corporate structure within the diegesis of the series. Certainly not one of the reach of Blue Sun; evidence from the series indicates that they produce numerous types of goods and services, from food products ("Shindig" 1.4) to medical equipment ("Ariel" 1.8). I have previously written about the ways in which River Tam was both created by and subverts the corporate structure (Giannini 2015) as an "embodied cultural jam" (that is, using a corporation's publicity and brand to expose their less-publicized and problematic aspects [Lasn 2000]), but it is important to acknowledge that despite the fact that the main characters live "off the grid"—they spend little time on terra firma, for obvious reasons—they can't actually escape the corporation.

Thus, in this chapter I'll be discussing how both *Angel* and *Firefly* represent early iterations of Whedon's focus on corporatism within his work. While the series *Angel* offered the first sustained corporate antagonist in the form of corporate law firm Wolfram and Hart, with only 14 episodes, *Firefly*, the third series Whedon developed, offers an acceleration of this with Blue Sun. In both, the protagonists are defined/define themselves in opposition to these corporate "evildoers," and yet, in both instances, it is rarely that black and white. It represents a starting point for the more layered interaction with corporations seen in Whedon's later works.

## *Gadfly to CEO in Only 88 Episodes*

The main characters of the series *Angel* exist on the social (and sometimes ethical) fringes. Angel, as stated above, is a vampire with a soul attempting to atone for centuries of evil, as well as a more recent relapse into his evil persona, Angelus (*Buffy*, "Innocence" 2.14 to "Becoming, Part 2" 2.22) and its effect on his relationship with Buffy. This reversion and its consequences led him away from Buffy's small town of Sunnydale and into the wider, and darker, canvas of Los Angeles. He is not alone in this: the first nine episodes of the series feature the half-demon, Francis Doyle (Glenn Quinn), who also has some darkness in his past (he abandoned members of his demon clan in need of succor, and they were killed) and subsequently dies to expiate it ("Hero" 1.9), and Cordelia Chase (Charisma Carpenter), a *Buffy* character whose parents have disappeared to avoid jail time for tax evasion, while she attempts to survive with a high school education and a dream of being an actress. Later in the first season, Wesley Wyndham-Price (Alexis Denisof) is also transitioned from the series' sister show, *Buffy*, having been fired from his previous job as a guide and trainer for Buffy (known as a "Watcher"), and making ends meet by killing demons on a freelance basis (or, as he styles it, "rogue demon hunter" ["Parting Gifts" 1.10]). Charles Gunn (J. August Richards) is added at the end of season one ("War Zone" 1.21), Lorne (Andy Hallett), a demon from a hell dimension, at the start of season two ("Judgment" 2.1), scientist Fred Burkle (Amy Acker) at the end of season two ("Belonging" 2.19), and

Angel's son Connor midway through season three (born in the episode "Lullaby" 3.9; returns from a hell dimension as a teenager in "A New World" 3.20).

The commonality between all of these characters is a shared outsider status. Cordelia and Wesley—the two characters, aside from Angel, that started on the series *Buffy*—despite originally operating from positions of wealth and privilege, struggle to find their place in an adulthood that did not turn out as intended or expected. "It was supposed to go home, hotel, hotel, husband," Cordelia insists as Angel and Doyle visit her filthy, low-rent apartment ("Lonely Hearts" 1.2). Wesley was the scion of a family of influence in the Watchers' Council (the organization charged with training and monitoring vampire slayers), only to be unceremoniously fired and blackballed when things didn't go according to plan ("Parting Gifts" 1.10). The Council did not give him the money to return home to England ("Sanctuary" 1.19), and his own father, Roger (Roy Dotrice) refers to him as the Watcher's Council's "most embarrassing failure," to which Wes responds, "Really? I beat out everybody dying in an explosion as most embarrassing failure?" ("Lineage" 5.7).

Rounding out the main cast is Winifred (Fred) Burkle, a physics student from Texas sent to a hell dimension in which humans were enslaved; since it is the same dimension from which Lorne escaped, it is implied that the portal that sent Fred to Pylea simultaneously sent Lorne to Los Angeles ("Belonging" 2.19). It is later revealed that the portal was opened by her mentor, Professor Oliver Sidell (Randy Oglesby), who was jealous of her intelligence; he attempts to do the same when Fred returns to the physics academic community ("Supersymmetry" 4.05). The trauma of that experience initially manifests itself in severe agoraphobia and social maladjustment; when she discovers Sidell is the author of that experience, she takes violent action against him, that is, creating a portal and sending him to a demon dimension.

Charles Gunn, the only African American main cast member in a Whedon series until the debut of *Firefly* in 2002, grew up in another type of hell dimension: poor and homeless in the shadow of Los Angeles's wealthiest neighborhoods. He is initially contrasted with David Nabbit (David Herman), a software engineer who hires Angel Investigations to retrieve some incriminating pictures ("War Zone") and who clearly longs to join the team; both Gunn and Nabbit are introduced in the same episode, and in "First Impressions" (2.3), they both display a similar work ethic; when Cordelia tells first Gunn and then Nabbit that Angel is sleeping, both respond with "I've been up since dawn." Yet it is Gunn who becomes a regular cast member, and Gunn who points out that while Nabbit may have made his "first millions" developing software for the blind and has a "foundation that donates 20 billion a year to countless charitable causes" (2.3), Nabbit clearly does not see those struggling and suffering closer to home: "You let me know when some of that coin trickles down to these parts," he responds. As Sara Upstone argues, *Angel* "focuses on … the dark underside of the wealthy Westside suburbs and glitzy entertainment industries, not the glamour of LA, but its dirty, violent, and divided urbanity"; scenes not generally shown in teen drama (Upstone 102). (In an interview, Whedon himself expressed weariness with teen television [Longworth 59].) Nabbit was initially meant to be a recurring character, but Herman's schedule could not accommodate multiple appearances (Stafford 145) and the character disappears following this episode. While it is a production-level issue that sidelines this character, the presence of Nabbit would have significantly changed the dynamic of the series; not only would concerns about money and work disappear for the Angel Investigations crew—Nabbit would have likely had connections to other wealthy clients, as well as his own considerable wealth—but Nabbit, as a representative of the corporate world (even with his reputation for philanthropy, noted above) would have been an odd fit with the struggling group dedicated to helping "the weak ones lost in the night, or the things that prey on them" ("In the Dark" 1.3). Early in the series, when Angel is presented with a magical object that allows him invulnerability and the ability to walk in sunlight, he destroys it, despite those he could help. They have help, he claims; it is those who are marginalized, "in the dark" so to speak, that need more assistance (1.3). That this mission statement—helping the helpless and vulnerable—is betrayed in the fifth season is a point I'll return to below.

Gunn, his sister Alonna (Michele Kelly), and a group of friends, however, are part of those "lost in the night"—homeless and struggling—although they work to defended their neighborhood against supernatural incursion. Gunn is in charge of the group until Alonna is killed ("War Zone" 1.20), and Gunn joins the Angel Investigations group. It is arguable that Alonna's death, for which Gunn feels responsible ("First Impressions" 2.3), drove him away from both his neighborhood and his friends; however, the idea that he holds his life cheaply and does not expect any marked change in either his circumstances or those around him is made manifest in the episode "Double or Nothing" (3.18) when it is revealed that he traded his soul for a truck. (He retrofits said truck with multiple demon- and vampire-killing apparatuses, suggesting a nobler motive.) It is Gunn's consistent undervaluing of himself—from his poverty to his lack of formal education—that makes him more vulnerable to the corporation's machinations at the end of season four.

Finally Lorne, a psychic demon from another dimension who runs a karaoke bar and reads peoples' futures when they sing ("Judgment" 2.1) is an occasional presence before becoming a part of the team at the end of the second season.[1] In his home dimension, one in which good and evil are defined in ways that allow no nuance, Lorne is an outcast because he can "hear music" and has no interest in fighting. Stan Beeler ties Lorne throughout the series into the camp aesthetic, as well as to the gay community (although Lorne's sexuality is never explicitly stated); this is underscored by his outcast status in his home due to his disinclination to join the warrior class and his ability to both recognize and live with moral ambiguity (Beeler 2005).

In contrast, Angel's son Connor, already supernaturally gifted due to being the offspring of two vampires, is honed as a warrior by Angel's sworn enemy Holtz (Keith Szarabajka) after Holtz kidnaps the child as an infant and jumps into a hell dimension; this is Holtz's revenge for Angelus (Angel's dark alter ego) and his sire Darla's (Julie Benz) killing of Holtz's family in the 18th century. Given both his physical and psychological environment—a hell dimension and a foster father bent on vengeance who views things in strict black-and-white-terms—Connor struggles with the moral ambiguity Lorne takes for granted. Once Connor escapes back into Los Angeles, it is clear that not only did Holtz use their time together in hell to turn Connor against his father, but hints dropped by Connor about his upbringing—such as Holtz tying a young Connor to a tree and leaving, in order to teach Connor how to "track" monsters ("The Magic Bullet" 4.19)—indicate that Holtz clearly took out his rage and animus for Angel on Connor as proxy. Holtz even kills himself to frame Angel, essentially a double abandonment, as Connor loses the only father he has known and is deprived of building a relationship with his actual one. These numerous manipulations mean that while Connor is part of the main cast in the fourth season, he remains an outsider even among this group of outsiders; neither Connor nor the team ever fully trust one another.[2]

The final season, which aired after *Buffy* ended its run, transitions the character of Spike (James Marsters), also a vampire with a (newly acquired) soul, to the series ("Conviction" 5.1). As the only person since Darla whose primary interaction with Angel was during both their evil pasts, Spike, particularly in the first part of the fifth season, takes Angel's former position as defender of the helpless and serves as the voice of dissent/conscience against the compromises the team makes within Wolfram and Hart. Spike is particularly well-suited to play this part for Angel, as he correctly accuses Angel of "making him a monster"—that is, taking pleasure in pain and torture as a vampire, rather than just feeding—when Spike was turned ("Destiny" 5.10). Further, Spike's position as non-corporeal for the first eight episodes of the season offers a tidy metaphor for the unseen, and unable to be physically touched, workings of the conscience.

The corporation as antagonist is present in the series' first episode, when Angel comes to the attention of Wolfram and Hart by killing one of their clients: a vampire, Russell Winters (Vyto Ruginis) who preys on young women ("City Of" 1.1). Winters, however, is not a run-of-the-mill vampire, as evidenced by the fact that he is a Wolfram and Hart client. He is an influential and successful CEO, with a cadre of kept women he uses, manipulates, and then (literally) devours; significantly, Angel is unable to save the woman, Tina (Tracy Middendorf), who comes to him for help. This sets a different and more ambiguous tone for the series, in contrast to *Buffy*; "[i]f *Buffy* was about 'growing up,' then *Angel* was about the pains of *being* a grown up" (italics in original) (Abbott 2014). That is, while the sixth season of *Buffy* focused on such adult matters as subsistence-level employment (which will be discussed below), it functioned primarily as the journey for both its heroine and her companions from childhood to adulthood, meaning that there were often older adults and authorities that could help guide or protect the characters from many of the issues the Angel team dealt with: money, shelter, survival, career, and consequences. Winters represents one of these consequences; he preys on the vulnerable, separating them into special "projects"—providing a high-end lifestyle until he becomes bored with them (Tina)—or food (Cordelia). Even his vampire make-up reflects this; in a radical departure from that seen in *Buffy the Vampire Slayer*, it makes Winters look both skeletal and diseased when he is feeding; an additional, if perhaps accidental, characterization of what he inflicts on those he targets: young women with few family ties and no options who are either literally or figuratively drained and discarded by Winters. He tells Angel that he is able to get away with this because he keeps a low profile and, most importantly, has enough power and influence to make both people and problems disappear, aided and abetted by the legal maneuvering of Wolfram and Hart. Indeed, despite airing more than a decade and a half ago, Winters claim that he can "do anything I want" sounds a bit like Trump's claim that "when you're a star, they let you do it" ("it" being sexual assault) (Fahrenthold 2016), offering a contemporary resonance to the ways in which money and power have been and continue to be used.

Winters may be the first, but he is certainly not the last, avatar for corporate greed and malfeasance within the series. Outside of Wolfram and Hart, Angel and his team have gone up against a CEO/warlock who plans to sacrifice his only daughter to a demon in order to gain more power and influence ("Guise Will Be Guise" 2.6), a vampire running a pyramid scheme ("Disharmony" 2.17), and a casino that engages in literal futures trading; one of the casino's games strips individuals of their destinies and trades them on the black market for massive sums of money ("The House Always Wins" 4.3).[3] While each of these are one-off episodes featuring antagonists who are eventually defeated, it speaks to the larger canvas on which the series is operating. Unlike *Buffy*, in which the majority of the action occurs in a small coastal town, the episode "Guise Will Be Guise" (2.6) reveals that there is a large network of cut-throat corporate players specializing in selling and trading curses, spells, and other supernatural items, as opposed to the single, small magic shop that serves the citizens of Sunnydale. I will return to these particular differences in size and economy in the next chapter.

While the first season of *Angel* was comprised of mostly stand-alone episodes (barring two separate "crossover events" with *Buffy the Vampire Slayer*), the continued presence of Wolfram and Hart ensured that the series itself would become more arc-heavy over time. Stacey Abbott points out that the original plan for the portrayal of Wolfram and Hart was to have Angel interact with a different lawyer each time, thereby "reinforcing its position as a faceless form of evil" (Abbott 5); however, as the series shifted gears to become more serialized, the law firm was primarily represented by the recurring characters Lilah (Stephanie Romanov) and Lindsey (Christian Kane) and the head of their department, Holland Manners (Sam Anderson), thereby personalizing the corporate relationship between Angel and the firm. Focusing on individuals within the corporate environment allowed the series to elucidate, using characters such as Lindsey, who grew up poor in a rural environment ("Blind Date" 1.21), and Lilah, as the sole provider for her mother, who suffers some form of dementia ("Sleep Tight" 3.16), the compromises that such an environment invites in those who operate within it.

Thus, starting with the second season of the series, not only did the characterizations of main characters Angel, Cordelia, Gunn, and Wesley deepen, but so too did the viewers' knowledge of lawyers Lindsey and Lilah, and the inner workings of their corporate law firm. The constant jockeying for position between Lindsey and Lilah, as well as the disconnect between corporate players feeling either cause or effect—elucidated in the quote that started this chapter—all particularly feature within the second season. The episode "Blood Money" revolves precisely around corporate charitable giving, and offers an excellent fit for economist Milton Friedman's contention that corporations should only engage in socially responsible initiatives if it makes an appreciable (positive) difference to the corporation's bottom line (Bakan 33–34).

Keeping with the second season's increased focus on the inner workings of the law firm, Lindsey and Lilah spearhead a charity ball for the East Hills Teen Center, a ball which features both celebrities and wealthy patrons; as Lilah says: "Rich people pay to touch famous people. Cameras catch all the not quite prostitutional action." Not only does the event serve to improve the reputation of the law firm, but it is explicitly a money-making enterprise; as Angel points out to shelter manager Anne (Julia Lee), once the firm deducts a series of expenses, the shelter will receive only 5 percent of the money earned from the event, approximately $100,000 to the firm's take of $2 million. This metric meets the guidelines of "worst charity," in which the majority of donations are paid to solicitors, with less than 10 percent of the monies actually given to those the charity claims to help ("America's Worst Charities" 2015). Anne claims not to care—the $100,000, she says, is more than the shelter could raise in two years—Angel rightly points out that the money Wolfram and Hart will earn will be used to underwrite the damaging and borderline illegal activities the firm is known for. While Angel himself is, at that point in the narrative, less interested in the morally questionable charity ball than in revenge on the firm that causes him so much grief, his point to Anne remains salient; is it moral to accept "blood money" even if it helps those in need? In a twist, Angel later steals the money and gives it to Anne; said money is now literally covered in blood from a fight with a demon, but Anne's only comment is "It'll wash." In this respect—and differing from the uses to which the law firm planned for the money—Angel's, and presumably Anne's, illegal acts (stealing and money laundering) are "cleansed" of the taint of its origins in a way that filtering it through the law firm would not have allowed.

The second season is also when, following the emergence of a prophesy regarding Angel hidden in the bowels of the law firm ("Blind Date" 1.21), as well as Wolfram and Hart's raising of Angel's dead sire Darla in the final episode of the first season ("To Shanshu in LA" 1.22), the series abandoned what are often referred to as "monster of the week"-type episodes in favor of the same season-long arcs that characterized its parent series *Buffy*. Indeed, in this respect the series surpassed *Buffy* in terms of the weight of its story arc; the raising of Darla is the beginning of an arc that would increasingly dominate the narrative until it came to fruition near the end of the fourth season ("Inside Out" 4.17) with the emergence of a "Power-That-Was" offering world peace to humanity in exchange for their unquestioning devotion. (This narrative domination is literal; the episode "Inside Out" suggests that every plot turn seen in the series, from Fred's journey to Pylea to Gunn's sister's death, led to that point in the story.)

The Jasmine arc itself, in which Jasmine, who uses (and discards) Cordelia in order to be born, offers an antagonist who can create devoted followers simply through the sound of her voice, whether in person or, increasingly, through various media outlets. Such a narrative offers a subtle dig at a media corporate structure with such reach that it takes only days for Jasmine to reach millions. She offers her listeners peace, fulfillment, and community; that the price of this is many of them will literally be consumed into the "body Jasmine" to maintain her power is a catch that her followers willingly accept, as is the fact that in the process of offering peace, she has stripped humans of their free will. It is only when Angel travels to a previous dimension Jasmine had visited, changed, and discarded (as she had done with Cordelia), that the group has the power to break her spell, barely in time to prevent Jasmine from appearing on national and international media and thereby making the entire world her personal fiefdom and abattoir. The cost of this victory, however, is the loss of Cordelia and Connor; Cordelia is in a coma, and for Connor, it is one lost too many; Angel makes a deal to remove Connor's memories of trauma and, in essence, given him up for adoption. (He is initially unaware that his deal has also altered the memories of his friends/coworkers, to everyone's detriment ["Home" 4.22].) Following the fall-out from that arc, Angel and company are offered the same corporation they had been fighting for four seasons, with the assurance that they can run it as they please ("Home" 4.22) in exchange for "ending world peace"; as with all contracts, however, the fifth and final season of the series focuses on the importance of reading the fine print.

*Angel*'s final season thus merges the outsider perspectives and insider corporate storylines of the second and third seasons of the show by placing its protagonists within that setting. Throughout *Angel*'s final season, the focus is primarily on the ways in which the corporation changes both the group's mission statement ("helping the helpless") and their selves. I touched on earlier that Angel initially rejected an opportunity to come aboveground, so to speak, claiming that those he could help "between 9 and 5" do not need it: "The whole world is designed for them, so much so that they have no idea what goes on after dark ... if I join them, maybe I'd stop seeing too" ("In the Dark" 1.3). Angel was more prescient than he realized; that is precisely what happens. As Janine Harrison argues, Wolfram and Hart, as "the epitome of a competitive, cut-throat environment based upon a masculine management style" (Harrison 119), cannot help but change those within it. This is literalized in the case of Fred, as I will address below.

In the first instance, the corporation's insistence on prioritizing profitability before any other concerns is evident from the season's opening episode ("Conviction" 5.1). Wolfram and Hart client Corbin Fries (Rod Rowland), accused of human trafficking, is close to losing his case; if convicted, he threatens retaliation: biological warfare using his own son as patient zero. The next episode ("Just Rewards" 5.2) has the team attempting to shut down the "interment acquisitions" department, a department that provides fresh corpses to a powerful and influential necromancer, Magnus Hainsley (Victor Raider-Wexler). What would have been straightforward for the team outside the corporate environment (the necromancer is instilling demons into fresh corpses, allowing the demons to escape detection) now must be balanced against the firm's profitability and laws designed to favor money and influence over justice.

Combining the shift in mission and in self is Gunn, who allows the corporation to implant legal knowledge into his brain, which he uses to exploit a legal loophole to get Fries freed ("Conviction" 5.1) and suggests the best way to fight Hainsley is freezing Hainsley's assets ("Just Rewards" 5.2). Such a decision builds on Gunn's arc from the previous season, in which his relationship with Fred fell apart; he questioned his place and importance within Angel Investigations ("I'm just the muscle"). The corporation exploits this vulnerability, under the rubric of Gunn as the individual with the "most unused potential" ("Conviction" 5.1). K Shannon Howard writes specifically of Gunn as "an ideal candidate for succumbing to L.A.'s corruption and materialism" even as the Angel Investigations team as a whole "battle a lack of selfhood in a culture that values commodities but not people" (Howard 147–148). This resonates on multiple levels; Gunn not only grew up in poverty, but was responsible for looking after his younger sister Alonna (Michele Kelly). When Alonna is turned into a vampire, requiring Gunn to kill her ("War Zone" 1.20), Gunn felt responsible for putting her at risk, and without the responsibility of watching over her, lost.

While Gunn gives up his "crew" to join Angel Investigations, Rejena Saulsberry argues that Gunn remains an outsider within the group, which, when coupled with his self-devaluing mentioned above, further contributes to his vulnerability to Wolfram and Hart's corporate manipulations; he is singled out by the "senior partners," which alienates him further from the rest of the original team; they are unsure they can trust him ("Unleashed" 5.3). The fact that this expression of distrust is coupled with a story in which the team attempts to battle a group of wealthy "foodies" who plan to devour a newly turned werewolf, only to allow the group to continue, clearly indicates that Gunn is not the only one in danger of corporate corruption. Gunn's alienation, however, which Abbott suggests turns him into a "form of cyborg," with "this artificial insemination of knowledge precipitat[ing] a change to his body and identity through technology intervention" that leads him to undermine both his ethics and identity (Abbott 57), is further exacerbated when Gunn makes a deal to make this upgrade permanent ("Smile Time" 5.14). This action results in the death of the woman he loves, Fred Burkle ("A Hole in the World" 5.15); while he knew the deal he made would have consequences, he tells Angel, "I didn't think it would be one of us" ("Shells" 5.16). This telling statement indicates how much the corporate mindset had invaded his thinking; as long as effects of his decision remained an "externality"—i.e., the consequences of corporate action felt by those unrelated to the business (Bakan 60–84)—he could live with the compromise. It also ties Gunn in closely with both River Tam in *Firefly* and the Actives in *Dollhouse*; all are (violently) technologically enhanced. Gunn subsequently attempts to atone for this by taking another character's place in a hell dimension, which on the surface looks like a pleasant suburban neighborhood, complete with a wife and child. This innocuous setting, however, is just a cover for daily torture, in which Gunn's heart is ripped from his body and discarded, only for his body to heal and his memory to be erased until the next day ("Underneath" 5.17). While this operates as a tidy metaphor for Gunn's loss of Fred, it also offers an interesting take on what the corporate setting attempted to do to the group. Actualizing this attempted emptying out allows Gunn to try and make himself whole, to restore his soul, or spark. (Indeed, "spark" is how Spike refers to his own soul (*Buffy* "Beneath You" 7.2.) That this might be working is evidenced in a few ways: Gunn refers to the torture demon as "Sparky"; the demon hands him a light bulb; and when the law firm offers him a deal to end this particular hell and mentions there was "not a lot of activity on the 'rescue Gunn' front," Gunn refuses ("Origin" 5.18).

Saulsberry argues that Gunn's arc as a permanent outsider to the primarily white Angel Investigations team represents "a step forward for the portrayal of black characters in that it avoids the post-racial, color-blind, class-blind narrative which is more prevalent and problematic" (Saulsberry 151). That is, the series, although it features demons and other fantastical elements, does not ignore the sociopolitical environment within which its characters move, including an episode in which undead cops target primarily black neighborhoods with a shoot-first, ask-questions-never approach ("The Thin Dead Line" 2.14) that both recalls the Los Angeles riots in 1992 (Upstone 101), as well as presciently resonating with the continued targeting of African Americans by police (Carbado 1479–1529).

It makes sense, then, that Gunn would be one of the two members of Angel Investigations that would be most affected by the corporate environment; the other, of course, being Fred Burkle. Kelsie Hahn analyzes what she refers to as the death of the "feminized body" within the Whedonverses, whether male or female, which includes "talk[ing] excessively, displaying a wide range of emotion and responsiveness, including moments of self-consciousness and emotional vulnerability, which are often coded as feminine" (Hahn para 3). Hahn argues that the deaths that occur (Wash [Alan Tudyk] from *Firefly* and Penny [Felicia Day] from *Dr. Horrible's Sing-Along Blog* are two examples she uses) to bodies coded as feminine "reinforces the cultural view that the female body is a vulnerable body, one that is fragile and in need of protection" (Hahn para 21).

Even before the protagonists take over Wolfram and Hart, the law firm itself invades the female (or "feminized," which in Hahn's definition can encompass both men and women) bodies of Angel Investigations. Cordelia, who already suffers from the mental invasion of visions sent from the Powers-That-Be (the "good" otherworldly counter to Wolfram and Hart's evil) has her visions "hacked" by the law firm to convince Angel to what they want; in this instance, release a half demon being tortured in a hell dimension, who just happens to be the nephew of an influential politician. Unlike the usual symptoms of Cordelia's visions (headaches), these Wolfram and Hart visions mark Cordelia with what she sees: a claw in one cuts her, a fire in another burns her skin ("That Vision Thing" 3.2). Significantly, this young man's demonic power is to release a "primordial misogyny" in men he touches; even Lilah, who is usually protected by virtue of working for Wolfram and Hart, is severely beaten when one of the male lawyers is affected ("Billy" 3.6).

Lorne, an empathic demon whose demeanor—and fashion sense—

is bright and campy, is also bodily invaded by Wolfram and Hart; agents sent by lawyer Lilah Morgan tie him to a chair and drill a hole in his head to remove his vision of an impending apocalypse ("Slouching Toward Bethlehem" 4.4). That this action ultimately saved his life was merely an unintended consequence ("Apocalypse Now-ish" 4.7). Thus, even before the team's takeover of the law firm, none of them were safe from its violation.

Fred, who is physically slight and is dressed in overtly feminine ways throughout the first part of season five, does in fact fit this pattern, as she is infected and killed nearly simultaneously to declaring her feelings for co-worker Wesley; in other words, when she is the most emotional vulnerable. Yet what differentiates Fred's fate from earlier "feminized" deaths within the Whedonverse is that she is reborn as "god-king Illyria," an ancient demon who literally grows a hard shell around Fred's body and is immeasurably powerful. I would argue that the "infection" of Fred by the god's essence offers a useful metaphor for the changes often required to work within a corporate environment, first embodied by Lilah, but also see in Gunn. The "devil's bargains" Lilah made allowed her to, in her own words "live somewhat dangerously and quite comfortably." When Angel warns her about her "game face" becoming a permanent part of her— hardening her, so to speak—she laughs and says: "The game face—the one I worked so hard to get—I became that years ago" ("Sleep Tight" 3.16). Lilah may not become a literal god in the same way as Fred, but given the immense power she wields as well as her ability, as a corporate player, to hold life and death in her hands simply by hardening herself bespeaks of the ways in which the intricacies of such power require an emptying out of those elements that make one vulnerable—or human. Similarly, the arrogance that Illyria displays ("I am Illyria, god-king of the primordium, shaper of things!" ["Time Bomb" 5.19]) does not sound out of line with the types of pronouncement one hears from CEOs.

It is worthwhile to revisit Harrison's analysis of traditional vs. non-traditional corporate climates in *Angel* and the way she contrasts the masculine management style and its effect on rising star Lilah (Harrison 118–125), with the more cooperative and integrated workforce of Angel Investigations (Harrison 125–131), particularly for what she leaves out. While Harrison touches on the effect of the group's takeover of Wolfram and Hart near the end of her analysis, concluding that had Angel and company continued in their roles within the corporate environment, they would have become completely corrupted, she does not address the significant way in which Fred was physically and psychologically changed within this time frame. Harrison argues, in terms of Lilah, that the masculanized corporate environment of Wolfram and Hart essentially devoured her; even after death, Lilah was beholden to the company ("Home" 4.22).

What Harrison does not address is the way in which Fred, the only remaining female at Angel Investigations, is similarly hollowed out due to her association with the corporation, and replaced with an ancient demon whose title ("god-king") implies a masculine origin, even as the ancient demon is considered to be beyond gender classification. The fact that Fred is human and therefore would have been unlikely to survive the protagonists' final battle with the corporation is likely is a factor in this change; her transformation into Illyria was the only way in which she could have participated in the defining battle that closed out the series ("Not Fade Away" 5.22). Yet there is a deeper implication here, which ties Fred into Harrison's analysis of Lilah. By the time Lilah is killed ("Calvary" 4.12), Harrison writes that Lilah "has surrendered possibilities of friendship and romance, even her own womanhood" in service of the corporation (Harrison 123). It is significant that when the original version of Wolfram and Hart is destroyed in season four by a minion of that season's antagonist (revealed as power-that-was Jasmine near the end of the season; Cordelia gives birth to Jasmine at the expense of her own life ["Inside Out" 4.17]), Lilah is not killed; instead, said minion punctures her abdomen, near where one of her ovaries would be located ("Habeas Corpses" 4.9), an injury that continues to bleed until Lilah's death ("Calvary" 4.12). Given the focus on birth through that season, such an injury does not seem coincidental.

Fred too is forced to "surrender possibilities of friendship and romance" (Harrison 123), but the difference is that Lilah displayed full awareness of the duties required and implications of her work at Wolfram and Hart. She is ruthless and ambitious, including engaging in corporate intrigue to keep her job via blackmail ("Dead End" 2.18), decapitating her former boss and taking his position ("Deep Down" 4.1), and both implicitly and explicitly causes the deaths of several people throughout her tenure at the law firm. When Wesley, in a futile act of chivalry, tries to burn her contract to free her from her post-death obligations to the corporation, Lilah, with a sad smile, reminds him that she knew what she was getting into when she signed ("Home" 4.22). That such sacrifices were ultimately not worth the cost is obvious.

Fred's fate, however, proves the insidiousness of the corporation as portrayed within the Whedonverse. While Fred was shown to be ruthless when either she or people she cared about were in danger (she attempts to murder the professor who had her sent to a hell dimension solely because of her intelligence and proficiency in his profession ["Supersymmetry" 4.5]; she tazes Connor when it is revealed he betrayed them and nearly killed Angel ["Deep Down" 4.1]), she was generally portrayed as kind, smart, and ethical; the occasionally violent action she takes are generally driven by her response to betrayals of her values. Like Gunn, the corporate environment invades her, emptying her out and replacing her with a ruthless and driven creature with an impenetrable shell. While Wolfram and Hart had an effect of each member of Angel Investigations— Angel was turned into an actual puppet ("Smile Time" 5.14), fellow vampire Spike (James Marsters), spent the first half of the season as a ghost due to an amulet given to him by the law firm, and head of the entertainment department/empathic demon Lorne allowed the firm to perform a dangerous procedure to increase his productivity ("Life of the Party" 5.5), which, as Beeler points out, was portrayed in a similar fashion to the effect on personality of such drugs as cocaine (Beeler 98), it is important to note that the two most affected by the corporate environment are the two most often excluded from positions of power within it: women and people of color.

*Angel* thus sets the stage for the portrayal of corporations throughout the Whedonverse as a toxic, invasive, and soulless environment that either discards or essentially damages those who operate within it. As Spike tells Wes and Gunn: "A place like that doesn't change ... not from the inside. Not from the out. You sign on there, it changes you" ("Soul Purpose" 5.10). The final episode, in which the group takes on avatars of the Senior Partners and jump-start an epic battle with demonic forces that they are fully aware they cannot win, elucidates the fact that when fighting against such monsters, sometimes standing up is more important than winning.

## *Running from the Blue Sun*

The corporate-inspired storyline was an explicit feature of season five of *Angel*; a corporate antagonist also made an appearance in *Firefly*'s single season, which aired the year prior (2002). While the fourteen episodes of the series did not allow this antagonist to be fleshed out in the same way as was possible with Wolfram and Hart on *Angel*, the actions of Blue Sun subtly inform the narrative of the series, as well as Whedon's subsequent series *Dollhouse*, as will be examined below.

*Firefly*, which is set in a 25th century in which China and the United States are the two remaining superpowers, follows the adventures of smugglers/criminals onboard the spaceship Serenity. The main narrative occurs six years after an interplanetary war between the Allied Planets (known as the Alliance) and the Independents (known as "Browncoats") over whether all planets should submit to the Alliance's central, controlling authority. The Alliance defeated the Independent faction. Two of the protagonists of the series, Malcolm Reynolds (Nathan Fillion), and Zoe Washburne (Gina Torres) were on the front lines of the war as Independents; they subsequently buy a ship so they can "live free" outside of the Alliance's control ("Out of Gas" 1.8), making money through both legitimate and illegitimate enterprises, including smuggling ("Shindig" 1.4, "Jaynestown" 1.7); illegal salvage ("Serenity" 1.1, "Bushwhacked" 1.3); theft ("The Train Job" 1.2, "Ariel" 1.9, "Trash" 1.11); and protection ("Our Mrs. Reynolds" 1.6, "Heart of Gold" 1.13). Their crew includes a pilot, Hoban "Wash" Washburne (Alan Tudyk), a mechanic, Kaylee Frye (Jewel Staite), and a mercenary, Jayne Cobb (Adam Baldwin). The mechanics of the plot begin when Serenity takes on four passengers: Shepherd Derrial Book (Ron Glass), a preacher, Lawrence Dobson (Carlos Jacott), later revealed as a government agent, and siblings Dr. Simon Tam (Sean Maher) and his sister River (Summer Glau). The crew is unaware that Simon and River are fugitives; Simon has rescued his sister from an institution that posed as a school for gifted children ("Serenity" 1.1), but in reality was creating psychic assassins using various neurological procedures ("Ariel" 1.9). While it is agents of the Alliance that the audience first see target River, it becomes clear throughout the season that they are not working alone.

River's story occupies much of the narrative of *Firefly*'s first and only season; its cancellation left many of the details unresolved, and the subsequent film adaptation shifted some of the narrative to focus on a government cover-up of a pharmaceutical treatment that left millions dead and was responsible for creating (in a small population percentage) extreme violence; those who suffered that adverse reaction are known as "Reavers." Christine Jarvis, in comparing the different pedagogical projects of the Whedon-helmed *Avengers* film versus Christopher Nolan's *The Dark Knight Rises*, concludes that "much of Whedon's work unmasks the workings of power in contemporary society, to show how the rhetoric of freedom and liberty is undermined by the machinations of global capital and the subjugation of democracy to the needs of powerful super-organizations hiding their power behind shows of benevolence" (Jarvis para 37).

In the film, this "show of benevolence" is an ill-conceived attempt to pacify the population using a drug intervention; the Alliance, working with an unnamed pharmaceutical company (which could be Blue Sun; it is never made explicit), infused the "air processors" throughout the planet with a drug to dampen aggressive responses. Such "benevolence"—trying to ensure peace—is itself an aggressive response on the part of the Alliance; as discussed above regarding Power-That-Was Jasmine, it erases human's ability to choose.

It is these types of "workings of power" by the Alliance that Mal and company are seeking to get beyond; however, there is a more insidious antagonist, in collusion with the Alliance, who seeks to retrieve River: the Blue Sun Corporation. Blue Sun easily fits into the definition of a megacorporation, along the lines of science-fiction writer William Gibson's (Gibson 1984) understanding of it: a large, multifaceted conglomerate that holds near-monopolistic market control. Whedon himself referred to Blue Sun as a cross between Microsoft and Coca-Cola and confirms that "practically half the government is Blue Sun" ("Serenity" commentary). The connections between Blue Sun and the Alliance are the very type of "machinations" that Jarvis refers to above. As I wrote in an earlier analysis of River (Giannini 2015), it is implied that the academy to which River was sent and subsequently tortured was either wholly or in large part run by Blue Sun. Such a partnership between academic and the corporate world has real world analogues, including exclusive contracts with schools to provide branded textbooks, drinks, and food. Such arrangements became fairly commonplace in the 1990s, particularly for cash-pressed public schools. Free soda and cash from cola companies, free pizza from Pizza Hut, and fast food franchises within school cafeterias are just the tip of the iceberg. As Eric Schlossser writes: "the spiraling cost of textbooks has led thousands of American school districts to use corporate-sponsored teaching materials" (Schlosser 55), including science books that taught "clear-cutting logging was actually good for the environment," texts from Exxon that dismissed fossil fuel-caused environmental problems, and study guides that indicated that the greenhouse gas was nothing to be concerned about, sponsored by the American Coal Foundation (Schlosser 55). The concept that Blue Sun would not only sponsor a school, but actually run it, does not require either a narrative leap or a particular suspension of disbelief on the part of the audience.[4]

Blue Sun's involvement with River's education is suggested in several ways. Two of the fourteen episodes ("The Train Job" 1.2 and "Ariel" 1.9) feature two men, both with blue hands, searching for (and in one instance nearly capturing) River. The connection is made more explicit in the graphic novel series that served as the bridge text between the series and the film, stating that they are independent contractors to the government from Blue Sun (*Those Left Behind*). Given their level of diversification, one could surmise that the blue-gloved agents could be part of a military contracting division of the corporation (an actuality in the later series *Dollhouse*); it is no surprise, however, that their accountability is not to the government but to Blue Sun. In the episode "Ariel," the two men kill several federal agents in their pursuit of River, with no apparent legal consequences. Finally, in *Those Left Behind*, when the Blue Sun agents are killed, the task of retrieving and neutralizing River is then passed on to the government, also indicating a level of collusion between the corporation and the Alliance, and touches on a long Western history of governments needing to clean up corporation-created messes, such as the recent bank bailout following the Great Recession (Gullapalli and Anand 2008).

Further, River herself frequently refers fearfully to "two by two/hands of blue" when faced with reminders of her time within the academy. As Ken Wharton also suggests, the inhumane treatment of River by the Academy bespeaks of a dehumanizing corporate logic, rather than a scientific, knowledge-seeking one (Wharton 149). River's aggressive strikes against even the Blue Sun logo underscore this; in the episode "Shindig," she tears off labels and tears apart boxes in Serenity's kitchen that bear the Blue Sun logo, mumbling to herself about the ubiquity of the corporation itself: "There it is, there it is. It's always there if you look for it. Everybody sees and nobody sees it.... These are the ones that take you!" (1.4). She is exactly right; it is always there. The Blue Sun logo appears twice in the pilot episode ("Serenity" 1.1): once on shipping containers and once on coffee cans, on the tops of the cans off of which River rips of the labels in "Shindig" (1.4), and three times in the episode "Ariel": on a t-shirt worn by Jayne, on a video phone, and on a neuroimager in a hospital (the implications of that last object will be addressed later on in this work). In this respect, Kahm makes the point that "the economic structure remains hidden in the background as an assumed part of daily existence, unremarkable in structure and practice, but critical to the overall framework of the lives of the characters and the development of the story" (Kahm 156).

River's reactions to instance of the Blue Sun logo clearly seek to expose this structure. Indeed, in "Ariel," River also reacts violently to the logo on Jayne's shirt, slashing his chest with a knife and saying, "He looks better in red." While Alyson Buckman primarily argues that River, who is revealed to be psychic in the final episode of the series ("Objects in Space" 1.14), is using this moment to avenge Jayne's eventual betrayal (he accepts payment to turn River over to the authorities) (Buckman 44)—a point with which I agree—I also find it significant that it is specifically the Blue Sun logo that River attacks.

In the film, River again resorts to aggressive action when she views a Fruity Oaty Bar commercial at a bar, a food product that is also manufactured by Blue Sun (the commercial, done in anime style, features a blue sun as one of several images). Given the aforementioned high rate of product placement of contemporary products in science fiction films such as *The Fifth Element, Demolition Man, Minority Report,* and *Total Recall,* triggering violence in River via a corporate logo thus combines two real-world analogues into the *Firefly* universe: corporate-sponsored schools and product-sponsored science fiction.

In an earlier article, I wrote about River Tam as representing the embodiment of a "culture jam" (i.e., "parodying advertisements and hijacking billboards in order to drastically alter their message" [Klein 280]), in the style of Kalle Lasn and Naomi Klein's work around branding practices (Giannini 2015). My particular focus was the way that her seemingly out-of-control behavior, as mentioned in the previous paragraph, could theoretically be considered an embarrassment to or reflect badly upon the Blue Sun brand. Yet, when factoring in *Serenity*, the film continuation of the series, with events within the television series—most notably in the episode "War Stories" (1.10), in which River displays advanced weapon skills with no prior training—one could logically conclude that the school imprinted or implanted particular weaponized skills within River for the benefit of both the government and the corporation. The abilities forced upon her by the academy she eventually uses to defeat the Alliance-created Reavers; it is not explicitly stated that was the purpose of her abilities, but it is suggestive (*Serenity* 2005). Further, the connection of both River's abilities and what was done with her (numerous neurological surgical procedures) suggests a link to Whedon's later series *Dollhouse*, in which the Actives undergo similar procedures in order to be of service to the corporate body. The connection between Blue Sun and Rossum, the corporation in *Dollhouse* is also hinted at in a commercial for Rossum (a paratext produced by Mutant Enemy), which shows a blue sun rising over planet Earth ("November Ad"). Further, the central narrative of the film *Serenity*, in which the crew discovers the planet on which the government hid the deadly results of a pharmaceutical experiment on the population, also offers thematic links between these two narrative universes, and offers another example in which the unintended consequences of such interventions require others to, in essence, clean up their mess.

To this end, Jeffrey Bussolini analyzes both *Firefly* and *Serenity* through a geopolitical lens. Of particular interest to the concerns of this chapter is Bussolini's arguments around the creation, mentioned above, of the Reavers through the pharmaceutical experimentation of the Alliance government. As the film explains, the (obviously non-consensual) dosing of the population of the planet Miranda with a drug called "Pax" (a gloss on the anti-depressant Paxil, according to Bussolini [145]) to promote stability and calm, had the unforeseen consequence of killing the majority of Miranda's inhabitants, as well as inciting madness and violence in a small percentage of subjects (also one of the adverse effects of Paxil ["Medication Guide"]). "[T]here is an economic and power dimension to [*Serenity*]'s critique, since the companies that make these drugs are major vehicles for neo-liberal, U.S.-led domination in the world market" (Bussolini 145). The misguided use of Pax in *Serenity*, Bussolini asserts, is a direct line to the behavior of drug companies in the real world, as is the "blowback" posited in both the film and in contemporary society, pointing to U.S.-led interventions in the Middle East as creating the very consequences the U.S. is still fighting.

Analyzing activist Ward Churchill's arguments about the events of September 11, 2001, Bussolini contends that Churchill is arguing that the U.S. government (and by extension, U.S. citizens more generally), should not be "unwilling to ignore the very real, misguided policies that had given rise to the hatred that motivated the attacks and that had ultimately provided the training and know-how to the people who carried them out" (149). Gerry Canavan also takes up the concept of "blowback" with regards to the Alliance, highlighting what the film makes explicit: those dead on Miranda are not the only victims; the Reavers are as well. "Reavers terrorize the Alliance at the edge of civilized space—but it was the Alliance that put them there" (Canavan 292). The fact that the Alliance is once again hiding or ignoring the consequences of their intervention on Miranda—going far enough to sanction even more destruction and murder in order to cover it up—indicates that the Alliance politicians have no more learned such lessons as their real-world analogues in the United States. Or, as Gareth Hadyk-Delodder and Laura Chilcoat convincingly argue, "by creating a monstrous Other, by actively repressing it from cultural consciousness, and by sublimating narratives of its existence by talking instead about the 'dangers' of the uncivilized outer planets who 'rejected' enlightenment, the Alliance is able to perpetuate and define its rule" (45).

In this respect, they tie the corporate/governmental creation of the Reavers directly to the aforementioned war; the collusion between the pharmaceutical industry and the government points to a concept explored in Whedon's later work with Marvel studios; in particular, the desire of former weapons manufacturer Tony Stark's (Robert Downey, Jr.) to create a "suit of armor around the world"—that is, trying to gain peace through the creation of a weapon, a point I explore in chapter three of this work.

The concept of "blowback" can easily be applied to River, the "uncontrollable" product of a corporate-sponsored school. As Gregory Erickson has pointed out, it is seemingly no accident that River and Reaver are nearly homonyms (Erickson 349). That either Blue Sun or the Alliance had a specific reason for their "treatment" of River is clear, as is the "blowback" in River's escape and subsequent actions against the governmental/corporate body that violated hers, a theme introduced in the seventh season of *Buffy* (the Slayer's origins are revealed to be the product of demonic rape ["Get It Done" 7.15]) and extended into the violations inflicted upon the Actives in *Dollhouse*. Like River, these women turn the violation around: Buffy subverts the "one slayer per generation" rule by sharing her power with all the potential Slayers ("Chosen" 7.22); Sierra/Priya avenges herself on the physician who put in under Rossum's control against her will ("Belonging" 1.4) and develops a relationship with Victor/Anthony even in Active state, and Caroline Farrell/Echo brings down the Rossum Corporation from the inside, despite multiple memory wipes (an action that has its own blowback, fitting with the darker tone and themes of that series, as will be addressed below).

While *Firefly*'s short televisual life did not allow these issues to be explored in the kind of depth that the 110 episodes of *Angel* did, one can see the same concerns are being addressed within both series. It is worth noting that while *Firefly*'s "big bad" was viewed by characters such as Mal as the Alliance government and their "meddlesome" ways—with limited awareness on the part of most of the characters of the corporation's involvement—*Angel*'s focus was more squarely on the effects of the corporate world, with little interest in U.S. governing practices. (There is the occasional off-handed joke aimed at the political area; indicating, for instance, that both the Bush and the Kennedy families were Wolfram and Hart clients, with the Bush family honoring their contract and the Kennedys not—suggesting the Kennedy tragedies were a consequence of breaking their contract with the law firm ["Conviction" 5.1]). Even within its short span, however, *Firefly* featured episodes that included the consequences of the use of indentured labor ("Jaynestown" 1.7); the environmental and economic effects of resource removal ("The Train Job" 1.2); powerful crime syndicates left to operate with impunity ("Serenity" 1.1; "The Train Job" 1.2; "War Stories" 1.10); and even an episode featuring an antagonist, Ranse Burgess (Frederic Lehne) who mixes wealth and power with a fundamentalist religious conviction that allows him a patina of morality over all his actions, including keeping the population under his control through poverty and violence and frequenting prostitutes ("Heart of Gold" 1.13).

The intersection between the corporate world and the U.S. government would not be explicitly addressed in Whedon's work again until *Dollhouse*. Taken together, however, both series paint a picture of an entity with little compunction against violating the rights—and bodies—of the protagonists. Both *Firefly* and *Angel* share the feature of a corporation that is both beyond conventional and accepted legal practices (Sutherland and Swan 2005), and hellishly, physically intrusive. Through Gunn, Fred, and River, Whedon and company clearly manifest the long and terrifying reach of the corporate body, even into the physical selves of the humans within its grasp.

CHAPTER TWO

# *A Stranger Comes to a (Small) Town*
## *Buffy*, *Roseanne* and the Long Reach of Corporate Culture

"You're not grown up enough to understand that your life doesn't always turn out the way you plan it to be" [Roseanne, played by Roseanne Barr, "Chicken Hearts"]

Long hours under fluorescent lights. Polyester outfits in day-glo colors. Bad skin from working the fryer and the grill. Fast food restaurants can be found everywhere, from the Malha Mall in Jerusalem to Hunt Road in Willard, Missouri (population 5288). If there is one type of corporation that is ubiquitous across the globe, it is the fast food industry. This ubiquity has become something of a trope within films with futuristic settings, with *Demolition Man* envisioning a near future in which the sole surviving chain is Pizza Hut, or *Idiocracy*'s 25th century, in which the world has fallen apart, but there is still a Starbucks, and everyone is named after specific brands (e.g., President Dwayne Elizondo Mountain Dew Herbert Camacho [Terry Crews] or Frito Pendejo [Dax Shephard]).

This very ubiquity, however, can render this corporation nearly invisible, and often hides the real-world consequences of the proliferation of fast food. Aside from the obvious health concerns inherent in the high fat, sodium, and sugar content of the food, there are social, environmental, and economic consequences as well. The concentration of food production to large factory farms and meat-packing corporations means that contaminated meat produced by even one corporate food producer can cause nationwide outbreaks of *E. coli* (Schlosser 194–196). In a World Health Organization study, it was revealed that the deregulation of industries that produce fries, ground beef, and soft drinks is a major factor driving the

45

obesity epidemic in nations in which fast food is prevalent (Kelland 2014). Another study found that fast food can impair the academic performance of children who regularly consume such products; the authors found that children who consumed at least four fast food meals per week in fifth grade still showed impaired cognitive development three years later (Purtell and Gershoff 871–877). This is a particularly disturbing finding given the ways in which fast food companies directly market to children, with 40 percent of McDonald's marketing aimed at children, and 79 percent of fast food ads airing on four networks that specialized in children's programming: Cartoon Network, Nickelodeon, Disney XD, and Nicktoons (Bernhardt et al. 2013).

From a production standpoint, the massive amounts of cattle, pigs, and chickens required for fast food production leads to overcrowded conditions, groundwater contamination, and overproduction of methane gases, which contribute to climate change (Goodland and Anhang 2009). Further, smaller farms and ranches either cannot compete or are absorbed by large conglomerates, creating production and economic monopolies and concentrating economic and social power with the few (Schlosser 133–147). This power and control of resources allows corporate-friendly lobbying and legislation to the extent that the vast majority of the population cannot hope to match, reducing them to merely living with the externalized consequences of these corporate policies, including poor wages, lack of health insurance, or environmental contamination. Or, in the words of former *Daily Show* host Jon Stewart, "Poor people have shitty lobbyists" ("Elizabeth Warren" 17.49).

Unlike the corporations discussed so far in this work—megacorporation Blue Sun, and the corporate law firm Wolfram and Hart—the fast food industry has a long-standing real-world relationship with television that stretches beyond simple advertising. Not only is fast food advertising prevalent during times when children are thought to be watching; restaurants such as McDonald's specially seek out that population through product placement in children's programming, and incentives, such as tie-in toys with popular films and television programs, included with items such as Happy Meals (Barraclough 107), but specifically target these populations with an emphasis on brightly colored advertisements and logos to a greater degree than those ads that are targeted to adult viewers (Bernhardt et al. 3). The presence of fast food franchises in high school cafeterias—as well as their sponsorship, as mentioned above, of sporting events, textbooks, and exclusivity contracts—means that even schools become vehicles for advertising and consumption (Peterson 17). Its prevalence across multiple facets of individual's experience makes it the perfect corporation to critique within the very medium that helped it rise to prominence: television.

The corporate structures that are so common in much of Whedon's later work are limited in his early oeuvre, such as Whedon's tenure as writer and story editor for the series *Roseanne*, and his first series as creator and showrunner, *Buffy the Vampire Slayer*. Both *Buffy* and *Roseanne* share a similar, small town setting, with smaller populations and less space for large corporate actors. Yet corporations still impact these series—particularly through the fast food industry—allowing Whedon and company to comment on this most prevalent global institution.

Thus, in this chapter I will focus on two episodes in particular: "Doublemeat Palace" from season six of *Buffy*, and "Chicken Hearts," a season two episode of *Roseanne* penned by Whedon, both of which are focused on the fast food industry, the likeliest corporate incursion into small towns. In both instances, the dehumanizing and paternalistic impulses of the corporation are on blatant display, a structure that even a superpowered Slayer cannot bring down; she can only survive it.

## *"No problem, boss": Taming the Domestic Goddess*

The series *Roseanne* still remains one of the few not created or directed by Norman Lear,[1] which focused on a working class family; indeed, one of the few portrayals of the working class on television more generally. As *Variety* wrote in 2008, the working class has all but disappeared on American television since its heyday in the 1970s, arguing that the current era showcases "the moral bankruptcy of the super-rich ... and the neurosis of well-educated professionals" (Littleton 1, 81). In a more recent *New York Times* article, Wesley Morris charts the disappearance of class consciousness, and therefore portrayals of the issues of the working class, on television, even as television expands beyond broadcast and cable and into streaming services like Hulu and Netflix, arguing that "[t]elevision is losing what work is and knows it ... the jobs are disappearing ... and the factories and mills and laundries are now lofts and cafes where characters sit around and talk" (Morris 2016). This "disappearance" from the media may have been a factor driving the successful candidacy of Donald Trump, who campaigned as a champion of those ignored by the establishment, which was defined by some as non-college educated white middle and working class men (Thompson 2016). Trump's status as a television star only underscores this; the coverage of and interviews of participants in his rallies offers them a visibility missing in narrative television. (*Roseanne* star Barr's support of Trump's candidacy seems to underscore this idea [Ross 2016].)

In a similar vein, Morris ties this representational disappearance with the rising struggles of the middle class and the desire for "fantasy," that is, people who are struggling to find work are thought to not want to watch reflections of that reality. The long-running genre series *Supernatural*, interestingly, offers both: the portrayal of working class/working poor individuals and escapism through the fantastical premise. Like its predecessor *Buffy*, the series uses metaphor to expose many of the horrors of the economically marginalized and the difficulties of upward mobility (see Wright 2008 for an analysis of these issues within the first two seasons of the series), and specifically places one of its antagonists as a corporate CEO, who manages to wreak significant financial and interpersonal damage on the protagonists (Giannini 2014). The series, renewed for an unprecedented thirteenth season as of this writing—making it the longest-running fantasy series in U.S. television history—remains one of the few portrayals of the working class/working poor on contemporary television.

Contrary to Morris' contentions, however, I would argue, however, along with Robert McChesney, that this lack may have more to do with advertising dollars than the supposed desires of the viewing public. As he writes: "Advertising accentuates the class bias in media. Advertising, on balance, tends to be interested in affluent consumers with disposable income. Hence, media firms find it far more rewarding to develop media fare for the upper middle class then for the poor and working class" (McChesney 19).

In other words, this particular representational lack may be due to the perception by advertisers that said viewers cannot afford to buy what is on offer during the commercials that support broadcast programs. Stephanie Coontz points out that "advertisers favored shows that presented 'universal themes' embodied in homogenized families without serious divisions of interest by age, gender, income, or ethnic group. The hope was that everyone could identify with these families and hence with the mass-produced appliances that were always shown in conjunction with the mass-produced sentiments" (Coontz 175).

*Roseanne* rarely showed identifiable products, clothing, or appliances; one episode, in which Roseanne substitutes for Darlene's (Sara Gilbert) home economics teacher, has Roseanne advising the students to buy generic instead of brand name products ("only the second best for my family") and showing them how to make cheap food in large quantities ("Home-Ec" 3.16). Given the controversy generated by the series' star, as well as the fact that the series itself portrayed a low-income family, it would not be a stretch to conclude that there was little incentive for either programmers or advertisers to place products or solicit advertising for expensive items within the series' diegesis, particularly if their assumption was that the audience for the series shared the same socioeconomic status as the Connors. (The fact that the series ousted *The Cosby Show*, which in contrast to *Roseanne*, featured a highly affluent family, from the number one spot in the Nielsen's during its second season, such an assumption would likely be incorrect; however, placing items like expensive televisions or cars would undermine the series' particular reality.)

*Roseanne* thus remains one of the few portrayals of the working class/working poor in late 20th-/early 21st-century American television. Indeed, for at least half of the series' nine seasons, Roseanne (Roseanne Barr), her husband Dan (John Goodman), sister Jackie (Laurie Metcalf), and friend Crystal (Natalie West) do not just struggle to find meaningful work, but any work at all. The first season ends with Roseanne, Jackie, and Crystal walking out of their jobs at the Wellman Plastics factory when new foreman Keith Faber (an early role for Fred Dalton Thompson, former senator and Republican candidate for president in 2008) demands an increase in productivity that is impossible to meet, as well as attempting to "break" the outspoken Roseanne, first through a series of infantilizing nicknames ("honey") and then by a soon-broken promise to lower quotas if she behaves the way he wants her to ("Let's Call It Quits" 1.23). Following this, Jackie decides to enter the police academy ("Little Sister" 2.2, also penned by Whedon)[2] and Crystal works for an Avon-type company; however, Roseanne works, at various times, as a telemarketer, a bartender, and a beauty shop attendant; she loses her one chance at a white-collar office job when she is forced to admit she has no computer skills ("Guilt by Disassociation" 2.3).

It is important to note at least two notable exceptions to more realistic portrayals of working class life in *Roseanne*. In season eight (1996), when ABC was purchased by Disney, in an orgy of cross promotion, numerous shows were seemingly required to send their characters to Disney World, including *Boy Meets World* ("The Happiest Show on Earth" 3.21), *Family Matters* ("We're Going to Disney World, Parts 1 and 2" 6.22/6.23), *Step by Step* ("We're Going to Disney World, Parts 1 and 2" 5.21/5.22), and *Roseanne* ("We're Going to Disney World" 8.17/"Disney World War II" 8.18). *Roseanne* in particular required a greater suspension of disbelief that a family who struggled for so long would use an unexpected windfall in such a way. Amusingly, the series mocks this studio-generated storyline in the following episode, "Springtime for David" (8.19), in which one of the character's job at a local theme park turns him into a mindless automaton. The other exception is the main arc for season nine, in which the Connor family wins the lottery; this is revealed to be fiction Roseanne (as character) wrote after the death of her husband ("Into That Good Night" 9.22/23).

No job Roseanne has throughout the course of the series is perhaps more humiliating than her brief tenure working fast food. Surrounded by coworkers and a boss who attend the same high school as her daughter Becky (Lecy Gorenson), Roseanne attempts to survive the circumstances with humor and sarcasm, which her boss Brian (Peter Smith)—known as "the little maggot" to her family—finds disrespectful; he tells her that her "attitude stinks." (His attitude, however, is never up for discussion.) He also assumes a physical position of dominance over her during a staff meeting: he comes up behind her as she is sitting down and grips her shoulders, physically holding her in place while he speaks. When he schedules her for Saturdays, despite the fact that she had explicitly said she couldn't work weekends because "I have a family," Brian lapses into the corporate speak that has become a cliché, both in the media and in the real world: "This is a family too."

The concept of the corporate family, especially as it supersedes other definitions of family, is something that Whedon addresses explicitly in *Dollhouse*, which I will address in chapter eight, but the appropriation of this type of language to describe workplaces and businesses was already commonplace in the late 1980s; witness the long-running slogan for the faux-Italian chain restaurant Olive Garden: "When you're here, you're family." While such language, on the surface, can be read as nothing but slick marketing to busy individuals, one does not have to dig deeply to understand that these "families" frequently shortchange certain "family members" in particularly abusive ways. A recent report found that Darden, the corporation that owns Olive Garden (among other chain restaurants), pays its employees using pre-loaded debit cards—which are subjected to a variety of fees for use that 63 percent of employees were not informed of—and allows no other paycheck disbursement options. This apparently generates a cost saving for the corporation of approximately $5 million per year (Restaurant Opportunities Centers United 2016). Combined with the numerous other pocket-picking of low-income individuals and families, including payday loans and check cashing services (Rivlin 21–59), it is easy to see the emptiness of the one-way "family" loyalty these corporations offer. Roseanne herself speaks for many in this situation when she tells her boss: "It ain't my family," while Brian allows a combination of necessity and favoritism to guide how he runs the franchise. He offers sycophantic fellow employee Andrew (Christian Jacobs) overtime that had been requested by another employee, simply because Andrew had offered him free washes at Andrew's family car wash; both young men, either through holding a managerial position or as the son of a business owner, have a privilege that neither Roseanne nor her coworker could aspire to. Given that the employee whose request for overtime was dismissed is female, and taken together with Brian's paternalistic attitude even toward a female employee literally old enough to be his mother speaks of an element of sexism alongside the favoritism, and touches on Barr's claims of paternalistic attitudes and outright sexism from both the studio and co-creator Matt Williams, which she asserts made the first season of her series "a living hell" for the actress (Barr 2011).

The Connors' socioeconomic struggles do not allow Roseanne to continue to speak freely, nor even to keep the corporate environment of the fast food chain from invading her home. Swallowing what pride she has left, she invites Brian to her home, ostensibly so Dan can help Brian with a shop project Brian is failing—he has to rebuild a carburetor; he owns a Mustang that he calls his "baby" but cannot perform maintenance—but primarily to humanize both Brian and herself. She tells him that part of her motivation in inviting him over is to offer him a glimpse of her non-work life—her family, her home—as if to give him the opportunity to consider that they are more than just employee and employer.

This fails, which is not surprising. Even as a teenager, Brian has clearly internalized the idea that the corporate family is the only one that matters. Brian's inability to be flexible (he fires Roseanne for refusing to work weekends) puts his own job at risk as the family dismantles the carburetor Dan put together for him; failing shop will drop his GPA and his high school requires a certain grade point average for students who work. While Brian is threatened with a loss of some social status—it is implied that without this job, he will not be able to afford to maintain his car, which he believes makes him an attractive social commodity (Becky refutes this)—it is nothing compared to the potential consequences for Roseanne and her family, as reflected in the quote that opened this chapter. Both Brian and the Connors understand that while Brian does not have the trade skills Dan has—car repair, home maintenance, etc.—Brian's are more valued in a technological/managerial economy. (Although such jobs are not necessarily safe either; the early 1990s saw massive layoffs of managers and technicians from such stalwarts as McDonnell Douglas [Stevenson 1990] that had an adverse effect on Midwestern towns and cities [Barringer 1991].) While Dan and Roseanne celebrate Roseanne's freedom from the drudgery of the job—Roseanne jokes that she would make a great diplomat—the reality of their situation is immediately clear. Dan calls the Brian a "loser" who will likely be a "lonely, bitter multi-millionaire" by the time he is in his 30s, while Roseanne sighs and says, "They're hiring over at Bucky Burger." It is a tidy way of summing up the difficulties of transcending the socioeconomic structures in which each lives; Brian works a managerial position before graduating high school; not to maintain a mortgage or feed a family, as Roseanne points out to him, but to maintain his Mustang.

"Chicken Hearts" aired a season and a half into the series; at that point, Dan and Roseanne had not been shown to work in any position of power. Indeed, when Dan attempts, later in the series, to open his own business (a bike repair shop), this coincides with the town's primary income driver—the plastics factory from which Roseanne quit—closing its doors. Dan's small business fails, the family is in danger of losing their house, and there is no money to send their oldest daughter to college, despite her good academic performance ("Terms of Estrangement, Parts 1 and 2" 5.1 and 5.2).

The Connor family fits fairly well into the socioeconomic category known as the "working poor," a term David K. Shipler considers an "oxymoron": "Nobody who works hard should be poor in America" (Shipler ix). "The poor have less control than the affluent over their private decisions, less insulation from the cold machinery of government, less agility to navigate round the pitfalls of a frenetic world driven by technology and competition" (Shipler 7); witness the earlier example of Roseanne unable to take a well-paying job because of her lack of computer skills. As the series made clear through numerous plot iterations: "their personal mistakes have larger consequences, and their personal achievements yield smaller returns" (Shipler 7). The Connors fret over tax returns, made more difficult by the sheer number of jobs Roseanne worked in a single year ("April Fool's Day" 2.22), have their electricity turned off for non-payment ("The Dark Ages" 5.3), and have to decide between clothes for themselves or their children—but not both ("Mall Story" 1.16). Even consistent medical/dental care is frequently out of reach; when a household accident breaks one of Roseanne's teeth, her only option is to get free care from the dental school ("Tooth or Consequences" 5.24). As Shipler points out, things like broken or missing teeth are not a matter of aesthetics for the working poor; they can be the difference between low- and high-wage jobs (52–53). There is no real safety net for the family, even in times of prosperity for much of the rest of the country (e.g., the mid–1990s, in which the series aired).

Significantly, the series also tackles the fraught dynamics of success, when daughter Darlene, who does manage to attend art school on a scholarship, reveals that she's been offered a well-paying job that she turned down in favor of finishing her degree, knowing her opportunities would be even greater if she was college-educated. Rather than displaying pride for their daughter's accomplishments, Dan, Roseanne, and the rest of the family feel threatened. Darlene's usual sarcastic and ironic comments are taken more personally; they assume that Darlene is joining a social class that considers the Connors to be "trash" ("The White Sheep of the Family" 8.13). That Darlene eventually ends up married and pregnant by the end of the season would indicate that the pressures and difficulties of transcending these social and economic limitations are all too real, although surprisingly for a series that tackled both feminist and class issues, Darlene's career prospects are never really discussed again ("Another Mouth to Shut Up" 8.20), and the final season veers into a fantasy in which the family wins the lottery. In keeping with some of their earlier concerns, however, they do use the money to pay off their house, as well as reopening the factory whose closure had such a deleterious effect on the town ("Lanford's Elite" 9.16).

Roseanne may have a voice, which she regularly raises to a shout, but it does little to transcend the socioeconomic issues under which she and her family labor. By using the fast food industry as a fulcrum to highlight these pressures, Whedon's script makes manifest the increased silencing of working poor/working class in both media and social situations: she can shout all she wants, but no one in power is really listening.

## "My hat has a chicken," or, with Great Power Comes Huge Economic Issues

*Buffy the Vampire Slayer*, a series about a young woman invested with power in order to fight the forces of evil that plague her small town of Sunnydale (situated over a "hellmouth," which itself either brings forth or draws the forces of evil to itself) is generically a far cry from the working-class situation comedy of *Roseanne*. While both *Roseanne* and

*Buffy* occur in small-town settings, the geographic locations are widely divergent: the fictional town of Lanford, Illinois, and the fictional town of Sunnydale, California. While a detailed analysis of the social and economic differences between the Midwest and the West coast of the United States is outside the scope of this work, it is worth noting that, like other Midwestern towns, such as Flint, Michigan, Lanford's primary economic driver is the aforementioned plastics factory from which Roseanne quits at the end of the first season and that shuts its doors at the end of the fifth; there is no analogous industry suggested to be driving the economy of Sunnydale. Roseanne's circle of friends primarily work in blue-collar industries: construction, car repair, dry wall, long-haul trucking, or the local police force. Indeed, one of the few within Roseanne's circle that works in a white-collar profession—Jackie's boyfriend Fisher (Matt Roth)—suffers from the same economic downturn that plagues his more blue-collar companions; he's less able to handle it, and becomes physically abusive to Jackie ("Crime and Punishment" 5.13).

In Sunnydale, Buffy's mother Joyce (Kristine Sutherland) owns her own gallery, her "Watcher" (an individual sent to train Buffy in her Slayer duties) Giles (Anthony Stewart Head) is Oxford educated and serves as the high school librarian (and later business owner), and Buffy's best friend Willow's (Alyson Hannigan, who also appeared on *Roseanne* following Whedon's tenure as story editor) mother Sheila (Jordan Baker) has a doctorate in psychology, leaving the third member of the friend trio (known as the Scooby Gang, in tribute to 60s-era cartoon), Xander Harris (Nicholas Brendan), as the sole representative of the working class within the series, although what his parents do beyond drinking and fighting is never addressed. Like the Connors, the social class in which Xander is from clearly precludes academic achievement or the ability to attend college alongside his friends; a factor that briefly drives a wedge between Xander and the rest of the group during the fourth season of the series, particularly when the vampire Spike, seeking to divide the Slayer from her friends, suggests Buffy and Willow have joked that Xander's best and only career option is military service ("The Yoko Factor" 4.20).

In the first five seasons of *Buffy the Vampire Slayer*, Buffy and her friends face an ancient vampire ("Prophecy Girl" 1.12), Buffy's evil ex-boyfriend ("Becoming, Parts 1 and 2" 2.21/22), an immortal mayor who becomes a full demon ("Graduation Day, Parts 1 and 2" 3.21/22), a human/demon hybrid created by the government ("Primeval" 4.21), and a hellgod ("The Gift" 5.22). In each instance, the monster is defeated. While each of these victories comes at a cost—Buffy dies (twice ["Prophecy Girl" 1.12/

"The Gift" 5.22), many of her classmates are killed at their high school graduation ceremony ("Graduation Day, Part 2" 3.22), Buffy has to kill her former lover ("Becoming, Part 2" 2.22), and the gang invokes ancient powers that nearly kill them ("Restless" 4.22)—peace is restored and life goes on for the Slayer, her friends, and the small town of Sunnydale in which they reside.

Season six, however, takes a more human-level approach to the troubles that Buffy and friends usually experience. The previous season showed Buffy reaching the heights of her powers as a Slayer; she was more focused and powerful, in large part due to the fact that she was facing her most powerful supernatural enemy: a god named Glory (Clare Kramer). This focus and power, however, was in tandem with personal upheavals, including the end of her relationship with boyfriend Riley (Marc Blucas) ("Into the Woods" 5.10), the sudden appearance of a younger sister, Dawn (Michelle Trachtenberg)—who was, in reality, a powerful mystical object that Buffy was tasked with protecting ("No Place Like Home" 5.5)—and the devastating loss of her mother Joyce to complications from a brain tumor ("The Body" 5.16).

Joyce's death, aside from the obvious grief at her loss, puts Buffy in the position of being a single mother/sole breadwinner for her family, in addition to her more supernatural responsibilities. She quits college and becomes Dawn's primary caretaker amid fears she would not be seen by authorities as a fit parent ("Tough Love" 5.19). Buffy managed to temporarily avoid the intricacies of this responsibility by sacrificing herself to defeat Glory ("The Gift" 5.22); however, when her friends perform a ritual to resurrect her (under the mistaken impression that she was suffering in a "hell dimension") ("Bargaining, Parts 1 and 2" 6.1 and 6.2), the necessity of financially (never mind psychologically or emotionally) maintaining the Summers family falls to Buffy. Within days of her return, she is not only informed that her inheritance from her mother is gone on basics such as food and shelter, but the basement floods and requires all the plumbing to be replaced ("Flooded" 6.4); due to Buffy's status as unemployed and the poor property values inherent in living over a hellmouth, she is unable to secure a loan for the repairs.

Like Roseanne and Dan, Buffy must find a way to support her family without the benefit of a college education. (Even auditing courses the local college proves unsuccessful.) Further, the intricacies of her duty as Slayer make conventional employment more difficult; even her interview with a loan officer at the bank is interrupted by a demon attack ("Flooded" 6.4). This is despite the fact that Buffy, unlike the Connors, has contacts in various professions that could provide more than poverty-level wages. Xander, who has found some degree of success in working construction, offers Buffy a job working on a construction crew. While her appearance—a petite blonde—and gender generate the expected sexist response in the all-male crew, her work ethic and strength ameliorate some of the crew's animus. Until, of course, the site is attacked by demons. The damage to the site—as well as the crew's lack of awareness of the attack—force Xander to fire Buffy, thereby cutting off that potential.

Later, she attempts to work in Giles' shop; like her attempt to reintegrate into academic life, this too is a failure. Unbeknownst to Buffy, the secondary antagonists of season six—a trio of young men who wish to "take over Sunnydale" using a combination of technology and magic to facilitate a crime spree—are testing her using magic and demons ("Life Serial" 6.5). Given the series reliance on metaphor to examine the challenges of everyday life (Little 282–293), the trio's tests operate as tidy metaphor for Buffy's school workplace problems. While auditing classes, the Trio uses a magical device to speed up time so Buffy cannot keep up; yet prior to this, she finds it difficult to get into the academic groove once again. At the construction job, Buffy annoys some of the other crew members by working faster and better, only to be attacked by demons that disappear when killed. The lack of tangible evidence of the demon attack bears a striking similarity to the outcomes of workplace sexism and harassment being dismissed as "he said/she said." When working retail, the trio casts a spell that puts Buffy in a time loop, doomed to repeat the same customer transaction until the customer is satisfied. The trapped feeling engendered by an endless parade of customers is certainly familiar to anyone who has worked in the retail sector. While Giles eventually agrees to pay the plumbing bill, the larger economic issues are not solved by this last-minute intervention, and Buffy seeks employment at Doublemeat Palace, a McDonald's-like fast food restaurant; this job she retains until the end of the season.

James South, in his analysis of the critique of the technological society that *Buffy* offers, focuses on two episodes of the series that focus on a corporatized, mechanized reality. The first, "Anne" (3.1), takes place in Los Angeles, and therefore is not entirely germane to my own analysis. The second, "The Wish" (3.9), takes place in an alternate reality Sunnydale, in which the first season villain, known as The Master (Mark Metcalf), was not killed by Buffy ("Prophecy Girl" 1.12), but had in fact succeeded in taking over the town. The Master unveils a machine that more efficiently extracts blood from victims; in his own words, using human innovation

## Two. A Stranger Comes to a (Small) Town    57

("mass production") for his own nefarious ends. South's Marxist analysis posits the familiar concept of capitalists as vampires; i.e., taking from the populace to feed an appetite that is never sated (South 97–98). In this context, The Master's appropriation of the techniques of human mass production underscores the connection.

Due to its publication before the end of the series, South's analysis does not cover *Buffy*'s final two seasons, in which Buffy's financial issues require her to undertake subsistence-level/minimum wage work. While Buffy, with the help of both new and old friends, and a reclaiming of her identity as "the Slayer" (and, as Rhonda Wilcox points out from South's analysis, wielding a hammer and sickle as she frees the workers [Wilcox 92]) succeeds in destroying the factory that uses up and discards the young in "Anne," in "Doublemeat Palace" (6.12) and the episodes following it, she is instead subjected to long hours, double shifts, and poor nutrition for both Buffy and her sister Dawn; she frequently brings home Doublemeat burgers for dinner, presumably because she gets a discount. Her work hours, too, leave little time for domestic duties or socializing. Buffy's work is monitored, and any deviation from the norm is frowned upon ("variety is the spice of bad, got it" is Buffy's response to her manager, Manny [Brent Hinkley]). Wilcox in particular draws on the way the series critiques global McDonaldization; the half-season Doublemeat arc explicitly addresses the ways in which "subsistence-level employment" such as the fast food industry requires no supernatural evil to reduce its employees to mindless automatons serving a corporation that does not serve them, all while McDonald's actually served as one of the sponsors for the series (Wilcox 93). Amusingly, despite complaints about the depiction of violence or same-sex relationships within the series, "Doublemeat Palace" was one of the only episodes for which sponsors threatened to abandon the series, due to the ways in which the fast food industry was portrayed (Pasley 264).

The episode in which this arc is introduced, "Doublemeat Palace," features Buffy's first week working for the franchise, in contrast with "Chicken Hearts," which focuses on Roseanne's last day at her job. After a brief interview, Buffy is left alone with an inappropriately cheerful video, which, from what the viewer overhears and Buffy's facial reactions, is a combination of training manual, sales pitch, and corporate farm exposure video (that is, showing the process by which the "double meat," supposedly a combination of chicken and beef, is created). She is then shepherded into the work area, in which she is trained on the broiler and fryer, and finds herself unnerved by her fellow employees' demeanor: slow-moving and seemingly mindless. When one of her co-workers, Gary (Thomas Michael Ferguson), who had apparently not been there long enough to evince the same hopelessness as many of the others, fails to show up for work, combined with Buffy's discovery of a human finger under the meat grinder, convinces her that, in the best *Soylent Green* tradition, the Doublemeat burgers "are people." After attempting to warn the patrons, she is fired and escorted out, but not before managing to grab a burger and bring it to her friends for testing. It turns out that the "meat" in the double meat is actually ground vegetables flavored with beef tallow; Buffy leverages this information to get her job back.

Given the nature of her calling, it is unsurprising that she assumes that something supernatural is involved; turnover is high, and nearly everyone seems as if they are drugged. Yet, as Xander, who has also worked in the fast food industry, tells her: "It's fast food.... There's the assorted creepiness, there's staring, there's the enthusiastic not showing up at all. I think you're seeing demons where there's just life." While it turns out that something supernatural is targeting the Doublemeat employees—a demon posing as a customer occasionally paralyzes, then devours the Doublemeat workers—it is not in fact the primary cause of the deadened affects and high turnover. The episode immediately introduces the primary division between various employees: those who work there for a short time before moving on to other opportunities (or being devoured), and those who refer to themselves as "lifers," complete with buttons on their uniforms indicating how long they have been with the company. The use of the term "lifer," most often associated with prison sentences, to describe these employees, does not seem accidental. Those lower on the ladder, like the middle-aged man who works the grill, scarcely talk to or interact with one another; the management is hardly better, speaking in clichés and platitudes, such as "Levity is the time thief that picks the pocket of the company."

As Wilcox writes, "the fact that Doublemeat is not involved in a conspiracy makes it clearer that there is a problem in the system—which, in the real world, does not have to be conspiratorial to be problematic" (Wilcox 93). While Wilcox puts this in the context of the series making a subversive point about the dangers of globalization, I would add that the phrase, repeated by management every time Buffy tries to dig deeper into what really constitutes the Doublemeat burgers: "It's a meat process" is equally significant. Eric Schlosser points out, in his polemic against the fast food industry, that these corporate entities rely on the Taylorist assembly line system—that is, the time management system developed by Frederick Winslow Taylor, supposed to increase productivity and lessen deviation—and particularly seek out unskilled workers willing to accept low pay: the young, recent immigrants, and the disenfranchised (70–71). In that respect, one of the most important qualities for fast food workers, according to management, is "obedience" (75). This viewpoint is referenced directly within "Doublemeat Palace" to such a degree that, as stated above, sponsor McDonald's was upset with the portrayal. Thus, when the Doublemeat managers are referring specifically to the "process" of burger making, there is a deeper point here: the global corporate system that Wilcox refers to, in which workers are easily replaced, identity-less, and hidden from view, is itself a process that grinds them into nothing. Buffy, who only months earlier defeated a god and who boldly claims midway through the episode that: "We need to bring down the whole corporation," ends up accepting her place in an economic system unfairly stacked against the most vulnerable. Demonic forces are nothing compared to the corporate structure.

## Conclusion

There are significant differences, on generic, period, production, and narrative levels (to name a few), between *Roseanne* and *Buffy the Vampire Slayer*. The series *Roseanne* takes place in a more familiar and mundane "reality" than does *Buffy*. They take place in geographically divergent areas of the country,[3] and despite some overlap in when the series aired (*Roseanne* debuted in 1987 and ended its run in May 1997; *Buffy* debuted in March 1997), there are significant culture differences in their respective eras, both politically (*Roseanne* started in the Reagan era and ended in the Clinton era; *Buffy* debuted near the end of the Clinton presidency and continued up to the onset of the Iraq War under George W. Bush; the seventh season of the series explicitly dealt with the ethics of war) and economically (tech boom vs. recession). Perhaps most importantly, Whedon served as story editor for a series created by Matt Williams and Roseanne Barr, in a television era rife with comedian-led series: *Seinfeld*, *Home Improvement*, *Ellen*, and *Grace Under Fire*; like *Roseanne*, these series were initially driven by the personality and comedy style of their respective stand-up stars, although in the case of *Roseanne*, creative development credit was a point of deep contention in its first season (Barr 2011). *Buffy the Vampire Slayer* was created and shaped by Whedon, even in its later seasons when he took a less active role (Q 138).

Despite these differences, the portrayal of the reality of the corporate fast food industry remains fairly unchanged between the two series. As social commentators such as Shipler (2005) and Barbara Ehrenreich (2001), have addressed, even during economic booms, those at the lower end of the economic, educational, and social ladder are often left behind. While analyses of corporate culture in both *Roseanne* and *Buffy* are limited compared to the other series examined in this work—in neither instance are they a continued driving force in the narrative, as they are in *Angel*, *Firefly*, and *Dollhouse*—the corporate conspiracy of low wage and unappreciated work is much closer to the quotidian reality of many of the series' viewers.

CHAPTER THREE

# *Who Owns the Show?*
## *The Avengers, Agents of S.H.I.E.L.D. and Marvel vs. Mutant Enemy*

Before both *Avengers* films and each episode of the series Marvel's *Agents of S.H.I.E.L.D.*, *Luke Cage*, *Daredevil*, *Iron Fist*, and *Jessica Jones*, is approximately a 20-second animated logo for Marvel, featuring pages from its decades of comic book production, and glimpses of the iconic heroes and superheroes it created, such as Iron Man, Nick Fury, and Captain America. While Whedon's other projects, such as *Buffy the Vampire Slayer* and *Dollhouse*, ended with the animated "card" for Mutant Enemy (Whedon's production company), no other Mutant Enemy production foregrounds itself (i.e., "Mutant Enemy presents..."). It is a not-so-subtle reminder that, even if Whedon serves as writer/director (*The Avengers/The Avengers: Age of Ultron*) or executive producer (*Agents of S.H.I.E.L.D.*), the property itself belongs primarily to Marvel studios. Whedon has since left Marvel, indicating numerous issues with his tenure there, including particular requirements within both films to shoehorn in certain scenes and characters, despite whether they "fit" into the story, in order to set up the greater Marvel Cinematic Universe (MCU) series of films (Keyes 2015).

In essence, the Marvel "brand," which extends across multiple platforms (and decades), is the driving force behind both the MCU and the associated series (*Jessica Jones*, *Luke Cage*, *Daredevil*, *Agent Carter*, *Iron Fist*, and *Agents of S.H.I.E.L.D.*). Both Matthew Pateman and I have written separately on the tensions between the Whedon brand and the Fox brand as exemplified by the studios' treatment of Whedon's short-lived series *Firefly*, with Pateman in particular focusing on Fox's desire for a "franchisable" property (Pateman 153-158), along the lines of Whedon's earlier series *Buffy the Vampire Slayer* and its spin-off *Angel*, two series that themselves are not wholly owned by Mutant Enemy; Fran and Kaz Kuzui, who produced and directed the original *Buffy* film, retain rights to both. This became something of an issue when it was announced the Kuzuis were seeking to reboot the series as a feature film (Kit 2009), without Whedon's involvement, a move that angered Whedon's fans (Holmes 2009; Anders 2010).

While there are some similarities that I will tease out on the course of this analysis, the relationship between Brand Whedon and Brand Marvel is not, in fact, a partnership of equals. While *The Avengers* films and *Agents of S.H.I.E.L.D.* offer certain aspects that have come to be associated with the Whedon brand, including "a kick-ass heroine; a certain genre playfulness and humour ... and a performance or questioning of identity that is at times quite serious and at others playful" (Abbott et al. 421–422), Whedon and company also must abide by the strictures imposed by Marvel, including the direction of the overarching MCU narrative for both the films and the associated television series.

While Whedon was at the forefront of the two *Avengers* films, *Agents of S.H.I.E.L.D.* seemingly has only limited involvement of Joss (his brother, Jed, and sister-in-law, Maurissa, serve as showrunners). Yet it is vital to look at both the films and the television show as both a part of the greater MCU and as a Whedon-associated property. While the previous chapters are focused primarily on particular series'/episodes' narrative in sociopolitical context, this chapter will also turn its gaze outward, to the ways in which both films and series operate with the Disney/Marvel corporate structure and its focus on branding.

Thus, in this analysis, I will examining not only the ways in which corporations are portrayed within the Marvel/Whedon texts, but also the way in which Marvel operates as one of the corporations that are so strongly vilified in many of Whedon's other properties, including the aforementioned directing of narrative, the controversy over the lack of Black Widow action figure as an erasure of female fans, and the ways in which its film directors, including Jon Favreau, Kenneth Branaugh, and Whedon himself are commodified and absorbed into the Marvel corporate structure.

Timothy Todreas asserts that branding is "a product that is differentiated from its competition by means of a design, name, mark, image, or a combination of any or all of these" (Todreas 173), which provides a good basic definition. That being said, I am following on Celia Lury's definition of a brand as "a set of relations between products or services" (Lury 1). Lury leaves this definition deliberately open-ended, because of the very intangible nature of the concept of branding, which seeks to create association between one thing and another. She then explicates the various ways in which these relations operate, are managed (by producers and consumers), and organized "in time and space" (Lury 2). In that respect, I am using Lury's definition as Lury does, which is as a building block to examine the operations, management, and organization of branding, particularly the many levels—economic, generic, quality, industrial—through which a series or network can draw its brand identity. While the overarching brand of, for example, a network is germane to which programs they air, the 2000s and beyond clearly disinterred series them from their broadcast context, creating, as Simone Murray argues, a shift from network and their programs as "household brands" to a "house of brands" (Murray 422), thus appealing to multiple niche audiences, building brand equity for multiple entities within the media conglomerates (Johnson 7), and "structur[ing] and stabiliz[ing]] global markets" (Grainge 6). As Barbara Selznick argues: "The brand filter employed by a network necessarily shapes the programmes that the network airs. Programming serves, like other forms of branding, to develop a network identity for both viewers and industry participants. In the mobile and portable post-network era, television shows—that are branded, sold internationally, and licensed to other manufacturers—are no longer merely what airs between commercials, but are now profitable intellectual property" (Selznick 183).

This is particularly apparent within streaming services such as Netflix and Amazon; not only do they provide broadcast and cable programming commercial free, but their original programming is both created to air sans commercials, and operate as a way to build these services' "house of brands." Indeed, given that the majority of the MCU television properties—*Luke Cage, Jessica Jones, Daredevil, Iron Fist*, and the forthcoming *The Defenders*, and *The Punisher*—have or will air on Netflix, Netflix seems to be outstripping the ABC network as Marvel's "house of brands." This is in direct contrast to the DC Comics television universe, of which five of its seven series—*Arrow, The Flash, Supergirl, iZombie*, and *Legends of Tomorrow*—air on the broadcast CW network. (*Gotham* and *Lucifer* air on Fox.) Indeed, four of the aforementioned series are connected to or spun off of the series *Arrow* (*The Flash, Supergirl*, and *Legends of Tomorrow*) and the CW has offered at least two cross-over events, one involving all four "Arrowverse" series; *Lucifer* and *iZombie* were developed from the more adult-oriented DC Vertigo comics imprint, and thus were excluded from those particular events. In essence, of the 11 dramas the CW currently airs, more than half feature characters from the DC comics universe, meaning that DC Comics represent the overarching identity of the network, despite the presence of non–DC series such as *Supernatural* or *Riverdale* (based on the *Archie* comic series).

For Marvel, however, neither the ABC nor the Netflix series, in fact, represent their first foray into either live-action television or an extended television universe; 1977 saw the debut of two series: *The Amazing Spider Man* (1977–1978) and *The Incredible Hulk* (1977–1982). While *The Amazing Spider Man* only last two short seasons and was widely considered to be poorly made and acted (Foster 2017), *The Incredible Hulk* was more successful; it ran for five seasons on CBS, as well as three follow-up television movies on NBC. Further, the television films, besides closing out the series narrative, also served as back-door pilots (that is, an episode of an existing series that features tie-in characters that are intended to be spun off into their own series) for ultimately unproduced *Thor* (O'Connor 1988) and *Daredevil* series. The third and final *Hulk* TV movie, "Death of the Incredible Hulk," was originally slated to feature both She-Hulk and Iron Man, who would then also be spun off into new series; however, star Bill Bixby's failing health made the film "a swansong" for the actor rather than an opportunity to franchise (McCoy 2011).

Perhaps given the respective lack of competition for viewer attention in the late 1970s—cable had yet to emerge as a significant force, home video was a decade away from widespread domestic use, and the Internet was still ARPANET—branding these series as explicitly "Marvel" was clearly deemed as unnecessary; *The Incredible Hulk*'s opening credits instead consisted of, by modern standards, a lengthy opening narration/origin story, presumably to continually catch up new viewers as to the series' background; in an era when personal archiving of series was mostly unheard of (see Kompare 335–60 for analysis of the shift in this practice with the introduction of DVD), and reruns the main venue for catching up on missed episodes, sequences such as this were a simple way for new or occasional viewers to catch up on the limited amount of serialization such series engaged in. It is equally as likely that CBS, which aired both Marvel series, did not want to brand itself as the "comic book" network. Such an action was similar to what was known as the "rural purge" (Hoyt 2004), in which CBS (as well as other networks) cancelled series such as *Mayberry RFD*, *Gunsmoke*, *The Beverly Hillbillies*, and *Hee-Haw*, known by some as "hayseed TV" (Fahri 2004) in favor of series deemed more socially relevant or urban (*All in the Family*, *The Mary Tyler Moore Show*); CBS in particular no longer wished to be branded as the "Country Broadcasting System" (Bedell 55). While branding did not assume the kind of prominence in the early 1970s as it has for contemporary programs and networks, audience and advertiser perception has always been television's focus.

The importance of branding to studios and networks is almost absurdly manifest within Marvel. Unlike the earlier Spider Man and Hulk series, the contemporary films and series under Marvel's corporate umbrella are clearly considered "profitable intellectual property" for which they wish to claim ownership. In that sense, the presence and length of the Marvel title card across the contemporary films, series, and even ancillary materials, such as featurettes and gag reels, underscores Marvel's ownership above all other contributors.

For television, the spring "upfront" presentation—in which networks present their fall schedules to advertisers—represents an ideal venue for networks to offer advertisers a particular brand identity (Curtin and Shuttac 48). The Upfronts provide an opportunity to examine "industry priorities, practices, and strategies of internal promotion" (Lotz 4), a proving ground for a broadcast network's branding strategy that can thus be migrated to viewers. In her analysis of the May 2003 upfront presentations, Amanda Lotz analyses the promotional strategies enlisted to introduce the first audience (advertisers) to programs; they are, she argues, inherently different from the branding strategies used to promote them to viewers. That is, they "make apparent the commodity status of the audience" as well as create "buzz," and, most importantly, "determine the textual forms that circulate" within the culture (Lotz 5–6). Examining these events can thus reveal "the complicated range of promotional efforts used to construct a perception of a network's programming, mission, and brand position" (Lotz 7) for the most important, initial audiences: advertisers.

Depending on the success or failure of the previous year, this brand identity can shift regularly, can assume a proactive ("we're number one among teens") or defensive (explaining away failures, pushing new and different programs) posture (Curtin and Shuttac 48). Thus the difficulties in broadcast branding are not just in their necessarily disparate offerings but also in the need to produce valued audiences year after year, as advertising prices can depend on these numbers. Further, as Johnson argues, the fact that many programs are co-produced by different companies means that a series can build the "brand equity" of a range of different entities (Johnson 7). With regard to Marvel, and given the numerous outlets on which components of the MCU are available (film, television, streaming), it is clear their primary goal is to build Marvel's brand equity above that of directors, producers, networks, or stars.

Paul Grainge argues that "branding assumed new currency in the attempt to manage the relationship between products and consumers and to structure and stabilize global markets" (6). Thus, his work, blending textual and industrial analyses, examines how the film industry adjusted itself, using various branding practices, to economic and technological shifts, in order to "better [understand] the contingencies of branding as a discursive and material practice" (Grainge 8). Grainge's engagement with the "politics" of branding in Hollywood films is also operative within television. Grainge separates these into three main points: the politics of commercial obviousness (that is, using the text to comment on the context of production); the politics of corporate obfuscation (i.e., using branding and promotion to distance a media work from its corporate genesis[1]); and the politics of global homogenization, through the lens of entertainment complexes and film exhibition (111). While questions of exhibition are obviously different with regards to television, both "commercial obviousness" and "global homogenization" are highly relevant entry points for examining the politics of the MCU's branding. Catherine Johnson's analysis asserts that "the programme as brand can also be understood to exist beyond the moment of transmission, and hence to transcend and exist separately from the network as brand" (Johnson 20). While Johnson was specifically addressing the exportation of HBO programs to Channel 4/E4 in the United Kingdom, I argue that her analysis is equally relevant with regard to the disbursement of the MCU across multiple platforms; however, I would assert that the individual programs' brand (of which the Netflix series share darker themes than the series developed for network television) are subordinated to the overarching Marvel brand; it is that brand that "transcend[s] and exist[s] separately" from the networks or streaming services on which the series appear.

Further, John Caldwell's analysis of the rise in available ancillary material is also germane to the "politics of commercial obviousness" within the context of television. He argues that the media industry is using ancillary products to offer "inside material" on media processes in order to "mediate knowledge" about the media industry for the viewer; in essence, taking control of the audiences' readings or perceptions of the text, as well as animating the audience into "consumer activity" in order to add value to the series (Caldwell 117–118), such as buying DVDs or action figures. (Note the aforementioned branding of even ancillary material such as gag reels.) Yet, in terms of Grainge and Caldwell's arguments, when applied to the relationship between Whedon and Marvel, can also cut in the other direction. That is, the text itself can use Griange's "politics of commercial obviousness" to critique its corporate genesis. This takes different forms depending on the medium. In this way, the Whedon-helmed films and associated series (*Agents of S.H.I.E.L.D.*) can comment on the corporate chains in which they struggle, something that the series *Angel* did quite explicitly in the episode "Smile Time," airing just as the series cancellation was announced, which is worth touching on briefly here. In that instance, the episode revolved around a failing children's series for which the team discovers its creator, Gregor Framkin (played by David Fury, one of Whedon's stable of writers) made a deal with a group of demons (disguised as puppets) to keep it on the air. While this deal made the series a number one show for its timeslot, said demons had total control over both its audience (children, from whom they sucked their life forces) and Framkin. In a scene both amusing and horrifying, the episode reveals that the puppets are literally pulling Framkin's strings: head puppet Polo (Victor Yerrid) has his hand up Framkin's back to make him talk.

This turn is rife with metanarrative commentary. First, the concept of making deals: this is the same episode in which Gunn, as mentioned in chapter one, makes a deal to keep the legal knowledge given to him by the firm, an action that results in Fred's death. Like Framkin, Gunn knew there would be consequences, but was clearly unaware of the ways in which these particular deals undermine both his body and his ethics, as they do Framkin's; the children Framkin wished to entertain were victimized by these demonic puppets stealing their life forces. Second, the fact that Angel himself is also turned into a puppet offers a dual commentary on both the diagetic narrative situation—Angel's sense that Wolfram and Hart have turned him into a tool and he has little control—as well as Whedon's own frustration at his own strings being pulled by the network with which he made his own deal (revising the series premise to gain another season). That the second Whedon-helmed *Avengers* film also touches on the idea of the Avengers themselves as "puppets"—going so far as to use the Disney (who owns Marvel) song "I've Got No Strings" to score the official trailer—may indicate that Whedon was also feeling a similar pull from Marvel Studios.

For the *Avengers* films, the subtextual commentary is most obvious in the good intentions/bad results of the actions of Stark Industries. In *Agents of S.H.I.E.L.D.*, these divisions are less grey, with at least two instances of corporations/industrialists in league with Hydra, the Nazi-infused nemesis of the Strategic Homeland Intervention, Enforcement, and Logistics Division (S.H.I.E.L.D.), a counter-terrorism/espionage-related governmental agency within the Marvel canon. As will be addressed in this chapter, the revelation in the first season of the series that Hydra had long infiltrated S.H.I.E.L.D. (a plot first introduced in the film *Captain America: The Winter Soldier*) speaks to the unholy alliance between the corporate world and the U.S. government. A later season also takes up a similar plot to that of the second *Avengers* film, which will be addressed below. Moving out to the "real world," both the Whedon-helmed *Avengers* films and *Agents of S.H.I.E.L.D.* can posit Marvel as the "big bad," using the avatars of Stark Industries and Hydra as different sides of the same problematic, branded coin.

## *"I want a suit of armor around the world": The Badness of Trying to Do the Right Thing*

One of the early scenes in the first *Avengers* film features billionaire inventor/CEO Tony Stark (Robert Downey, Jr.) using alien technology to power his building; a green energy initiative that guarantees his building uses no fossil fuels. A noble goal for the 21st century, certainly, but Stark's real goal is revealed almost immediately, when the first indication it is working is the lighting of the word "Stark" on the side of the building. Not unlike Donald Trump, this moment seems to suggest that Stark's first instinct is to brand everything with his name, a desire that will have dire consequences in *Avengers: Age of Ultron*. Such a maneuver is not uncharacteristic to how Stark is portrayed in the films leading up to *The Avengers*; *Iron Man 2*, with its subplot of Stark legally battling the U.S. government because of his refusal to turn over the weaponized Iron Man technology, has a undeniable libertarian streak (something P. Gardner Goldsmith also applies to Whedon's series *Firefly* [Goldsmith 55–65]). At best, Stark's work here on green energy could be characterized as enlightened self-interest, making his distaste with the film's reveal that S.H.I.E.L.D. is using of the same technology to build weapons more than a little disingenuous.

Throughout the first half of the film, in fact, Stark himself emphasizes how he is "volatile, self-obsessed, and does not play well with others"; as a self-proclaimed "genius billionaire playboy philanthropist," he believes he has both the intelligence and the resources to operate (mostly) on his own. His shift to green energy rather than the arms/munitions development that is responsible for his family's wealth, is further underscored, as Samira Nadkarni argues, by the fact that "Stark's own market value is largely predicated on the amassed wealth from this previous arms dealing, and later, from the continued creation of Iron Man suits and his deliberate use of them as a visible advertisement for Stark Industries" (Nadkarni 2018). In essence, the existence of Iron Man, and the fact that, unlike superheroes such as Batman or Superman, Stark outs himself as the man in the suit at the conclusion of the first film, makes Iron Man an ongoing "brand ambassador" for Stark Industries itself.

On the macro level, the fact that the current MCU's origins start with the release of *Iron Man* in 2008 means that both diegetically and extradiagetically, Iron Man/Tony Stark serves this ambassadorial function for both Stark Industries and the MCU. Marvel Studios, created in 2005 with funding from Merrill Lynch, one of the players in the subprime mortgage crisis that created the late-aughts Great Recession, was focused on developing films with their existing properties that had not been licensed to other studios (such as Spider-Man to Sony, or The X-Men to 20th Century Fox) for which they would assert creative control and reap the majority of profits (Waxman 2007). This funding from Merrill Lynch offers another parallel to Nadkarni's argument regarding Stark Industries' funding. Much as Stark's munitions profits fund not only his green energy initiative, but, as is revealed in *Avengers: Age of Ultron*, the Avengers Initiative itself (providing training and transportation for the individual Avengers, and humanitarian relief for countries affected by alien invasions), so Marvel's films are financed with the profits from the market crash and sub-prime speculation that threw the global economy into a tailspin and rendered millions homeless and/or bankrupt (McLean and Nocera 2011).

The blending of the problematic genesis of Stark's fortune, his access to technology and money, and his belief that he is brilliant enough to solve any problem by combining these particular elements leads to the events of *Avengers: Age of Ultron*, in which Stark uses alien technology, combined with his own created artificial intelligence (J.A.R.V.I.S. or "Just Another Rather Very Intelligent System"), to create a peace-keeping weapon; what Stark envisions as "a suit of armor around the world." Operating from what appears to be some level of post-traumatic stress to previous events (he nearly dies in *The Avengers* after carrying a missile into a wormhole), exacerbated by an implanted vision of a future in which the world (as well as all of the Avengers) is destroyed, is what leads Stark to unintentionally create Ultron (James Spader), who interprets Stark's desire for peace as only achievable through domination and war; Ultron determines that humans are responsible for war, and thus must be exterminated. Stark proceeds with this project despite the concerns expressed by others, most notably Steve Rogers/Captain America (Chris Pine), who experienced first-hand the Second World War. "Every time someone tries to end a war before it starts, innocent people die," he tells Stark, a moment that does seem to penetrate, albeit too late to avoid the fallout from Stark's creation.

Yet the creation of Ultron is not the only Stark-related fallout; the alliance of two super-powered individuals—Wanda Maximoff/Scarlet Witch (Elizabeth Olsen) and Pietro Maximoff/Quicksilver (Aaron Taylor-Johnson)—with Ultron is directly related to Stark's arms and munitions sales and his penchant for branding; as children, the Maximoff siblings' parents were killed and the pair held hostage by the presence of a Stark-labeled, unexploded missal, nearly starving to death before they were discovered and rescued. The film implies that they allowed Hydra to create (or enhance) their abilities through experimentation so they would not feel so vulnerable again.

My argument here is not to say that the MCU can destroy the earth, but rather to draw a comparison between the ubiquity of Stark's branding and the Marvel brand, as well as company's seemingly dismissive attitude towards many of those who have worked under the Marvel umbrella. In the 8 years since the debut of *Iron Man*, the MCU has made $2.43 billion from the 13 films that have been released thus far. Yet, Whedon has been quoted as saying that he actually made more money with his self-financed Internet musical *Dr. Horrible's Sing-Along Blog* than as director of the first *Avengers* film (Littleton 2015). Numerous reports have surfaced as to the difficulty of working within the Marvel system, with directors dropping out and being replaced at an alarming pace (Keyes 2011); the most notable was Edgar Wright, who'd been working on the *Ant-Man* script for more than a decade, only to drop out just as filming commenced (Keyes 2014). While Wright's "quirky" vision of the film was appropriate for Marvel before the success of films such as *Iron Man* and *Captain America: The First Avenger*, the Marvel of 2014 was less likely to take risks, ordering numerous rewrites without input from Wright (Masters and Kit 2014).

In an interview with *Wired* magazine, Whedon confirmed that Marvel had particular guidelines as to how the first *Avengers* film should be structured and what (and who) precisely should be included (Rogers 2012). Working under particular strictures is not unfamiliar to a writer who has worked on network television; with regard to, as per example, the burgeoning relationship between Willow and Tara Maclay (Amber Benson) on *Buffy*, the network's constraints on what could be shown were a challenge Whedon accepted: "There are things the network will not allow us to show.... Restrictions are often a writer's best friend—they force him to be CREATIVE" (Whedon 2002).

There were indications, however, that Marvel's restrictions were tiring. Whedon had to fight to include the character of Black Widow (Scarlett

Johansson) in the first *Avengers* film, and Marvel itself excluded the character from the product lines, claiming that boys (whom they still wrongly assume are the primary purchasers of action figures; 52 percent of their audience is female) would not buy female figures, as well as releasing related t-shirts in which the male characters were labeled "Hero" and Black Widow, "Needs a Hero" (Romano 2015). The mixed critical reception to *The Avengers: Age of Ultron* (*Avengers: Age of Ultron*, Rotten Tomatoes), which required Whedon to introduce three new characters—the Maximoff twins and new Avenger Vision (Paul Bettany)—and set up the next phase of Marvel films, seemingly bespeaks of creative exhaustion rather than creative challenge on Whedon's part.

It is thus clear that whether creating entertainment (Marvel) or "peace in our time" (Tony Stark), both Marvel and Stark want the world to know precisely who is responsible for it; they are "defining the contours of what the brand can mean," so that "consumers are free to produce the shared meanings and social relations that the branded good will help create in their life" (Arvidsson 245). The lengthy title cards that begins each Marvel product, the protective suits of armor that look precisely like the well-known Iron Man suits, let both audiences and the diagetic world of the MCU know who precisely is in charge of the narrative. The promotional materials for the first *Avengers* film emphasized Marvel over Whedon, despite their assertions that Whedon was chosen precisely for his cult and comic credibility (Rogers 2012), and could (theoretically) entice an audience segment that would attend because of Whedon rather than Marvel.

Yet, the second *Avengers* film directly problematizes both Stark's and Marvel's branding through Stark's peacekeeping desires and actions. The fact that Stark's plan to create peace, already fundamentally flawed, is further undermined by the actions of two who were directly affected by what created Stark's fortune in the first place (weapons and munitions) means that where the money came from cannot be so easily erased or fixed. Extending that outward into Marvel's own genesis, their initial funding from Merrill Lynch could, in some respects, implicate them in the backlash of the sub-prime mortgage crisis and subsequent recession; the films are thus funded by the broken lives of those on the front lines of the recession's consequences. On a narrative level, this resonates with the significant plot turn near the end of the first season of *Agents of S.H.I.E.L.D.*, in which it is revealed that the agency had been long been infiltrated and its resources and goals shaped the very organization it had been developed to fight: its nemesis Hydra.

## Hydra Is S.H.I.E.L.D. Is Hydra, or What's in a Logo?

Near the end of a struggling first season of *Agents of S.H.I.E.L.D.*, the debut of the film *Captain America: The Winter Soldier* finally offered the series an arc along the lines of Whedon's earlier series.[2] In *The Winter Soldier*, it was revealed that Hydra, the long-time nemesis of S.H.I.E.L.D., had infiltrated the organization decades earlier in an attempt to warp it to its own ends. To emphasize this takeover, the episode "Turn, Turn, Turn" (1.17) replaces the S.H.I.E.L.D. logo that appears at the final commercial break of each episode with the Hydra logo. (This replacement occurs again in season four, in which an alternate reality has the series characters working for Hydra ("What If..." [4.16].) The agency was discredited and disbanded, as Hydra operatives carried out terroristic acts in the name of S.H.I.E.L.D. ("A Hen in the Wolf House" 2.5); it is not until the fourth season ("Uprising" 4.3) that S.H.I.E.L.D. is again acknowledged as a functioning governmental agency. In the second season, it must operate primarily under the radar, as the agency and its operatives are considered enemies of the state; in season three, it operates as a shadow agency under the aegis of the Advanced Threat Containment Unit (ATCU), which is also later revealed to have been created by the remaining members of Hydra, most notably industrialist Gideon Malick (Powers Boothe), first seen in *The Avengers* as a member of the World Security Council advising Nick Fury (Samuel L. Jackson), and advisor to the president within *Agents of S.H.I.E.L.D.* These multi-level infiltrations of a single entity operate as Hydra's modus operandi; their logo (or brand) of the many-headed mythical creature underscores their precise methods, with the motto "If a head is cut off, two more will take its place."

Shatley Q argues that *Agents of S.H.I.E.L.D.*, more so than other Whedon properties, represents Whedon's "translating real-world geopolitic into the fictive landscape" (Q 79), particularly that of governmental surveillance and counter-terrorism efforts, although I would argue that it does no more than other Whedon series have done. Season four of *Buffy* introduced the Initiative, a military project that sought to "harness the otherworldly threat" for its own ends. The use of surveillance is highly associated with the Initiative; not only does the Initiative require its employees to undergo facial and voice recognition to access their facility, but "The I in Team" (4.13) reveals that Initiative head Maggie Walsh (Lindsey Crouse) monitors her soldiers with hidden cameras, including in their bedrooms; she is show spying on Initiative soldier Riley (Marc Blucas) during an intimate moment with Buffy, leading her to make an attempt on Buffy's life. This action, as Samira Nadkarni points out, positions Walsh her as one of the Whedonverses' "transgressive mothers" (89), a point I will return to in chapter eight. On *Angel*, the corporate law firm Wolfram and Hart enacts digital surveillance on Angel Investigations headquarters ("That Vision Thing" 3.2), as well as those associated with it ("Slouching Towards Bethlehem" 4.4). While this type of surveillance was limited in *Firefly*, the follow-up film *Serenity* both directly addressed the ways in which the Alliance monitors the population and engaged with those who subvert it. As examined in chapter one, the Alliance uses embedded code in an advertisement to trigger River's violent impulses, tapping into the security feed of the bar in which the violence occurred. More importantly, the crew exposes the Alliance's nefarious cover-up on the planet Miranda by broadcasting a video exposing their crimes across the galaxy, using the equipment of hacker Mr. Universe (David Krumholtz). Whedon's short-lived series *Dollhouse*, of course, is a place in which nearly everything is monitored; even the showers the Actives use are under surveillance. The only significant difference is that S.H.I.E.L.D. represents the first governmental agency to serve as the primary setting for both characters and narrative action.

The first season also features the machinations of Ian Quinn (David Conrad), CEO of Quinn Worldwide, a megacorporation that funds many of Hydra's initiatives throughout the season. Quinn, in many respects, acts as both a caricature and an indictment of a selfish, bottom-line obsessed CEO in the Friedman vein; at no point do his more nefarious actions, including his near-fatal shooting of S.H.I.E.L.D. agent Skye/Daisy (Chloe Bennet) in the episode "T.R.A.C.K.S." (1.13) seem to trouble his conscience, nor is he a true believer in Hydra's mission—as are, to a limited extent, S.H.I.E.L.D. double agents Grant Ward (Brett Dalton) and John Garrett (Bill Paxton)—he chooses self-preservation over ideology in every instance. While he claims that certain actions, such as shooting Skye, were made under duress, it does not keep him from attempting to negotiate with the Department of Defense for a large government contract to create "super soldiers" using technologies he has developed and/or appropriated ("Beginning of the End" 1.22). With Quinn's focus on selling "security" in troubled times, his corporate actions are in keeping with similar real-world corporate deals following September 11, 2001, when defense contractors and security corporations were given no-bid contracts to provide surveillance and weapon technology in the name of national security (Klein 299–308). It also presages the narrative in *Age of Ultron*; while

Stark's action, as a point of view character, comes across as more understandable, Quinn is essentially promising the same thing: "a suit of armor around the world"; his super soldiers would be impervious to pain and nearly unkillable, allowing a reduction in military personnel. Unlike Stark, however, who, as pointed out above, seems to operate from a place of fear and desire to help (however misguided), Quinn's sole motivation seems to be the lucrative government contract he will receive for developing this "suit of armor." This characterization is repeated in the character of Malick in season three, during which it is revealed that he betrayed his own brother to avoid his family's near-religious crusade to rescue a creature from another dimension that his Hydra faction had worshipped for centuries ("Paradise Lost" 3.16); his own self-interest was more important than even family bonds.

Minus any obvious corporate trappings, the specter of developing these types of "peacekeeping" initiatives idea is revisited in season four of *Agents of S.H.I.E.L.D.*, with scientist Dr. Holden Radcliffe's (John Hannah) development of a "life model decoy" (that is, androids) to protect those in the field—the LMDs are programmed to take any means necessary to preserve human life—prompting S.H.I.E.L.D. director Jeffrey Mace (Jason O'Mara) to say, with some degree of frustration: "Doesn't anyone remember Ultron?" ("Laws of Inferno Dynamics" 4.8).

Mace's words are not just a clever callback to the MCU; as the plot progressed, it became clear that the LMD Aida (Mallory Jansen) was perhaps even a greater danger than Ultron. Programmed to protect at any cost, and infused with the near-mystical power of a text called The Darkhold, Aida interprets (alongside Dr. Radcliffe) safety as creating an alternate reality (known as "The Framework") in which those inside live an existence that does not include their greatest regret. That this is achieved by either killing or putting into a coma-like sleep the physical bodies of those inserted within it does not strike Aida as problematic, nor does she concern herself with issues of consent or free will; with few exceptions, none of those in The Framework are there by choice. In this respect, the series was able to tease out the implications of the interpretive differences between human perception and cognition with that of an artificial intelligence, in a way that *Age of Ultron* was unable to do in its shorter running time.

In something of a shift from the earlier machinations of Quinn in season one, Radcliffe is not tied to a corporation; indeed, his work and outlook on human enhancement was considered too radical for the corporation he worked for, and he was fired. Instead, the narrative reveals that Radcliffe's motives for creating both Aida and the Framework are intensely personal; he had been seeking a way to cure the woman he loved of a terminal brain tumor. When conventional medicine failed to find a solution, he offers her a place within his created alternate reality; her body will die, but her consciousness will live forever ("BOOM" 4.14). (The idea of individual consciousness living beyond the death of the physical body was also a significant feature of Whedon's earlier series *Dollhouse*, with apocalyptic results, as will be examined below.)

The series does offer some Whedon-esque qualities, in particular a cast that features several equally, if differently, strong, intelligent, and capable female characters: a scientist (Jemma Simmons [Elizabeth Henstridge]), a hacker (Skye/Daisy), a spy/biologist (Bobbi Morse [Adrianne Palicki]), and pilot/muscle Melinda May (Ming Na-Wen). Lorna Jowett points out that the casting itself bears hallmarks of the "Whedon brand"; most notably, the casting of Whedon regulars such as J. August Richards (*Angel*) as Mike Peterson/Deathlok (multiple episodes); Ron Glass (*Firefly*) as Dr Streiten ("Pilot" 1.1; "The Magical Place" 1.11); Amy Acker (*Angel/Dollhouse*) as Coulson's love interest Audrey Nathan ("The Only Light in the Darkness" 1.20); and Patton Oswalt (*Dollhouse*) as brothers Billy, Sam, Thurston, and Eric Koenig (multiple episodes), and seemingly deliberate casting of UK actors (all of Whedon's series, with the exception of *Firefly*, have featured actors either from the United Kingdom or spent a significant amount of time there) (Abbott et al. 422).

Further, the series offers a repudiation of, as Scott Interrante argues, traditional masculinity through the valorization of the more "beta" qualities of scientist Leo Fitz (Iain Caestecker) as opposed to the more traditional alpha qualities of Agent Grant Ward, who is later revealed to be working for Hydra; Interrante argues that this particular betrayal proves that Fitz's version of masculinity is preferable (Interrante 84–89). It also avoids certain characterization traps, including the trope of having a female character sympathize with or fall for the "bad guy" because of his tortured past, despite his current actions. (While season six of *Buffy* features a subplot in which the newly resurrected slayer embarks on a sexual relationship with "bad boy" vampire Spike [James Marsters], the narrative makes it obvious that this only occurs because of Buffy's trauma and depression upon being resurrected.) When Ward is revealed as a traitor, Skye/Daisy rejects all of his attempts to play upon her sympathy; her disgust with him even seems elevated because of the low-key flirtation and understanding between the two throughout the first season. Like many (if not all) of Whedon's series, the show consistently passes the Bechdel test.

In terms of Whedon's association with Marvel, Leora Hadas analyzes the ways in which Marvel used Whedon's name not to promote *The Avengers*, but rather *Agents of S.H.I.E.L.D.* This makes sense, as Whedon's primary medium has been television, but Hadas goes further, tracing "the writer-director's function in validating the brand extension, acting as the glue that holds the transmedia universe together" (7). That is, Marvel/ABC was clearly banking on Whedon's name as a draw to viewers that might be fans of his earlier work. (Which may have bearing on why many of the early reviewers of the series were harsher than expected; those familiar with Whedon's trademarks would be hard pressed to discover them in *Agents of S.H.I.E.L.D.*'s early episodes.)

Hadas' analysis of the promotion of the TV-associated Whedon brand was written early in *Agents of S.H.I.E.L.D.*' run, although her points with regard to Marvel's use of Whedon's name as brand remain relevant. Hadas points to Whedon's uncredited rewrites of many of the Marvel films leading up to *The Avengers*, as well as promoting *Agents of S.H.I.E.L.D.* as a Whedon-authored text to "establish a tone and style that ties other products ... back to the tremendous success of the 'tent pole' *The Avengers*" (Hadas 10), that is, the studio determined that merely promoting *Agents of S.H.I.E.L.D.* as a Marvel production was not sufficient to draw television audiences (Hadas 11), particularly given that it predated the release of the more critically acclaimed Netflix series, such as *Jessica Jones*. Particularly since the DC comic-created productions, such as *Arrow*, *Gotham*, and *The Flash* had gotten a head start over Marvel in creating successful (read: renewed for multiple seasons) television properties, Marvel certainly seemed to think that touting Whedon as author of *Agents of S.H.I.E.L.D.* would provide an edge over their DC competition.

But is Whedon truly the author? Mary Ellen Iatropoulos contests this idea, indicating that Marvel head Kevin Fiege, as well as the large corpus of Marvel comics, could claim a share of the vision for both *The Avengers* films and *Agents of S.H.I.E.L.D.* (72), certainly to a greater extent than other Whedon-helmed series, which regular Whedon writer Jane Espenson asserts were more hands-on for Whedon than *Agents of S.H.I.E.L.D.* appears to be (Q 138). Iatropoulos does note that Whedon's productions are known to be collaborative ventures, both in the writing room and on the set. "Authorship is not just about the authoring acts of one individual, but rather is a part of a collaborative, meaning-making process" (72). Somewhat counter to Iatropolous' argument, Abbott contends that Whedon himself is "as much an object of fandom as *Buffy*, *Angel*, and *Firefly*— perhaps more so now as he is the link between these shows as well as the many productions and transmedia tie-ins that have followed. His work—no matter how collaborative—is, therefore, often viewed through the prism of his authorship" (Abbott et al. 422). Jowett agrees, asserting that Whedon "is a single figure who handily embodies the varied characteristics of the Whedon brand, as created in practice by many contributors and different teams" (Abbott et al. 422).

While Hadas acknowledges the roles of others, her argument regarding the centrality of Whedon as brand ambassador for *Agents of S.H.I.E.L.D.* was that Whedon's "authorship stands as a reassurance of viability for this form of transmedia expansion," that "through his presence and the centrality of his authorship Marvel is not merely selling the MCU as a transmedia brand. They are selling a new kind of transmedia storytelling *as part of* the MCU brand [italics in original]" (Hadas 11). There is something hollow in this, however, that Whedon acknowledges, albeit jokingly, in the musical commentary to his Internet series *Dr. Horrible*. Whedon sings about how "Homer's Odyssey" was not subjected to behind-the-scene glimpses and author promotion and test audiences; Homer "is not the story." Whedon's series *Dollhouse* touches on this as well, in the episode "Belle Chose," in which a medievalist college professor discusses how medieval texts also had no concept of the author (2.3)—although Cynthea Masson points out that this was emphatically not the case for the author the professor is discussing: Geoffrey Chaucer (Masson para 12). Yet for Marvel's promotion of *Agents of S.H.I.E.L.D.*, Whedon *is* the story, which not only reduces him to figurehead, but seems to ignores the contributions of the actual showrunners and writers in a way that Whedon's other series did not; Whedon frequently acknowledged the contributions of his coworkers (both writers and crew) in multiple venues, including interviews and DVD commentaries. In four seasons of *Agents of S.H.I.E.L.D.*, Whedon has written a single episode ("Pilot" 1.1), and yet, as Hadas points out, Marvel very purposefully puts him front and center, "as a figure for fandom to rally around following the medium transition" (Hadas 13), rather than actual showrunners Jed Whedon and Maurissa Tanchereon. Bronwen Calvert has a more positive reading of this relationship, however, arguing that reads such positioning renders "the Whedon brand as potentially distinct from Whedon authorship ... and is perhaps the most transparent example yet of the Whedon brand as founded on teamwork and creative collaboration" (Abbott et al. 429). In this respect, one could view Whedon's influence as an inspiration for the staff of *Agents of S.H.I.E.L.D.*, rather than merely representing an empty suit.

As stated above, its narrative must be in service to the MCU, and by extension, the Marvel brand that is so prominently displayed at the start of each episode. Numerous reviewers of the series' first season complained of its slow pace, meandering plots, and lack of Whedon's signature style (Sternako 2013; Valentine 2014; Goldman 2014), but the pace and plot had to be subordinated the MCU; as stated above, it was only after the April 2014 release of *Captain America: The Winter Soldier*, that the major narrative arc of the season could be revealed, giving the 15 episodes that preceded it the impression of marking time. On the other hand, however, most debut series are not giving the majority of a television season to draw in viewers; clearly *Agents of S.H.I.E.L.D.* benefitted from being under the Marvel umbrella in that respect. Calvert also points out that all of Whedon's previous series have used a "slow arc" for the narratives; in which early episodes are tasked with building up the season-length or longer stories (Abbott et al. 428).

Further, while early press materials and interviews indicated that *Agents of S.H.I.E.L.D.* was part of and would benefit from the larger MCU in terms of crossover with the films (implying certain stars may make appearances within the series [Goldberg 2013]), only Cobie Smolders, who plays Agent Maria Hill in *The Avengers* films, and Samuel L. Jackson, as S.H.I.E.L.D. Director Nick Fury, have appeared on *Agents of S.H.I.E.L.D.—* and both were confined to *Agents of S.H.I.E.L.D.'* first and second seasons. This gives the (perhaps unintentional) impression of *Agents of S.H.I.E.L.D.* as the lesser media property, rather than what it is: an opportunity for the MCU to extend and expand upon plots and ideas brought up in the MCU. The lead up to and fallout from *Age of Ultron* was referenced directly in the second season of the series; a psychic sees "men made of metal" raining destruction ("The Dirty Half Dozen" 2.19), and it is revealed that the Coulson was the lead in creating the heli-carrier that rescued thousands at the end of the film ("Scars" 2.20). The linchpin of the plot of the recent *Captain America: Civil War*—i.e., governmental registration of those with superpowers—is one of the major plots of the latter part of the third and beginning of the fourth season of *Agents of S.H.I.E.L.D.*, allowing the implications of such a ruling to resonate beyond the 120-minute running time of the films. Yet the films themselves show no narrative awareness of the events occurring within *Agents of S.H.I.E.L.D.*, from potentially (and literally) earth-shattering events as alien invasions that threaten to turn humans into monsters ("Ascension" 3.22) to even the fact that Coulson (killed in *The Avengers*, but resurrected through alien technology) is still alive.

In this respect, one can see that the MCU, then, prioritizes itself over its broadcast cousin; even the Netflix streaming series, such as *Daredevil* (which, in all fairness, actually was an early Marvel film, although years before Marvel created its own independent studio), are given "Easter egg" moments in the MCU (e.g., the appearance of a truck in *Captain America: Civil War* bears an uncanny resemblance to that driven by Frank Castle/ The Punisher [Jon Bernthal] in the series). Yet, the ongoing storyline of seasons two to four of *Agents of S.H.I.E.L.D.*—that of a worldwide uptick in the presence of "Inhumans" (i.e., those with superpowers granted by the presence of alien DNA) due to an industrial accident—is given no mention within the MCU, even though it relates directly to the plot of *Captain America: Civil War*.

Whedon himself is clearly not unfamiliar with the challenges of working within the corporate media structure; with the exception of *Agents of S.H.I.E.L.D.*, all of Whedon's previous television projects have been developed under 20th Century Fox studios, a studio in which he, at times, had a contentious relationship with regard to the direction of his later series *Firefly* and *Dollhouse*. His public declaration, however, of ceasing to work within the "crushing" system of the MCU (Keyes 2015), is seemingly indicative of an environment in which the brand trumps all, and actors and directors alike are subordinated to its will. If Whedon is the "story" for Marvel, he is only a single chapter.

In the next chapter, I'll examine the ways in which operating within the belly of the corporate beast is examined both from a production and narrative level in *Dollhouse, Dr. Horrible's Sing-Along Blog,* and *The Cabin in the Woods*.

CHAPTER FOUR

## *In the Belly of the Beast*
### Dollhouse, The Cabin in the Woods and Dr. Horrible's Sing-Along Blog

"My nemesis is Captain Hammer. Captain Hammer: Corporate Tool." Thus says Billy (Neil Patrick Harris), aka Doctor Horrible, about the buff, branded "hero" who defends the nameless town in which superheroes and supervillains are known and recognized (and organized; there is an "Evil League of Evil" as well as a "Henchman's Union"). This world looks much like our world; many of the heroes and villains are not seemingly invested with superpowers per se (although there may be some exceptions to this); instead, they have some mental or physical skill that they can use for either their own, or society's, benefit. *The Cabin in the Woods* offers another nameless town with striking similarities to those in the real world; much like *Dr. Horrible*, there are initially only small differences that point to an alternate reality. *Dollhouse*, on the other hand, situates itself quite firmly in the real world; not only does it declare itself as set in modern-day Los Angeles, but also references contemporary events within its text, such as the 2008 election of Barack Obama as the first African American U.S. president ("Omega" 1.12) or the war in Afghanistan ("Stop-Loss" 2.9).

What these three texts share is a particular connection to the corporate world. In both *Cabin* and *Dollhouse*, the characters act within, and/or are acted upon, a corporate environment. *Dr. Horrible's Sing-Along Blog*, on the other hand, owes its existence to the fact that Joss Whedon and company wanted to comment specifically on the entertainment corporation in which television is created.

In this final chapter of part one, then, I'll be examining these three texts in which the corporate structure, both in and outside of the narrative, plays the strongest and most insidious role. Starting with *Dr. Horrible* as a response to corporate media (an extra-diagetic force, rather than directly engaged in the narrative), I'll move on to a deeper examination of both *Cabin* and *Dollhouse*, both of which also engage with deconstructing/subverting the corporate media structure within their separate narrative worlds, represented by their antagonists: The Facility and the Rossum Corporation, respectively. These texts represent the apotheosis of the anticorporate thread within Whedon's work.

## *"And lose we did, impressively": Striking Out with* Dr. Horrible

On November 5, 2007, the Writer's Guild of America (WGA) went on strike, following a breakdown in negotiations with the Alliance of Motion Picture and Television Producers (AMPTP). One of the issues at stake in the strike was the residual payments due writers for both DVD releases and ancillary materials, as well as whether web content (such as webisodes or graphic novels) should be classified as publicity (the AMPTP's position) or content (the WGA's position). With the former, the AMPTP claimed that it had not yet determined the cost-benefit of this additional content; the WGA, having been burned over VHS residuals during the 1987 strike, were determined not to lose the fight over DVD and Internet content residuals (Verrier 2007).

Complicating the issue was the fact that many of the executive producers, such as Greg Daniels of *The Office*, also served as writers on their series, putting them in the unfortunate position of not being able to strike with the writers, nor align themselves with the AMPTP. While showrunners such as David Letterman, who owned the production company for his show (Worldwide Pants), immediately negotiated with the WGA and was back on the air, other series were forced to air their remaining episodes and go off the air (or return with limited staffs, particularly late-night talk shows), meaning that most of the programming between November 5, 2007, and February 12, 2008, was either reruns or reality series (which were not covered under the WGA; another reason for the strike). That this strike occurred during two of the "sweeps" period—that is, when the Nielsen company collects viewing information from a percentage of households (November, February, and May), in order to determine series' popularity and determine advertising prices—was intentional on the WGA's part; networks were forced to refund a significant amount of money to advertisers who were not getting what they paid for, that is, first-run comedy or drama programs (Consoli 2007). By the time the strike ended, it was estimated to have cost $2.5 billion in wages, damages to entertainment-adjacent businesses, and abandoned projects, which was less than the anticipated $5 billion early estimates had given (Lewinski 2008).

Joss Whedon, who at the time of the strike was in talks with actress Eliza Dushku to develop the series that would eventually become *Dollhouse* through her Boston Diva production company (but did not have a series on television at that time), was one of the many writers who used the Internet and fandom to counteract the message in the media regarding the WGA members. When the *New York Times* referred to writer's strike as "having all the trappings of a union protest.... But instead of hard hats and work boots, those at the barricades wore arty glasses and fancy scarves" (Cieply, Barr, and Barnes 2007), Whedon responded to the subtextual dig implied by "trappings" with "Oh my God. Arty glasses and fancy scarves. That is so cute! My head is aflame with images of writers in ruffled collars, silk pantaloons and ribbons upon their buckled shoes.... The entire writers' guild as Leslie Howard in *The Scarlet Pimpernel*. Delicious. Except this is exactly the problem. The easiest tactic is for people to paint writers as namby pamby arty scarfy posers, because it's what most people think even when we're not striking.... (And Hollywood writers are overpaid, scarf-wearing dainties.) It's an easy argument to make. And a hard one to dispute" ("More Joss Strike Talk" 2007). The fact that this dismissive attitude was coming from fellow writers clearly rankled Whedon.

The long-standing website Whedonesque.com, which aggregates continuing coverage of series and actors both created by and/or related to Whedon's work, was, in the days before Twitter, the venue in which Whedon chose to address his fans. In the lead up to the strike, he posted: "I don't think of the studio heads as a bunch of grinning tycoons sitting in a smoke-filled club and drumming their fingers like Montgomery Burns. I know some of those guys. I think they're worried about the future as much as anyone. But they are beholden to their corporations, and that inevitably causes entrenchment and shortsightedness" (Whedon 2007).

As I have striven to show throughout this work, Whedon's portrayal of corporations within his work does, for the most part, offer the type of nuance suggested in terming them "entrenched" and "short-sighted."

Online posting to fans were not Whedon's only arguments or actions regarding the strike; he also sought to prove that online content could be monetized and generate profit in order to undermine one of the AMPTP's central arguments. Out of this desire was born the self-funded, three-part web series *Dr. Horrible's Sing-Along Blog*. The web series debuted for free on July 15, 2008, with Acts 2 and 3 released on July 17 and 18, respectively. In its first week, it was viewed 2.2 million times, crashing the server at drhorrible.com; when it was released on iTunes the following week, it became the number one purchased/downloaded item for the week, and continued to sell briskly when released on the then-new option of print-on-demand DVD. Whedon used his own money to finance the production; collaborated with family members to write the music and lyrics; and both the production staff and actors Neil Patrick Harris, Felicia Day, and Nathan Fillion agreed to participate and forego salaries, with only the promise from Whedon that they would receive something if the musical was financially successful.

As stated in the previous chapter, Whedon claims that the profits from *Dr. Horrible* exceeded what he was paid to direct the first *Avengers* film (as well as uncredited rewrites on other MCU films). While the creation of the musical was construed by Whedon and his associates as an act of protest conceived during the writer's strike, it also generated enough money and views to underline the WGA's claim that Internet content was narrative rather than publicity, and obviously monetizable, even if not before the strike was resolved. While its release pre-dated that of the first *Avengers* film by nearly four years, *Dr. Horrible* origin story, if you will, speaks directly to the challenges of working within a corporate media setting. It seeks to prove that "the old Hollywood power system is unethical, unacceptable, and, in the face of new media and strong fan works, unsustainable" (Williams para 1).

The narrative of the series is the conflict between Billy, or Dr. Horrible ("I have a PhD in Horribleness"), as he prefers to be called, using his brain and technical skills to become a supervillain in the "Evil League of Evil"—the trials and travails of this goal he shares on his video blog (or vlog)—and his nemesis, Captain Hammer (Nathan Fillion), whom he considers to be a "corporate tool" and who frequently thwarts Dr. Horrible's exploits. Not surprisingly, Hammer is always dressed in what seems like his version of "superhero" attire: cargo pants and a t-shirt decorated with a logo in the shape of a hammer; this offers a nice meta-moment: the logo of the "corporate tool" is an actual tool. Yet it is soon revealed that Billy's real goal is to be able to talk to the woman he sees at the local Laundromat, Penny (Felicia Day); as the series opens, he sings about developing a "Freeze Ray" so he can stop time long enough to muster the courage to introduce himself. The first act ends with Billy, in his Dr. Horrible guise, narrowly pulling off a successful heist of "Wonderflonium" (which he'll used to power said freeze ray) while inadvertently both endangering Penny and introducing her to Captain Hammer. Hammer and Penny hit it off, leaving Billy to slink off alone.

Act two opens on a duet between Billy and Penny; Billy sings of his unhappiness over Penny and Hammer developing relationship; Penny sings about her happiness over the same. Despite his loathing for Hammer, the development of Hammer and Penny's relationship seemingly frees Billy to talk and connect with Penny over the frozen yogurt he brings for them to share; this moment of connection, however, is undermined both by the fact that Billy only knows Penny likes the dessert because he's been stalking her, as well as the eventual arrival of Captain Hammer, who clearly notices Billy's affection for Penny and claims he is only interested in her to take her away from his nemesis. Amy Williams points out that while Hammer's sense of entitlement is obvious, Billy/Dr. Horrible is no less problematic: he "believes he *deserves* certain things—respect, success, the girl he has been trying so hard to win. He feels slighted and that the world is against him" (Williams para 34). In this, she draws a cogent parallel between Billy—the picked-on nerd—and some of the recent mass shootings, in which such behavior as Billy/Horrible displays, theft and stalking among them, are ignored as warning signs (Williams para 37). Indeed, the episode ends with Billy fantasizing about killing Captain Hammer, and retreating to his "lair" to plan Hammer's downfall.

The final episode is when everything comes to a head; Billy/Dr. Horrible infiltrates a ribbon cutting/unveiling honoring Captain Hammer's good works—including convincing the mayor to convert an abandoned building into a homeless shelter (Penny's pet cause)—with a death ray. While his plan initially seems to work, freezing Hammer long enough for Dr. Horrible to sing about his prowess as a supervillain, it all falls apart when the freeze ray fails and Hammer grabs the death ray away from him. When fired, however, it explodes, injuring Hammer and killing Penny. The series ends with Hammer retreating and Billy becoming Dr. Horrible permanently, singing about how he's gotten "everything I've ever wanted": "all the cash/all the fame" and entrance into the League; all of which is rendered meaningless due to the cost.

Alyson Buckman has written about how the series itself represents a communal event; not only on the production level—the series was written by brothers Joss, Jed, and Zach Whedon, as well as Jed Whedon's fiancée Maurissa Tancharoen; actors and crews donated their time; and Universal allowed the use of their lot for minimal cost (Vary 2008)—but in the ways it was consumed and publicized by Whedon fans. She compares it to the 19th century serials, arguing that its "individual, non-simultaneous consumption ... still connects to a sense of community" (Buckman 30). While Whedon fans did not fund the project, they were integral to its success. In many ways, the fan mobilization to publicize (and purchase) the self-funded web series presaged the crowd-funding sites such as Kickstarter; in one of Kickstarter's biggest success stories, Rob Thomas (co-showrunner/co-creator of the series *Veronica Mars* and *iZombie*), and Kristen Bell, star of *Veronica Mars*, convinced fans to fund a large percentage of the creation of a *Veronica Mars* film; the goal set on Kickstarter by Thomas was met in less than two days; the project was filmed and eventually distributed by a major studio (Dickey 2013).

On a narrative level, the tension between Billy, who is creating online content for a small but seemingly invested viewership (a fairly accurate representation of many of Whedon's loyal viewers), and Captain Hammer, a superhero that Billy (and the narrative) characterizes as a vainglorious bully, speaks directly to that between Whedon and the corporate studio system the WGA was striking against. Each of Whedon's four television series encountered some level of network interference in either content or scheduling. His first, *Buffy the Vampire Slayer*, not only was required to tread carefully and hide under metaphor the burgeoning relationship between two female characters (Robinson 2001), but was nearly cancelled over a fight regarding licensing fees between Fox (the studio that produced the series) and Warner Brothers (the studio that distributed it for broadcast) (Rice 2001). *Angel*, a spin-off of *Buffy*, was moved several times during its five-year run and frequently paired on the WB network's schedule with series of such radically different tones and genres that it could not build off the previous series audience[1]; *Angel*'s noir-ish tone and subject matter, including atonement, free will, self-loathing, addiction, corporate culture, and a cast that physically looked more adult than the more fresh-faced casts of series such as *Popular*, *Roswell*, and *Felicity* meant indicated that it would always be a strange fit for the teen-oriented network. It was subsequently cancelled mid-way through its fifth season when Whedon requested an early notification of its renewal prospects, despite the fact that at that time, its ratings were second only to ratings stalwart *Smallville*, a significant achievement for a series in its fifth season (Adalain 2004).

The issues around *Firefly* have been written about extensively (Pateman 2014; Giannini 2015; Buchanan 2004), but Fox, who invested millions into the series, nonetheless scheduled it on Friday nights (known colloquially as the "Friday Night Death Slot," which refers to the high cancellation rate of series scheduled on Friday evenings, under the assumption that most 18- to 34-year-old viewers would be otherwise engaged at that time ["Friday Night Death Slot"]), showed its episodes out of order, did not send advance screeners to advertisers, and requested a new pilot (Frutkin 2002); it ended up being cancelled with three of its filmed episodes left unaired in the United States. Finally, *Dollhouse*, which received a surprise second season renewal because Fox president Kevin Reilly claimed he did not want "10 million angry e-mails" from Whedon fans, but in reality primarily driven by the good sales numbers of Whedon's other series when released on DVD (Fienberg 2009), nonetheless dealt with a network that requested a new pilot, was queasy about the concept, and scheduled it yet again on Friday nights. The idea that *Dr. Horrible* not only served as a message to studios on a production level (Internet content was worth paying for), but as a story of frustration with the corporate media more generally is not a stretch.

Whedon suggests as much in the (musical) commentary that accompanied the DVD release of *Dr. Horrible*. In his song "Heart, Broken," he sings that his heart's "broken by the endless loads/of making-ofs and mobisodes/the tie-ins, prequels, games and codes/the audience buys/the narrative dies," to which his brother Jed responds with "Why do you rail against the biz/you know that's just the way it is." Yet Billy, if viewed as an avatar for Whedon himself, is seemingly invested in creating his own brand, of becoming a "corporate tool" in the same way he is seemingly disgusted by in Captain Hammer. The quote, said to friend/henchman Moist (Simon Helberg), "I have a PhD in Horribleness," is met by an eyeroll and an on-point comment from Moist: "Is that the new catchphrase?" Indeed, his first lines in the series are about him working on his evil laugh ("it's about standards"), highlighting the perfomative aspects of his quest for recognition. While Billy claims in the beginning of the series that "the status is not quo," he also later lists enacting "social change" as an afterthought to "all the cash/all the fame"—a point Williams addresses when she writes about the sense of entitlement Billy displays throughout the musical, equal to that of Hammer, even if the genesis of that sensibility in both men is wholly different (Williams paras 34–35)—while instructing reporters at the unveiling the proper way to spell his name. While Billy serves as the point-of-view character the audience could identify with, his goals are not antithetical to those of Hammer; he wanted to be branded and known more than he wishes to change the world. In essence, he wants to make "Dr. Horrible" a corporate brand.

This is obvious even in the attire Billy dons at the end of the series: a red lab coat and black goggles. Previous to this, Billy had only donned his Dr. Horrible attire (a white lab coat and large silver goggles) when he was either vlogging or committing his latest crime; in a riff on Superman, he ducks into a stairwell in his street clothes, only to emerge seconds later fully dressed as Dr. Horrible ("Act One"). Hammer, however, is never out of costume; he clearly feels no need to hide from the public his "other" identity as Hammer (indeed, it is not clear he has any other identity). As an avatar of law and order, he does not necessarily need to hide; as a brand, he is a walking advertisement for himself. At the end of the third act, however, after Penny is killed, "Billy" is not seen in public again; the Hammer "groupies" have switched their allegiances to Horrible—complete with Horrible-branded items—banks just hand money over to him, and he is shown hob-nobbing with the "elite" Evil League of Evil. In essence, he got, as he sings, "everything I ever wanted": cash, fame, and social change. The only glimpse of the man behind the mask appears at the very end of the series; alone in his apartment, he admits that none of it means anything.

As I wrote in the previous chapter, Whedon's later association with Marvel, particularly *Agents of S.H.I.E.L.D.*, positioned him as a brand ambassador for a series in which he had significantly less involvement than his other properties, arguing that such a position is essentially hollow. It is telling that Whedon himself, in ending *Dr. Horrible* with the "successful" supervillain out of costume and staring blankly and bleakly into the camera highlights the emptiness of such a role. Combined with the fact that the antagonist of the musical is Captain Hammer, a so-called superstrong superhero, adds to the irony of Whedon's later relationship with Marvel Studios.

This point is driven home by the next two Whedon properties I'll examine: *Dollhouse* and *The Cabin in the Woods*.

## *"They want to see us suffer"*: Appeasing the Corporate Gods

The second half of this book will be dedicated to examining *Dollhouse* as a case study of corporatism within Whedon's work, so to conclude this chapter, I'll be examining *Cabin* and *Dollhouse* together. While *Dr. Horrible* was created and distributed outside of the usual channels, both *Dollhouse* (a television series) and *Cabin* (a film) were distributed by major (or mini-major) studios, and both had a rather circuitous path before they made it to air/cinema. As stated earlier in this work, Whedon had been in discussions with Eliza Dushku to co-produce a series (a co-production of Whedon's Mutant Enemy and Dushku's Boston Diva production companies) that could serve as a vehicle for the actress (Tobias 2009). *Dollhouse*, a series in which individuals are stripped of their identities and personalities (known as being "wiped") and given new ones ("imprinted") made to order for high-paying clients, was set to debut on Fox in 2008; instead, due to the 2007/2008 writer's strike, it was pushed back to the 2009/2010 season. Similarly to *Firefly*, Fox requested a new pilot episode after the first version ("Echo" 1.0, included as an extra on the DVD release) was filmed; as Whedon phrased it: "the network pretty much wanted to back away from the concept five minutes after they bought it" (Ryan 2009). *The Cabin in the Woods*, about a group of five young people who visit a remote cabin and are tormented by monsters as part of a ritual (and ritualized) sacrifice to prevent the apocalypse, filmed in Vancouver in March 2009, was initially supposed to be released in February 2010, only to be delayed nearly a year in order to be converted to 3D. This delay fell squarely in the midst of studio MGM's financial difficulties, and the film's release was shelved as the studio sought to find a new distributor for *Cabin* and other unreleased projects (Fleming 2011). The film was finally released by mini-major studio Lionsgate approximately six weeks before the Whedon-helmed *The Avengers* film hit theaters, and one year after *Cabin* star Chris Hemsworth appeared in the film *Thor*. It did moderately well upon opening; it was the third highest grossing film the week it opened, beaten only by *The Hunger Games* and the *Three Stooges* (not bad for a delayed release from a mini-major studio) (Subers 2012).

*Dollhouse* and *The Cabin in the Woods* share a particular feature: the main action occurs within a corporate setting, and in neither case are the protagonists are aware of it. In *Dollhouse*, protagonist (of a sort) Echo (Eliza Dushku), as well as Sierra (Dichan Lachmann) and Victor (Enver Gjokaj), are Actives (or Dolls, colloquially), that is, they have "volunteered" for five-year contracts with the Rossum Corporation to have their personalities removed and continually replaced with new ones at the behest of high-paying clients. As the series makes clear on numerous occasions, the term "volunteer" belongs in scare quotes; one of the many ethically questionable elements of the sponsoring corporation (Rossum) is the pointed targeting of vulnerable individuals to serve as Actives. While Echo's developing awareness is part of the overall narrative of the series, even she is initially unaware of much beyond the most rudimentary aspects of her surroundings: she knows that she is in the place she eats and sleeps and does child-like activities or exercises, but not the reasons why or who is responsible for maintaining this particular existence. This is typical of all the Actives.

In *Cabin* as well, the five young people who travel to the cabin in question for a weekend of relaxation and fun are unaware that their actions, setting, and (eventual) deaths are being managed by a shadowy corporate group, known as The Facility. Indeed, the film starts within the sterile environment of the Facility, rather than with the protagonists, as two coworkers, Hadley (Bradley Whitford) and Sitterson (Richard Jenkins) shift between discussing the successes and failures of previous years and Hadley's wife's fertility treatment; the white sterility of the setting offers an ironic contrast to the discussion (Giannini para 7). In her analysis of *Cabin*, Deanna Day argues that this discussion answers the question Whedon himself posed in an interview about why horror focuses so strongly on killing the young; by "beginning with a discussion of reproductive technologies, and continuing to focus as much on scientists and engineers as on cavorting coeds," Whedon offers "an indictment of the real-world institutions of modern science in all of their bureaucratic, banal, and globally destructive glory" (Day 2013). Hadley, Sitterson, and the rest of the employees of The Facility are tasked with appeasing the "Old Ones"—ancient monsters who allow humankind's continued existence only as long as a yearly sacrifice is enacted to appease them—with the latest technology available to them. While neither Day nor Whedon are seemingly arguing for a technology-free existence, Day reads this yearly ritual, facilitated by technological progress, as the film's expression of "the cost of doing business" tacitly accepted by society at large, similar to the ways in which events such as industrial accidents are considered Friedman-esque "externalities"; unfortunate, but not surprising. Indeed, Day continues, the technocracy in which we live makes these deaths "written so completely into the functioning of modernity that to remove them would mean death for all, the death of our future" (Day 2013), which is precisely what happens at the end of the film.

Given the global nature of this sacrifice—the film shows that numerous countries around the world have their own scenarios, as long as one succeeds, the world is saved—L. Andrew Cooper offers a reading of the film as a critique of American exceptionalism. Throughout *Cabin*, Hadley and Sitterson make several disparaging remarks regarding the ability of other countries to "deliver" on the sacrifice; that America will come through as both success and global savior is, to them, never in doubt. Cooper writes: "[T]he film creates an analogy between the unrepresented (and unrepresentable) post-human planet hinted at by the apocalypse with what is, for some Americans, the equally unimaginable idea of a planet beyond American domination. When the Americans fail, too, then,

America is reduced to the same level as the rest of the world, and this reduction potentially contradicts exceptionalist elements in core American ideologies … the end begins with America and Americans taking their rightful place in the world: on the same level as everyone else" (Cooper para 4).

In essence, Cooper argues, *Cabin* critiques the idea that America does (and should) dominate global markets, both in film and in other industries—the non–U.S. scenario the viewer sees, for instance, is from Japan, and is as stylistically similar to Japanese horror as the Cabin scenario is to U.S. horror—both through Hadley and Sitterson's dismissive attitudes towards their allies and counterparts in other countries, and through their ultimate failure, which serves to topple U.S. dominance (and possibly human existence). The failure means "the end of American exceptionalism" as "a condition of the apocalypse," but perhaps most importantly, "such a radical ending may be necessary in order to 'give someone else a chance'" (Cooper para 4), to use Marty's words at the end of the film.

The pervasiveness of The Facility's involvement with the "sacrifices" (or "horror-producing bureaucracy" [Cooper para 4]) is made clear in the scene following the film's opening: college students Dana (Kristin Connolly), Curt (Chris Hemsworth), Jules (Anna Hutchinson), Marty (Fran Kranz), and Holden (Jesse Williams) set off in an RV for Curt's cousins' cabin, only for the scene to cut to a man on the roof of a nearby apartment building, dressed in black with an ear piece, who communicates, "The nest is empty; we're right on time." Later, when the surviving members of the group—Dana, Holden, and Curt—attempt to escape, not only does The Facility trigger an explosion to block the only escape route (a mountain tunnel), but when Curt attempts to jump over the canyon, he is stopped (and killed) by the presence of an electrical-type wall, invisible until it is interacted with, offering a not-so-subtle metaphor for the pervasiveness of corporate culture within American society.

While it first becomes clear to Marty—an inveterate pot smoker and the designated "fool" who later convinces Dana, "the virgin"—that the group's actions are being controlled by these outside forces ("puppeteers" as he calls them), the presence of the man on the rooftop is the first indication that this control is as thorough-going and invisible as the aforementioned wall that kills Curt. Even before we actually meet this group, the employees at The Facility reveal precisely how they have exerted their will on these young adults: Jules, who appears as a brand-new blonde when we first meet her, had the hair-dye she used chemically enhanced to increase her libido and lower her critical thinking skills, and Marty's marijuana was altered in order to leave him in a compliant fog.

Sitterson claims that once at the cabin (the site of the ritual sacrifice), the five can only be killed if they "transgress"—that is, both finding and activating a particular object that brings forth any number of monsters, as well as, presumably, having sex—and yet this is revealed almost immediately as an illusion. In a scene in the woods, through which Curt and Jules cavort, trying to find a place to get intimate, Jules' reticence to Curt's advances ("I'm chilly") is overwhelmed by the staff adjusting the temperature and treating the air with pheromones. Later, when Curt suggests they stick together, a drug is released into the cabin to convince the group that splitting up is a good idea. All of these interventions are in the service of making these five individuals into the stereotypes required for a yearly sacrifice: a jock, a whore, a scholar, a fool, and a virgin. That none of them fit into these particular molds is irrelevant; the corporate body has no use for their individuality. Indeed, they will go to any means necessary to reassure their particular goals are met to please the ultimate shareholders: the Old Ones.

At least the young people in *The Cabin in the Woods* have names; in *Dollhouse*, they have only designations. For the Los Angeles Dollhouse, their names are military codes: Echo, Sierra, Tango; in Washington, D.C. (the only other "Dollhouse" the series visits during its two seasons), they are named after Roman gods. What the characters in both *Dollhouse* and *Cabin* share is that they are reduced to abstractions: codes, gods, sacrifices, victims. Much like the assignments that the Actives are sent on, the Facility in *Cabin* is constructing a narrative in which each of these individuals must play a particular role, even if it does not fit who they really are. As per example, Curt is slowly turned into a brainless jock, even though earlier in the film he's portrayed as intelligent and scholarly, attending university on a full scholarship. Dana, who has been designated the "virgin," is not; she had an affair with one of her professors. In a more subtle moment, Holden, designated "the scholar" admits that he has not studied Latin since high school, and yet is able to translate a Latin text on sight. "Weird how it all comes back," he says; like the hair dye and pot, the Facility likely made additional tweaks to the others. Further, when Dana and Holden start kissing, she finds herself saying, "I've never..." before stopping, shocked. It is clear from the context of the scene that she was about to say, "I've never done this before," which she knows is not true. She recognizes, if only briefly, that her words are not her own.

This awareness is not immediately available to Echo or the other

Actives within *Dollhouse*. It is important, however, to note what Eve Bennett has written, in her analysis of the series. She points out that, of the purchased scenarios we see between clients and Actives, many if not most are predicated on pre-existing media/textual narratives. Both "Ghost" (1.1) and "Echoes" (1.7) feature romantic comedy scenarios (boy meets girl for a crazy weekend); "The Target" (1.2) is a direct gloss on the short story "The Most Dangerous Game"; "Omega," similar to the film *Natural Born Killers*; and "Belle Chose," a play on *My Fair Lady*, in which an older male teacher provides private lessons for a beautiful, if untutored, young woman. Bennett makes the point that the clients, as much as the Actives, are trapped inside the corporate media narratives they've been exposed to; even their fantasies are not original (Bennett 2011), a point I'll address in greater depth later in this work.

What *Cabin* and *Dollhouse* also share is the source of their power. In *Cabin*, it is revealed near the end of the film that five young people are chosen each year as a ritual sacrifice. This sacrifice, enacted worldwide but generally dominated by the U.S. contingent, requires that at least four out of the five individuals selected must be sacrificed to "the old gods"; if not, these old gods will destroy the world. I have written previously about the ways in which these "Old Ones" can be read as a gloss on the 1 percent; a small contingent of immensely powerful individuals who have the power to destroy communities, cities, or countries if their demands are not meant (Giannini 2015). That is, there is a parallel here to corporations that require tax breaks and other concessions (fewer inspections, self-regulation, etc.), under the threat that they will leave if their desires are not met. One can see a kind of hell that departing corporations have left in areas of what is known as the "rust belt" of the United States: massive unemployment, high crime, crumbling infrastructure, and despair among residents (McClelland 2013). In this scenario, the five individuals trapped in the Facility's Cabin are the "externalized consequences" of a corporatized world (Giannini 2015), that is, their deaths are the cost of a world forced to do business with these powerful creatures, if only to avoid their own deaths.

Unlike the Facility, whose main goal is global survival, Rossum's main goal is an unlimited amount of power and potential immortality ("Epitaph One" 1.13). This is not to say that the employees at the Facility, particularly Hadley and Sitterson, do not take pleasure in their work, particularly their prowess at making the sacrifice run smoothly; however, the executives at Rossum operate differently. Milton Friedman, the University of Chicago economist whose economic ideas—moving into areas in which disaster has struck and tasking the rebuilding solely to corporate bodies—have been tested, to the detriment of millions, in struggling states and countries around the world (including the United States) (Klein 2007), told Joel Bakan in an interview that the only responsibility a corporation has is to its shareholders (Bakan 34). Friedman was speaking particularly about the so-called green initiatives by companies like British Petroleum, indicating that unless these initiatives increased the bottom line, they were de facto economically immoral (Bakan 34), an idea in which one can see the outlines of a Rand-ian objectivism point of view. This type of thinking pervades the actions of the Rossum executives we see throughout both seasons of *Dollhouse*. They install a pedigreed senator (who is unknowingly an Active), as a rising political star that will rubber-stamp any favorable legislation the corporation suggests. Such an idea has been proposed, in the real world, by conservative lobbyist Grover Norquist, in 2012, who suggested at the 2012 Conservative Political Action Conference that all they required was "a Republican with enough working digits to handle a pen ... we just need a president to sign this stuff. We don't need someone to think it up or design it" (Frum 2013). Further, as is revealed in the penultimate episode of the series, even protagonist Echo's growing awareness, which seemed to be positioned as a way in which to bring down the corporation, was actually just another way in which the corporation was attempting to use her to protect their investments (so to speak), a point I will return to within the case study.

Yet, as both *Cabin* and *Dollhouse* make clear (as well as earlier series *Angel*), one cannot descend into the corporate "belly of the beast" without paying the price. Thus far, I have spoken primarily of the Actives in the Dollhouse and the sacrifices in the cabin. Yet employees of both the Facility and Rossum play an equal role within their respective texts, as the narratives are so squarely set within the corporate environment. Despite their work to ensure that these five young people die to save their lives and the lives of others (see Parker's [2013] analysis of *Cabin*'s examination of penal substitutionary atonement threaded through its text), the employees of The Facility are massacred by the creatures they planned to use to enact the sacrifices of the five people in the cabin; that this wholesale loss of life is not enough to appease the Old Ones is never addressed. The corporation in *Dollhouse* is destroyed from the inside by the technology that they used on the Actives; by the end of the series, many of the Rossum employees who were a vital part of the story arc, including scientists Topher Brink (Fran Kranz) and Bennett Halverson (Summer Glau), Dollhouse physician Claire Saunders (Amy Acker), Rossum head Boyd Langton (Harry Lennix), and FBI agent turned Rossum hire Paul Ballard (Tahmoh Penikett), are all dead. That fact that the roster of the dead is a mixture of those who were resisting the corporation's agenda and those who were promoting it indicates that the consequences of the unchecked corporate environment do not discriminate.

The sad fact of both narratives, however, is that the fates of the employees are the least of the damage that these corporations enact, and the wholesale slaughter of those in both the film and the movies, regardless of their ethics or morals (or lack thereof) underscores this. In both *Cabin* and *Dollhouse*, the wounds and death inflicted on the central characters is merely a foretaste of what happens to the rest of the world. In essence: an apocalypse. While *Cabin* ends as the Old Ones rise up and destroy the world (represented by a monstrous hand emerging from the earth and slamming down on the titular cabin as Nine Inch Nails' "Last" begins to play), *Dollhouse*, as a television series, had the narrative and temporal space to take viewers beyond the point of no return. Rossum's dreams of power ended up with a world population of people who were either empty or violent, with cities destroyed around the globe.

In both the extradiagetic corporate media discourse of *Dr. Horrible*, and the diagetic corporate antagonists of *The Cabin in the Woods* and *Dollhouse*, Whedon plants a firm foot into the anti-corporate camp, merely by showing where unchecked corporate power leads: domination, despair, and death.

# PART II
# Subverting Tropes, Corporations and Media
## *A Dollhouse Case Study*

CHAPTER FIVE

# "That is their business, but that is not their purpose"
## Dollhouse as a Subversive Text[1]

SECURITY GUY: "Oh god, you're a thief?"
CAROLINE: "Relax. I'm not a thief. I'm a terrorist."

In the episode "Getting Closer" (2.11) as the series *Dollhouse* was wrapping up its broadcast television life, a flashback of the series protagonist, Caroline Farrell (later known as Echo) is revealed manipulating her way into the office of a subsidiary of a corporation called Rossum. Rossum (its name a nod to Karel Capek's play *RUR*),[2] funds their medical research and development around the world with illegal underground human trafficking. This trafficking takes the form of removing the personalities of young, attractive individuals, and "imprinting" them with new ones at the behest of wealthy clients. Known as "Actives" or "Dolls," these individuals are targeted when they are at their most vulnerable, sign a contract, and, once wiped, are literally stored underground, in facilities known as Dollhouses. Caroline (Eliza Dushku) lures a Rossum security guard (Rick Otto) into the office of Adelle DeWitt (Olivia Williams), who runs the Los Angeles Dollhouse, with a promise of sex, only to handcuff him to a wall fixture and proceed to rifle through DeWitt's desk, prompting the above exchange.

There is a significance within this dialogue that goes beyond the episode's narrative; indeed, beyond the narratives of several episodes of the series *Dollhouse*. It is the use of the word "terrorist" within this context, as well as numerous instances within the series of the protagonists bombing or suicide-bombing their perceived enemies ("Getting Closer" 2.11; "The Hollow Men" 2.12; "Epitaph 2: Return" 2.13) that is simultaneously interesting and troubling. That such a series aired on the Fox network, whose most successful series of that era, *24*, was set within the fictional Counter-Terrorism Unit of the US government, adds another layer of resonance on *Dollhouse*'s willingness to own both the term and the actions of what some would consider terrorist acts.

That is just one of the ways in which the series *Dollhouse* subverted accepted narratives and expectations within its brief network run, a series that has been described as a "mind-bending, deeply subversive exploration of identity and corporate power" (Boulware 2). In particular, Boulware argues, *Dollhouse* takes on what Henry Giroux terms the "virulent and brutal form of market capitalism" (Giroux 2, qtd in Boulware, para 6). "Under neoliberalism, corporate interests dominate the nation state, to the extent that the nation state itself becomes little more than the political and social arm of corporate interests" (Boulware para 6). This is the type of world in which Rossum operates, a point I will examine in greater depth in chapter seven.

While the narrative itself interrogated larger questions, such as the nature of the distinction between body and mind (Rennebohm 2011), issues of connection and trust (Alvi 2011; Souza 2011), and the entertainment systems from which it sprang (Tresca 2011; Bennett 2011), both the series production and narrative also did not always follow the usual trajectory on either a story level, or the ways in which it attained and sustained its broadcast life. This case study is an attempt to examine the idea of the series from multiple angles: the corporate setting and postapocalyptic narrative endpoint and the ways in which employees, Actives, and others act and react to the context, the series interrogation of technological advancements and enhancements in ways that neither wholly embraces nor outright condemns them, and its interaction with and subversion of familiar tropes with creator Joss Whedon's canon. While others have examined some of these elements,[3] the layers of this comparatively short-lived series lend themselves to an even more thoroughgoing examination of its complexities.

## "How long have we been off the air?" Subverting Production Paradigms

The advent of Netflix-produced series or reboots such as *House of Cards, Stranger Things,* and *Gilmore Girls: A Year in the Life,* Amazon's collection of Internet-only productions such as *The Man in the High Castle,* or the much-anticipated *The Handmaid's Tale,* debuting on Hulu—

many of which boast big names such as David Fincher, Winona Ryder, or Jane Fonda—is only the latest shift in the large-scale changes in the distribution of television. While broadcast television has previously faced competition from cable and satellite programming, the netlets of the 1980s and 1990s (Fox, the WB, UPN, or the CW), or the introduction of the VCR, the rapidity of new format and platform adoption and use since the mid–1990s—television on DVD, digital video recorders facilitating greater time-shifting capabilities, online and streaming services—theoretically posed a greater threat than previous, possibly because the speed at which these innovations occurred. To put it in context, DVD players reached 87 percent penetration into American homes by 2007, only seven years after they were introduced into the mass market. Compare this with VCRs and televisions, which took 15 and 25 years, respectively, to reach similar penetration levels (Cardona and Fine 2003:1; MPAA Inc. 2007:17). In the 2000s, consumer electronics seemingly left television playing technological catch-up.

Digital video recorders and DVDs are simultaneously discussed in both the network and advertising publications as the "end" of television as they (and the viewer) know it, and sold as a liberating technology that empowers the viewer to create their own schedule and free themselves from the advertising-based model of network (and the majority of cable) programming, with network executives often embodying the former (McClellan 19) and advertisers frequently touting the latter. A column in *Advertising Age* argued, "[T]his is not a time for fear, resistance, denial or defensiveness—despite the natural inclination to protect an existing pile of cash. It's the most exciting time ever to be in or around the businesses of media, marketing and communications" (Donaton 26). What seems most clear is less a fear of technology then a struggle for control of the technology and its implications on the part of both the advertising and entertainment industries.

The advent of television on DVD, a format which allows viewers to more easily collect and store their favorite programs (Kompare 2006)—one of the factors that ushered in what critic David Bianculli has termed "the platinum age of television," which he determines from the debut of *The West Wing* on broadcast and *The Sopranos* on HBO (1999) to the present (Bianculli 3)—initially took the entertainment industry by surprise. Even as early as 2003, industry analysts were predicting that sales of television series on DVD would top $1 billion; they had already started to affect development. Series such as *Family Guy* were brought back from cancellation when its initial final season was the top-selling television DVD for that year (Goldman 2008); high-cost series such as *The Sopranos* recouped the costs of earlier seasons based on DVD sales; and many of the purchasers were younger than those who viewed the series on terrestrial television, garnering the all-important youth demographic (Hettrick 1).

It also aided in reviving the "mini-series" (or "limited series"), as "DVDs let consumers undertake such commitments on their schedule, not the network's," something not possible with older mini-series such as *Roots* and *The Winds of War*, which was no doubt a greater concern in this era, given the amount of channel choice (Lowry 15). To tie this in with the concerns of this chapter, the low-rated *Dollhouse* was renewed for a second series based on anticipated sales of the first series on DVD— given the popularity of Joss Whedon's other series in the DVD format— and its high ratings in DVR and online viewing (Feinberg 2009).

Whedon has clearly made use of these shifting paradigms, not only with the aforementioned release of the web-only musical *Dr. Horrible's Sing-Along Blog* as a self-funded, collaborative effort of Whedon's family, friends, and coworkers, but because of the general trend of his programs to be generic hybrids aimed at niche audiences. That is, *Buffy* combined comedy, horror, and melodrama in a bildungsroman narrative (Wilcox 8), *Angel* combined horror and noir (Abbott 22–45), and *Firefly* explicitly combined the western and the space opera. Despite the fact that *Dr. Horrible* was initially distributed for free in the U.S. and abroad, ancillary products such as its soundtrack, the DVD and iTunes releases, and the musical commentary track (known as "Commentary: The Musical!"), both covered production costs and made a profit (Bercovici 2012). As discussed in chapter four, the series was written and filmed during the 2007–2008 Writer's Guild strike, with the avowed purpose to indicate to skeptics that online content was both profitable and television-quality, something, as the examples above elucidate, of which the industry no longer needs to be convinced. Whedon's next project, *Dollhouse*, was distributed in a more traditional fashion (it aired on the Fox network), but on a narrative, canon, and technological basis, it too subverted both expectations and established models.

According to *Dollhouse* producer and star Eliza Dushku and creator Joss Whedon, the series was conceived over a Gouda cheese pizza lunch; Dushku referred to this lunch meeting as "the best investment I've ever made" (Tobias 2009). During this meeting, Dushku described her life as both an actress and a woman to Whedon, leading Whedon to the idea of narrativizing her experiences through the creation of a series in which programmable people are kept underground and available to the highest bidder, who decides what that individual will be. In other words, actors so deeply invested in their roles they no longer realize they are playing parts; Stanislavski "method acting" approach gone wild, so to speak. Dushku wanted the series to be explicitly "political" in the way that it tackled subjects such as feminism, technology, socioeconomics, and sexuality ("Finding Echo"). The way that this was clearly at odds with the network's (Fox) conception (and branding) of *Dollhouse* will be addressed below, but on Fox it did air, since Dushku's production company, Boston Diva, had signed a production deal with them.

The series was slated for production in 2008, only to be derailed (temporarily) by the writer's strike. Whedon had previously stated he would not work with Fox studio any longer, after his series *Firefly* was treated poorly—episodes shown out of order, a last-minute pilot replacement, and no screener sent out before the series' debut, limiting the ability of the series to gather either reviews or the type of high-priced advertising such an expensive series would require (Frutkin 2002)—and cancelled after 11 of 14 filmed episodes had aired. Despite that, Whedon seemed initially optimistic about *Dollhouse*, claiming that there was "a completely new bunch of people over there and they seem really intelligent and supportive" (Hibberd 2007). *Dollhouse* (along with sci-fi series *Fringe*) was also tapped for Fox's short-lived experiment "Remote-Free TV," which offered series with longer running times and fewer (if more expensive) ads, as a response to the proliferation of DVRs and their abilities to skip or fast-forward past commercials. Fox's thinking was that the fewer commercials would thus stand out all the more because the advertising field was less crowded (Stelter 2009).[4]

Despite this seeming vote of confidence, problems occurred almost immediately. The original pilot episode ("Echo") was scraped (in what Whedon indicated was a mutual decision [Hibberd 2009] and portions of the original pilot were incorporated into later episodes), the series was scheduled for the infamous "Friday Night Death Slot," and rumors abounded regarding network interference, mirroring similar reports around *Firefly*. In an interview with Maureen Ryan near the end of the series, Whedon claims that *Dollhouse* was initially going to explore sexuality and intimacy in greater depth, but the Fox network seemed to "back away from concept five minutes after they bought it" (Ryan 2009), insisting on more action-oriented storylines (much as they insisted on a more action-oriented pilot for *Firefly*). When the series finally debuted in 2009 to lackluster ratings and so-so reviews, fans of Whedon's other series feared the worst.

The series got off to a narratively slow start—something not atypical with Whedon series (see Abbott et al. 422)—and both Whedon and Dushku asked fans to stay with it despite the tonal and narrative issues. Of particular concern was the way each engagement was, on a meta level, a different genre, within its first five episodes (Tobias 2009), including action-adventure, thriller, heist caper, and musical, seemingly making it difficult for viewers to connect with either the protagonists or the plot. The ratings peaked at an average of four million viewers for the first season ("2008–2009 Primetime Wrap"), considered a low figure for a major network at the time.

Whedon and Dushku were correct, however, in their assessment that the series itself really started its narrative drive with the sixth episode ("Man on the Street"), which directly addressed, in both its storyline and the vox pop interviews that were interspersed throughout the episode, the complicated nature of the series, while also building on the narrative elements that had already been established, including Echo's adaptability and increasing self-awareness, and the ethical implications of embodied fantasy, through the perspectives of clients, Actives, and ordinary citizens. Unfortunately, the ratings were still poor, and it seemed likely that *Dollhouse* would be cancelled, particularly when the final episode of the season, "Epitaph One" (1.13) was left unaired. Whedon explained that the series had been contracted for 13 episodes, but since a pilot had been filmed and then scrapped, "Epitaph One" would actually represent episode 14, and thus did not indicate that the series' fate was decided (Goodwin 2009).

Reviewers and fans, however, seemed resigned to the idea that *Dollhouse* was yet another Whedon series that would never get a chance; when it was in fact renewed for a second season, nearly every headline reporting it expressed shock and surprise. As Fox Entertainment president Kevin Reilly joked when it was announced that *Dollhouse* would be renewed: "[I]f we cancelled Joss' show, I'd probably have 10 million e-mails this morning from fans" (Fienberg 2009) referring to the efforts that surrounded the WB's cancellation of Whedon's series *Angel* and Fox's own cancellation of *Firefly*. Reilly's contention aside, the introduction and acceptance of the C3 Nielsen ratings (commercial and live plus three, a metric that provides ratings for whether a commercial had been watched and includes "live plus three" [programs recorded and viewed up to three days from broadcast]) and the aforementioned robust sales of previous Whedon series on DVD, both played a significant role in *Dollhouse*'s renewal. For the second season, however, the series could not garner the kinds of numbers could ensure a third season renewal. When the series was pulled during the 2009 November sweeps period and the remaining episodes burned off in double airings between December and January, it was clear there would be no third season, both to fans of the series and the writers and production staff. The series thus compressed what was a five-year plan (according to Whedon) into a handful of episodes, making for a rushed but intriguing final run of the series.

## "There is no me. There's just a container": Subverting Character Paradigms

*Dollhouse*, as mentioned above based on series star Dushku's description of both the pressures of her career and the numerous roles she is required to play as both an actor and a woman. The basic premise of the series is that an underground organization—both funding and funded by the corporation Rossum—known as the Dollhouse, offers wealthy clients programmable people. These programmable people—both men and women—are divested of their personalities and left an empty shell, in order to minimize conflict and maximize authenticity when new personalities are "uploaded." As DeWitt tells a client who wishes for someone who will "pretend" she is in love with him, he is "out of luck": "If you engage an Active ... he or she ... will see you and totally, romantically, chemically fall in utter and unexpected love with you" ("Epitaph One" 1.13). Such a narrative conceit means that from episode to episode, the series could play with genre. An Active could be engaged as a love interest ("Ghost" 1.1; "The Target" 1.2; "Man on the Street" 1.6; "Echoes" 1.7; "A Spy in the House of Love" 1.9; "Vows" 2.1; "Belle Chose," 1.3; "Belonging" 2.4; "A Love Supreme" 2.8); hostage negotiator ("Ghost" 1.1); master thief ("Grey Hour" 1.4); social worker/abuse counselor ("Echo" 1.0; "Briar Rose" 1.12); back-up singer ("Stage Fright" 1.3); or new mother ("Instinct" 2.2). This allowed the series to engage with disparate genres such as thriller, domestic drama, science fiction, horror, and romantic comedy, sometimes within the same episode. While this in theory could work to keep the series "fresh," many of the initial reviews and reactions to *Dollhouse* focused on its lack of a cohesive narrative identity (Stanley 2009; Lowry 2009; Shales 2009). Such a lack of cohesion was built into its premise, but the focus on branding televisual properties across multiple media in contemporary broadcast television makes such a series a risky proposition. The fluidity of the series premise made it difficult to classify, at the very least, and nearly impossible to brand. There is a particular irony here, that in (initially) doing precisely what networks had asked Whedon to do with previous series such as *Buffy* and *Angel*—that is, make them less arc-heavy and serialized and more "stand-alone" (Colvin 24–25)—lead to critiques by viewers and reviewers that the series lacked depth and coherence.

Further, not only does the main protagonist switch identities from episode to episode—from a dominatrix ("A Spy in the House of Love" 1.9) to a wealthy woman trying to solve her own murder ("Haunted" 1.10)—depending on the assignment she's been hired for, but when not on assignment, Echo, as well as the other Actives, is an empty vessel; they are supposed to have no identity beyond what is given them. The rationale is that such an identity would undermine the fantasy or function they are hired to perform, yet it is difficult, from an audience perspective, to invest in characters who have no will of their own, who speak in and desire only the most basic human needs—food, shelter—and are so seemingly devoid of independent brain function that they can no longer read.[5] The LA Dollhouse looks like a cross between a spa—with massage facilities, work-out rooms, and pool—and a kindergarten class, with picture books and a craft corner where Actives paint child-like watercolors of birds and houses. This is notably different from the DC Dollhouse, which is harsh and white and resembles a laboratory; as DC programmer Bennett Halverson (Summer Glau) says: "You let them roam. They roam like free-range chickens. We keep ours more like veal" ("Getting Closer" 2.11). Such differences—spa vs. utilitarian laboratory—could reflect the differing cultures of Los Angeles vs. Washington, an analysis beyond the scope of this chapter.

The non–Actives, however, even those not employed by Rossum, operate in such a morally grey area that audience identification also poses a challenge. Characters such as Paul Ballard, an embattled FBI agent investigating the Dollhouse, who could nominally act as the "hero" of the series, was already making questionable ethical decisions before being appropriated by Rossum, including offering no witness protection for a mob informant to draw out those he works for ("True Believer" 1.5) and sleeping with his neighbor even after she had been revealed as a "sleeper" Active ("Haunted" 1.10). His obsessive search for a single individual (Caroline Farrell), rather than exposing corruption or trafficking within a major corporation, leaves him little room to occupy an ethical high ground against those he is fighting, as pointed out by a Dollhouse client ("Man on the Street" 1.6). Certain characters are introduced only to be later revealed as Actives, including Ballard's Russian mob informant, Ballard's neighbor Mellie (Miracle Laurie), and in a major plot point of the second season, Senator (and later president) Daniel Perrin (Alexis Denisof).

Echo's handler (i.e., the person who watches out for Actives while they're on assignment and pulls them out in case of trouble), Boyd Langton (Harry Lennix), also seemed poised as nominally heroic, despite his association with the Dollhouse, particularly in "Man on the Street," when he exposed another handler's rape of the Active Sierra (1.6), in addition to the fact that he is viewed by those around him, including Echo, as a "swell guy with a trustworthy brow" ("A Love Supreme" 2.8). While Boyd was never revealed as an Active, the "swell guy" actually turned out to be the main antagonist of the series. As Christopher Souza argues, this narrative turn was an excellent example of the "metaphor of the Dollhouse"; Boyd's trustworthy looks and demeanor revealed that our own programming tends to judge on externals (Souza 211–212).

This lack of identification is one aspect of the way that the series itself inverts and subverts narrative tropes associated with both broadcast television and creator Joss Whedon, one that can be viewed as a particular endpoint for the issues and concerns raised in his previous works: *Buffy the Vampire Slayer, Angel, Dr. Horrible's Sing-Along Blog*, and *Firefly*. That is, if *Buffy* was a (relatively) straightforward bildungsroman and hero's journey (Wilcox 8), such a concept was already being interrogated in *Buffy*'s spin-off *Angel*, in which the eponymous hero often made wrong choices and operated in moral and ethical grey areas. In this, *Angel* shares particular features with *Dollhouse*, particularly its fifth season, in which Angel and his team take over the corporate law firm Wolfram and Hart, who had been their antagonist throughout the previous four seasons, trying (and failing) to turn that particular corporate behemoth into a force for good. By *Firefly*'s debut in 2002, the nominal protagonist Mal (Nathan Fillion) was an opportunist and smuggler who had given up hope in change (and faith in a higher power) after his heroic achievements in war had not only resulted in defeat, but in massive loss of life and even abandonment by the forces with which they fought; a deleted scene in the pilot indicates that the survivors of the final battle were left for days on the battlefield while those in charge of both factions came to terms ("Serenity" 1.1). *Firefly*'s follow-up film, *Serenity*, explicitly deems "heroes" as "someone who gets other people killed," and indeed, the crew's heroic actions in exposing Alliance (and corporate) malfeasance resulted in the deaths of numerous Alliance soldiers, Reavers, and two Serenity crew members: Shephard Book (Ron Glass) and pilot Hoban Washburne (Alan Tudyk). In the web musical *Dr. Horrible's Sing-Along Blog*, the disillusioned villain/protagonist, Dr. Horrible (Neil Patrick Harris) sings that "heroes are over with," and, indeed, in terms of audience sympathy, the "hero" Captain Hammer (Nathan Fillion), is portrayed as an arrogant bully, while Billy (alias Dr. Horrible) is easier to identify with, particularly since his villainy seems driven by a sense of powerlessness both physically (being beaten up by Captain Hammer) and socially (his inability to talk to Penny [Felicia Day], the girl of his dreams).

Instead, by making the majority of the characters within *Dollhouse* either severely morally compromised or empty vessels, the onus then reverts to the audience to examine their own complicity in requiring narrative sustainment of their own fantasies that asks actors to empty themselves to take on a character that may be morally, ethically, or socially different or abhorrent to the actors themselves. To cite examples from Whedon's own oeuvre, James Marsters, who played Spike on both *Buffy* and *Angel*, had to film a scene near the end of the sixth season in which he attempts to rape Buffy ("Seeing Red" 6.19), a type of scene Marsters indicated he personally cannot bear to watch, as well as "the hardest day of my professional life" (Zuckerman 2017). Robia Lamorte, the actor who played Jenny Calendar—a self-described technopagan of Romany ancestry—in seasons one and two of *Buffy the Vampire Slayer*, became a born-again Christian in 1998, not long after her character was killed off the series ("Passion" 2.18). She appeared once in the third season as a manifestation of the First Evil ("Amends" 3.10), that is, the source of all the evil in the world. She claimed to be unaware of why her character returned, and was upset that she would be playing what was essentially a satanic role, as that violated her beliefs. In a similar vein, Amber Benson, who played Willow's girlfriend Tara, turned down an opportunity to return as the character for a similar reason: the character would be used in the service of evil, which she felt would betray fans already hurt by the character's death ("Interviews: Amber Benson").

Thus, by making the Actives empty vessels to be filled at the behest of paying clients, *Dollhouse* offers a metanarrative look at the "backstage" of the profession of fantasy creation. The third episode actually dealt with this issue directly, through the lens of a pop star courting death and attention simultaneously because she no longer knew who or what she was outside of the context of her fan base or the corporate entity that brought her into prominence. This entity is, not surprisingly, "The Mouse" (that is, Disney) according to her manager, which ties her explicitly, and obviously, with pop stars such as Brittany Spears, Justin Timberlake, and others who got their start on the Mickey Mouse Club ("Stage Fright" 1.3). Such an idea remains the subtext of the series more generally, however, with a "programmer" who "imprints" the Actives with personalities he's created, with little initial regard for their own self-hood, referring to them at one point as "bison" ("Grey Hour" 1.4), a concept that Don Tresca ties directly to creators/showrunners treatment of actors (Tresca 2012). The fact that the Active Echo consistently goes off-task (or script) is thus a cause of concern for the corporation, although they also find a way to use it to their advantage. (Even when she disrupts and undermines Rossum's paramilitary wing, Rossum is thrilled; in Adelle's words, they were "devising ways to turn you into a weapon" ["Stop-Loss" 2.9], much as Blue Sun later does with River.)

This is an element that both Madeleine Muntersbjorn and Rhonda Wilcox have addressed in their analyses of the series. Not only does Muntersbjorn argue that *Dollhouse* offered "no one for whom to cheer," as explicated above, but points out the obvious, but pertinent element: "The show is about a place, not a person or a crew, and a nasty place at that" (6). This is an important distinction, as Whedon's first two series (*Buffy* and *Angel*) as well as his web-only musical *Dr. Horrible's Sing-Along Blog* and Marvel co-production *Agents of S.H.I.E.L.D.*, indicate in their titles that the narrative's main focus is people; indeed, for most, one particular person—Buffy, Angel, or Billy (aka Dr. Horrible)—and their narrative journey. It is interesting to note that, with the exception of *Dr. Horrible* and *Agents of S.H.I.E.L.D.*, later Whedon (television) work seems primarily concerned with a setting's effect on an ensemble of characters, as reflected in the series titles: Firefly is a class of ship the nine main characters travel in, the Dollhouse is essentially both a "secret prison" and a "shopping mall" (Klein 306) where most of the characters live and work, and the cabin in the Whedon-penned film *The Cabin in the Woods* is a manipulated set for a ritual sacrifice. In the latter two, these environments are controlled by a corporate entity, a point I will address explicitly in the chapter seven, especially as it applies to the transubstantiation of corporate entities into corporate persons. Thus, the "nasty place" of the Dollhouse allows us "to see ourselves more clearly, especially those sides of ourselves we are not in the habit of including as part of our personal identities" (para 13). In Muntersbjorn's words, *Dollhouse*, in essence, makes the audience into "complicit perverts" (para 4); after all, we are the ones watching. Wilcox also makes this point, as she argues that actors, creator, writers, and the audience "all share in the creation of and engagement with illusion; all are complicit" (5).

Five. "That is their business, but that is not their purpose" 107

## "Now I know how Blockbuster feels": Subverting Narrative Paradigms

Breaking the fourth wall and other metafictional devices have become relatively commonplace in genre television, with perhaps the series *Supernatural* (2005–present) making the most use out of such elements throughout its run.[6] These particular narratives can be used to highlight both the constructed nature of television, as well as interrogate aspects of production, writing, and characterization. Whedon's previous series have contained metafictional moments: the musical episode "Once More With Feeling" (*Buffy the Vampire Slayer* 6.7), in which the characters are forced to sing their innermost feelings, with Buffy looking directly into the camera as she sings, "And you can sing along," and "Smile Time" (*Angel* 5.14) in which corporate puppet Angel is turned into a literal puppet (see Masson 2013 for an in-depth analysis of the episode, and Angel himself, through the lens of puppet theory), are particular standouts for their sustained metafictional constructs. It is rare, however, to see a series for which the entire premise is constructed on a metafictional level. As I will address in greater depth throughout this work, this is one of the many subversive elements of the series, and, as Bennett argues, "yields several layers of commentary on the American entertainment industry and the capitalist infrastructure that supports it" (2). Further, the series does not stint at only critiquing the "capitalist infrastructure," but also the creators,' writers,' and actors' complicity within that system.

Dan Tresca offers a point-by-point analysis of the series as an overarching metaphor for television economics and politics, meticulously matching each element with its corresponding one in entertainment in general and television in particular: the Actives as actors, programmer Topher Brink (Fran Kranz) as creator/writer, head of the Los Angeles Dollhouse Adelle DeWitt as producer, and the evil corporation Rossum as the network (Tresca 412–413). (Tresca is not the only one to associate Topher with Whedon, but Whedon likens himself to Adelle, who is forced to make "hard choices" ["Vows" commentary]). Yet if these correspondences were all there was to *Dollhouse*'s metafictional construct, it would certainly not lend itself to a full-length analysis, nor could it be construed as being more than a shallow subversion, a game for Whedon fans and viewers to parse out over its run. My opening example of the nominal "hero" of the series referring to herself with a loaded word such as "terrorist"; the lack of an unproblematic protagonist for audience sympathy or identification; the complicated parsing of corporate malfeasance, government complicity, and physical and technological abuse; the specter of audience complicity in objectification and fantasy creation; and even the ways the series structure, narrative, and concerns deviate from particular tropes associated with Joss Whedon's work, all exist within *Dollhouse* as series, and are worth examining in greater depth.

In this introduction, I have striven to examine the various ways that *Dollhouse* operates as a subversive text. The next chapter analyzes the use and misuse of technology within *Dollhouse*, with a particular focus on two elements: the ways in which technological creation and advancement, even when for noble ends, can be abused and twisted when the profit motive is involved, and how the imprinting technology and its uses simultaneously offer redemption in the most unlikely places. Using the pharmaceutical industry as a significant example, this chapter will examine the ways in which the narrative elucidates contemporary culture's problematic relationship with technological progress without necessarily (or simplistically) advocating for an "off-the-grid" lifestyle. From there, I will more closely examine how Topher's interaction with this technology—particularly his role in developing its most dangerous aspects—help him create an ethical and moral sense within himself.

Following that, I will discuss the way the series interrogates the intersection of corporate America and the government. This represents a major arc of the narrative in the first half of the second season, as the agenda of the Rossum corporation, including the installation of an Active in the position of senator in order to enact favorable legislation, is revealed as particularly nefarious. While this is an increasingly common feature in Whedon's later oeuvre (see Giannini 2014), particularly in the series *Firefly* (and its accompanying film *Serenity*) and its overlap between the Blue Sun Corporation and the Alliance government, *Firefly* differs in that it is set 500 years in the future. *Dollhouse*, on the other hand, engages with elements and concerns that have contemporary and real-world analogues, such as the Citizens United decision (Kennedy 2010) that gave corporations unparalleled financial access to policy makers, or the recent Hobby Lobby decision that allowed corporations to claim religious objections to governmental policies they don't agree with (Alito 2014). The way in which *Dollhouse* engages with this makes a fascinating case study in how genre television can incorporate critique between the fiction.

Fitting *Dollhouse* into Whedon's oeuvre is the focus of the next section, particularly the way it undermines particular aspects associated with his work. Whedon's use of language—particularly neologisms and slang—

has been extensively written about, especially with regard to his debut series, *Buffy the Vampire Slayer* (Peters 2006; Kirchner 2006; Adams 2003). Other elements, such as the notion of "created" family within Whedonverse series—the Scooby gang in *Buffy*, the Angel Investigations team in *Angel*, and the crew and passengers of Serenity—are also considered a hallmark of Whedon's work (Battis 2005). So too is a focus on feminist-centered themes. *Dollhouse* deviated from all three in significant, and to some, off-putting ways, with early reviews citing the lack of the usual Whedon slant to the dialogue (Goodman 2009) and narrative (Lowry 2009). Perhaps more devastating is the continued question of whether the series undermines Whedon's avowed feminism, something Whedon himself has contested. He claims that a narrative of a woman who literally builds her sense of self from scratch, despite the forces aligned against her struggle—both social and political—*is* feminist ("Defining Moments"). Thus, this section will focus on the ways in which *Dollhouse* knowingly subverts much of what has been associated with Whedon's work, particularly the "chosen family" trope, in a way that reconfigured the narrative of the series in toto, as well as its approach to feminism and objectification, which is both fascinating and problematic.

It is in these numerous ways that *Dollhouse* operates as one of the most subversive series to be aired on a major network in the contemporary era.

CHAPTER SIX

# *Curiosity or Arrogance?*
## *Dollhouse* and the Troubled Relationship with Corporate-Sponsored Technology

In the best Frankenstein tradition, nearly every Whedon project addressed in this work has had at least one storyline in which technology, and the attendant arrogance in creating it, has gone awry. In *Dr. Horrible's Sing-Along Blog*, Billy's inventions range from pathetic (a "transponder ray" that accidentally reduces gold bars to liquid during transit) to deadly (his "death ray" actually kills Penny [Felicia Day], albeit by malfunctioning). As examined in chapter one, *Firefly*'s Alliance government and Blue Sun Corporation collude to create psychic assassins through torturous medical procedures performed on children—as well as an extinction-level event on the planet Miranda—and the technological enhancements the law firm offers the Angel Investigation team are shown to have consequences ranging from insomnia/madness to death. Yet even before the team joins the law firm, *Angel* showed an awareness of our questionable relationship with technology; in the second season, a physicist nearly ends the world when he creates a machine that freezes time. While Gene (Matt Champagne) only wants to hold onto a moment with his soon-to-be-ex-girlfriend, the technology gets out of control ("I can't emphasize enough how sorry I am about that," he tells Angel) ("Happy Anniversary" 2.13). In season four of *Buffy*, the Frankenstein metaphor becomes actual, as the U.S. government attempts to "harness the otherworldly threat" ("Primeval" 4.21) through creating soldiers that are a combination of human, demon, and machine, an experiment that leads to a massive, high casualty battle within the facility in which the experiments take place, and an abandonment of the program itself. Finally, as discussed in chapter three, the recent episodes of *Agents of S.H.I.E.L.D.* address many of the same issues Whedon's *Age of Ultron* did: a scientist creates an android to serve in a peace-keeping capacity who quickly becomes a bigger threat than what they were seeking to avoid. Previous to this, the series also interrogated the questionable use of alien technology, both as weapons and as life-saving or -restoring interventions ("The Magical Place" 1.11; "T.A.H.I.T.I." 1.14; "Love in the Time of Hydra" 2.14).

*Dollhouse*, however, represents the apotheosis of this particular narrative/social concern apparent throughout Whedon's work, in that the use and abuse of this technology is the overarching theme of the work. As elucidated above, his previous series (excepting *Firefly*, which did not run long enough to encompass multiple story arcs) did not stint at plots that either subtextually or obviously offered viewers a window into the United States' relationship with technological progress that often showed little regard for potentially terminal consequences; in the case of *Buffy*, *Angel*, and *Firefly*, however, I would argue that these series interactions with such stories serve as a prequel to *Dollhouse*'s hyperfocus on the ethical and environmental consequences of individuals "playing" with tech toys that they either refuse to or unwittingly do not understand.

Therefore, in this chapter, I will examine the ways in which the narrative of *Dollhouse* critiques the use and misuse of technology. As Lesley Chow argues, "the idea [is] that an organization can manufacture conviction—no matter how small or seemingly trivial—might be the most powerful of institutions" (Chow para 2). The association of rapid technological advancement and abuse of these discoveries is familiar territory within genre series, whether it is cyborgs, sentient computers, or radiation, and has the unfortunate taste of social conservatism in the way it pines for a more natural past. Instead, *Dollhouse* gives both points of view equal weight, both through dialogue and the narrative itself: from imprinting technology as a method to "steal" a person's soul ("Omega" 1.12) to the same being used to offer counseling to a traumatized child ("Briar Rose" 1.11) or treat psychological or neurological diseases ("Briar Rose" 1.11; "Omega" 1.12; "Belonging" 2.4; "Stop-Loss" 2.9). The episode "Man on the Street" in fact uses interspersed interviews with Los Angeles citizens to offer both the pros and cons of the technology, from offering closure for problematic relationships to the Actives' situations as human trafficking and slavery. What remains an open question throughout the series is whether the problem is the technology itself, or the humans that oversee it. As an interviewee says in the episode "Man on the Street": "Imagine this technology ... being used on you. Everything you believe, gone. Everyone you love, strangers, maybe enemies. Every part of you that makes you more than a walking cluster of neurons, dissolved at someone else's whim.

If that technology exists, it'll be used. It'll be abused. It'll be global. And we will be over. As a species we will cease to matter" (1.6).

Indeed, that prediction comes to fruition by the end of the series, but the interviewee's final comment—"I don't know. Maybe we should"— is resonant not only with the apocalyptic endgame in *Dollhouse*, but also the world-ending conclusion of *The Cabin in the Woods*. This ambiguity of moral responsibility for technological abuse keeps the series from devolving into a polemic against either technology or humanity. Instead, it clearly comes from a similar narrative place as that seen in the series *Firefly* and follow-up film *Serenity*, that is, a clear examination of the concept of "blowback" (Bussolini 147–150).

## *"Did I think of that?" When Technology Meets Profit*

In the first episode of the second season, the viewer is introduced to the character of Daniel Perrin (Alexis Denisof)—a junior senator bent on taking on the Rossum corporation—via a press conference watched by Adelle and Boyd ("Vows"). Adelle assumes that the only reason Perrin is taking on Rossum is to make a name for himself, guaranteeing re-election and perhaps a place on an important congressional committee. Perrin himself, however, states that the reason he is taking on Rossum in particular is because he believes they withheld vital treatment that could have ameliorated or even cured his mother's Alzheimer's dementia.

While later revelations call into question Perrin's motives—even to Perrin himself—a vital element of corporate-based research and development is the proprietary nature of their outcomes. To put it simply: it is about the patents. While Jonas Salk famously did not patent the polio vaccine, forfeiting an estimated $7 billion ("How much…" 2012), others who have developed vaccines, medical equipment, and medication did not follow Salk's precedent. The most famous recent example of this, of course, would be that of Martin Shkreli, the CEO of Turing Pharmaceutical. Turing bought Daraprim, an anti-malarial drug currently used to treat toxoplasmosis in patients with AIDS. While Shkreli garnered a great deal of attention (and rage) over raising the price of a single dose from $13.50 to $750 (Pollack 2015), his is neither the first nor the only pharmaceutical company to institute this type of purchase and subsequent price hike. While drug companies have claimed that such price hikes are necessary due to the amount of money sunk into research and development, they are hesitant to offer any precise accounting to justify their drug pricing (Pollack B1). This hesitancy, coupled with the numerous suits regarding how such medications are marketed to both the public and physicians, failure to report safety data, kickbacks to physicians, and Medicare fraud, to name a few ("GlaxoSmithKline to Plead..." 2012) are some of the numerous reasons why pharmaceutical corporations' reputations are "not much better than that of the financial sector or tobacco companies" (Kessel 983). Mark Kessel cites a recent survey of patients' views of the pharmaceutical industry, in which patients cited several damning indictments: "[A] failure to assist patients in securing medications in a difficult economic environment; offering drugs with only short-term health benefits; not serving the needs of neglected patient groups; inappropriate marketing of drugs; a lack of fair pricing policies; making drugs unaffordable to many patients; a lack of transparency in corporate activities, adverse news about products; not having a patient-centered strategy; and not acting with integrity" (Kessel 984).

Further, while many pharmaceutical industries offer philanthropic donations of drugs to developing countries, these programs come with a heavy price tag for U.S. taxpayers (the corporations can write off the donations); are generally are limited to drugs whose donation would benefit the company (whether through opening new markets or as public relations); and are under no obligation to continue the program if it no longer benefits the corporation (Bakan 47–48).[1]

Most importantly, however, for the concerns of this chapter, is the particular choices pharmaceutical and other medical technology companies make with regard to precisely what drugs and treatment they choose to research and develop. A 2014 study found that it takes approximately 12 years and $2,558 million to develop and market a new drug (DiMasi 2014); the industry has adjusted itself to make up these research and development costs through numerous channels, including what is known as developing "incrementally modified drugs"; i.e., making small changes to the formulation that allows drug companies to extend the patent. One can see this in drugs such as fluoxetine (Prozac), which has been tweaked to treat mental illnesses such as depression, used as a component in weight-loss medications, and sold as a treatment for premature ejaculation ("Fluoxetine Hydrochloride"). There is less incentive, therefore, to create drugs to treat illnesses that disproportionately affect the developing world (tuberculosis or malaria, among others), than to create new or improved medications used in markets such as the United States, such as the aforementioned anti-depressants ("Research and development in..." 45) or treatment of erectile dysfunction.

It is the overwhelming use of direct-to-consumer (DTC) advertising, however, that aligns most closely to the concerns of this chapter. In 2015, the pharmaceutical industry spent $2.6 billion on television advertising alone, flooding the airwaves with commercials for medications that primarily treat depression, erectile dysfunction, bowel and digestive disorders, and heart diseases. This overwhelming amount of DTC drug advertising, combined with the public relations disasters brought on by both Skreli and Mylan Pharmaceuticals' price hike for Epi-Pens (Willingham 2016) led both the American Medical Association and Congress to call for a ban on pharmaceutical advertising on television (Birkner 2016), a call Kessel echoes as one way to restore the industry's problematic reputation of putting profits before patients (Kessel 988).

It is the use of this advertising, however, and the resulting spikes in demand for advertised medication, that bears a close relationship to that of advertising and the programs it interrupts. Advertising, of course, is what supports the programs aired on television; further, more successful programs allow networks to charge more for the advertisements that interrupt said programs "flow" (Williams 66–67). To put it simply, in both instances, it is demand and supply: consumers will often ask for medications advertised on television (McKinlay et al. 294–299) just as networks can set prices on advertising based on both programs and networks' success (Lotz 3–24). For both industries, advertising is the support system for the development of new products, whether it is a drug or a drama.

In this respect, then, *Dollhouse* offers an intimate (and subversive) look into this particular process. As Eve Bennett elucidates so clearly in her analysis of the relationship between the series and the entertainment industry, *Dollhouse* as a metaphor for the entertainment industry works on numerous levels. While I will address Bennett's work in greater depth below, it is important to note that the way in which the series works as a deconstruction of this construct: "the narrative mounts an increasingly apparent and hostile critique of the Hollywood dream factory and the corporate power behind it," Bennett writes, one that intensifies as the series faced greater pressures from producer/network Fox (Bennett para 2). That is, much as the Dollhouse itself fund Rossum's research, so too does the network and its advertisers fund series such as *Dollhouse*, as well as the audience that watches the series and could potentially buy the products advertised between acts. While it is easy to view Rossum as exploitative, Rhonda Wilcox points out that the fact we the audience are watching these individuals being put into constantly exploitative situations shifts some of the onus on the audience for the ways in which we are complicit in this exploitation (Wilcox para 4).

Further, as Bennet points out: "The entertainment industry is fueled by the imaginations of the creative people who work within it, not to mention the imaginations of the audience who consume their output. However, anyone who believes that they enjoy playing a part in this system is deluding themselves, because ultimately they are nothing more than cogs in a vast corporate-capitalist machine from which there is no escape" (Bennett para 39).

It is not just complicity, then, between creators, network, advertisers writers, actors, and the audience, but collusion; just as the clients' purchased scenarios from the various Dollhouses fund Rossum's necessary research and development, so too does the fantasy creation of series such as *Dollhouse* fund the multivariate activities of the media companies that produce them. One does not have to fall far down the rabbit hole of media companies' ownership tangles, as per example, to find that until 2013, General Electric owned NBC Universal. This means that the same corporation that designed—and ignored reports of significant flaws for more than 30 years—the Fukushima reactors (Zeller A14) profited off of every *Friends* or *Seinfeld* rerun or DVD sold. Does that therefore make the creative staff (actors, writers) or the audience share responsibility for such devastation? Is participating or viewing propping up a corrupt system?

*Dollhouse* does not necessarily have the answers to these questions, but the questions themselves are baked into the series' premise. One, for instance, might not look too closely at the conditions under which laptops or jeans are made; the question might not even occur to said person. Yet, by subbing Rossum for Fox (Tresca 2012; Bennett 2011), by subbing Dolls for actors, and programmers/executives for writers and production staff, makes these questions manifest. Like many corporations, both the charitable work they do and the useful inventions they produce have a hidden cost. The example of pharmaceutical companies donations of life-saving medicines to developing countries mentioned above is one such cost; Doctors Without Borders turned down Pfizer's donation of a medication to treat trachoma—an infectious disease that causes blindness—because of the unreliability of depending on corporate generosity for necessary medications (Bakan 48). That Rossum's technological developments within the series significantly depend on the high income generated by what is essentially human trafficking implicates both the corporation and those who benefit from Rossum's technology. This is not to say, to use a particularly egregious example, that an individual should turn down a treatment for a disease such as syphilis because of the horrors of the Tuskegee experiments ("The Tuskegee Timeline" 2016). Instead, the series seems to be asking the viewer to at least consider that many of the innovations we take for granted have a shadow side of misery and profiteering over human rights.

As Tami Anderson writes in her analysis of the series, those who work within Rossum have numerous ways of dealing with the ethical dilemmas such work engenders, including focusing primarily on the good the corporation does (Adelle, Topher), such as helping abused children ("Briar Rose" 1.11) or helping cure illnesses such as schizophrenia ("Belonging" 2.4). These stories allow those who work within the Dollhouse—Anderson excludes the executives in these justifications, for good reason—to believe they were "sheltering those who needed it, counseling others who were missing something in their lives, all while making money that went toward vital medical research to help even more people" (Anderson 168). This is in line with Bakan's analysis of how corporate employees can engage in what can be viewed as psychopathic behavior at work—crushing competition through any means necessary, producing things that could cause harm to the general population, etc.—and still lead normal lives; "they go home, they have a warm and loving relationship with their families, and they love their children, they love their wife, and in fact their friends are friends rather than things to be used" (Hare, qtd in Bakan 56). They compartmentalize and rationalize their work as "work," keeping them from becoming as psychopathic as the corporation they work for (Bakan 56).

The difference with *Dollhouse* is that almost none of the employees have lives outside of the corporation; it goes without saying that the Actives do not either. While I will address this point in greater depth below, I am not arguing that characters such as Topher, Ivy (Liza Lapira), or Adelle are somehow more prone to psychopathy because of the inability to disengage from the corporate structure; however, having no clear division between the personal and the professional does, in fact, leaves them nearly as vulnerable as the Actives in their care. When things start to go badly, particularly Adelle and Topher's discovery of just how much they had been fooling themselves—and others—as to Rossum's real agenda (as with many hubristic villains, the end game seems to be immortality), there is no outside life to which they can turn for even something as basic as comfort. Indeed, as Adelle points out, a former Active who made a reference to Rossum's Dollhouses in his blog was literally terminated: "That was his last entry" ("The Public Eye" 2.5). Rossum has therefore cut off most possibilities for any interaction with non–Rossum employees, meaning their fates are thus inextricably tied in to that of the corporation itself. Topher in particular, given that he develops the world-ending technology for Rossum, is particularly vulnerable, and it is the numerous effects of the technology on its developer and programmer that I turn to next.

## "Then we put 'em in a glass jar with our fireflies": Topher Brink Gains a Soul

In discussing his works, such as *Firestarter* and *The Stand*, Stephen King indicates that, as a novelist, one of his thematic concerns is "how difficult it is—perhaps impossible!—to close Pandora's technobox once it's open" (King 2001, 207). This "box" metaphor indeed appears in *The Stand*, in which one of the survivors of an apocalyptic flu virus likens the recent destruction of society to dropping a cherry bomb into a toybox, and his (and others) job being to gather said toys together again, pruning out those that are too damaged or too dangerous. The question he cannot answer, however, is whether humans are capable of throwing away the "bad" technological toys that caused such destruction in the first place (King 1990, 830).

In the case of *Dollhouse*, it is difficult for many of those working within Rossum's corporate environment to admit that there is any problem with the technology they so freely use on their so-called volunteers. To both Actives and clients, DeWitt pitches the Dollhouse's technology as what these individuals "need," putting both the emptying of the Actives and the filling of client desires in the same psychological basket. That is, the wiping and imprinting process helps the Actives, as any psychological pain/mental illness is removed by the process, while simultaneously helping clients fulfil (often troubling) fantasies or rewrite parts of their own personal lives with different, more psychologically satisfying endings.

One of the more in-depth views of why clients frequent the Dollhouse occurs season one, through client Joel Mynor (Patton Oswalt). Mynor hires an Active once a year to recreate a moment that his wife's tragic death did not allow her to share: his first big success and subsequent house he purchased for her. This is the first real insight we get into a client's point of view, appropriate for an episode that splits its time between the Dollhouse itself, Paul Ballard's FBI investigation, and a series of "man on the street" interviews. "Man on the Street" (1.6) is precisely at the midpoint of the first season; while the first five episodes laid the narrative and character groundwork—both from Rossum's perspective and from those aligned against it—it is this episode in which the overarching themes are both deepened and critiqued. When Paul's investigation leads him to interrupt Mynor's engagement, the two of them have a lengthy discussion focused primarily on motivations: Mynor's for hiring an Active, and Paul's growing obsession with bringing down the organization. Mixing Mynor and Ballard's conversation with the vox pop interviews sprinkled throughout the episode deepens the viewer's understanding of the implications of Rossum's technology. While Mynor's reasoning is understandable—he actually heard the car accident that took his wife's life as he waited at the house—it does not follow that his actions are not problematic (to put it mildly). Yet, as Mynor points out, he knows these engagements are ethically questionable; on the other hand, Ballard, Mynor claims, is just as lost in fantasy as Mynor himself, without the same degree of self-awareness: the fantasy of the brave knight (or FBI agent) rescuing the princess (or Active) from "cash-wielding losers," causing said Active to then fall in love with him. "There's no room for a real girl, is there, when you can feel Caroline beckoning?" he tells Ballard. (This fairy-tale subtext will come to fruition in the aptly titled episode "Briar Rose," in which Ballard finally enters the Dollhouse to rescue Caroline.)

Scenes such as this allow the type of nuance associated with Whedon's previous work, in which most, if not all, the characters operate within ethically grey areas. As Devon Anderson writes in his analysis of technology in the Dollhouse through the lens of the Frankenstein myth, the technologies themselves are not "inherently evil, but ... possess a potential for unthinkable destruction, or unthinkable evolution" (Anderson para 36). That Anderson pairs "destruction" and "evolution" as "unthinkable" excellently encapsulates Whedon's own approach to humanity's relationship to technology within *Dollhouse* and his other series, and avoids the potential Ludditian implications of critiques of technology. In the episode "Haunted" (2.10), for instance, a wealthy woman has her brain mapped in the eventuality that she either dies or is killed. When she is in fact murdered, her personality is uploaded into Echo, giving her the opportunity to solve her own mysterious death. "Eternal life? Is that a service we offer now?" Boyd asks Adelle. "Because if it is, you realize that's the beginning of the end." Adelle's response, "I'm not planning on presiding over the end of Western civilization," becomes layered with irony given subsequent events. In this instance, the good (solving a murder) and the bad (offering wealthy clients immortality) are so entwined that it is difficult to separate them: destruction AND evolution in a single scenario.

The unthinkable is not that these technologies exist, perhaps, but that in each of the Whedonverse portrayals of technological modifications, such as the hybrid Adam in *Buffy* or the Actives themselves, is what Jeffrey Bussolini argues operates around issues of consent. That is, these modifications often "instrumentalize subjects rather than treat them as autonomous agents," resulting in feelings of betrayal from those affected (Bussolini 339). The amount of time that Rossum employees, particularly Adelle DeWitt, spend emphasizing that the Actives consented to the erasure and subsequent uses to which their bodies are put seemingly indicates that they are trying to convince themselves more than either their clients or their critics. Madeleine Costly (Miracle Laurie), formerly the Active November, is an excellent case in point: she is horrified when she sees a video of herself killing a man; the Dollhouse had installed a "sleeper" protocol that turned her into an assassin when she heard the right combination of words. That the man she killed was a rapist clearly does not alleviate her guilt, and it is obvious that whatever level of consent she gave to become an Active, she had no idea her body would be put to that kind of use.

The "Epitaph" episodes that close out seasons one and two do prominently feature those for whom technology is the greatest evil: "No tech, isn't that our motto?" While this is an understandable reaction to a world that technology has destroyed, it is only when this anti-tech group enters the Dollhouse itself and uses said technology that they finally understand the reasons why the technology spiralled out of control. Most importantly, they are neither the only voices to which the viewer is exposed, nor necessarily the series' final word on the place of technology in human society. "Epitaph 2: Return" reveals that many of the survivors have created what they refer to as "Safe Haven" within the shadows of Rossum's former corporate headquarters, poaching Rossum's remaining technology to keep its residents safe. Further, it is the same technology that caused the apocalypse that reverses its effects.

It is instructive, then, to look at the character of Topher Brink. When he is first introduced ("Ghost" 1.1), the most accurate descriptor for his ethics would be "amoral" (Jones 80). He is fascinated by the technology available at the Dollhouse, and in a flashback to his initial hiring ("Epitaph One" 1.13), it is revealed that the reason the technology works so well is because Topher immediately recognized a way to make it work more efficiently. He is, in many respects, a "Mozart" of imprinting, with a "near-intuitive understanding" of the process (Jones 81). The downside of this, however, is that for Topher (at least initially), the technology trumps the humans upon whom it is used. Topher himself is the embodiment of Rossum's corporate goals; as a paratextual advertisement for Rossum states: "Your mind is our business" ("November Ad" 2009). That is, all of the personalities with which Topher works with are merely tools for creating what Lesley Chow terms "conviction": a convincing mother ("Instinct" 1.2); a cured veteran ("Stop-Loss" 2.9); a back-up singer/bodyguard ("Stage Fright" 1.3); or even the healthy adult version of an abused child ("Briar Rose" 1.11); as Adelle points out to clients, not only are the Actives convinced of these roles, but the goal is that the clients should be similarly convinced. Topher (along with other programmers at other Dollhouses) is the one who is tasked to make sure this happens.

Rossum's seemingly innocuous motto, however, hides its real agenda, just as Topher is slow to realize both the humanity of the Actives and the implications of the technology. Not only is the obvious interpretation factual—Rossum produces neurological and other medical equipment and treatments, so the mind is literally their business—but the subtextual one as well: what is *in* your mind is also their business, a point that resonates in environment of ubiquitous surveillance and targeted ads. Rossum is not speaking merely of client preferences, akin to Facebook ad feeds or Amazon's tailored suggestions based on purchase history; all the brain scans conducted by Rossum equipment are part of their database, used for what are called "personality builds" ("Epitaph One" 1.13). Even more insidious, however, is the fact that the Rossum mainframe is *also* powered by the minds of human beings; as will be discussed in greater depth below, problematic Actives and employees are consigned to a place known as The Attic, in which they are kept in a comatose state of constant fear, which produces the adrenaline they use to maintain the mainframe's power. Thus, in an endless loop, Rossum builds its database of brains, Topher and other programmers create personalities, Adelle and other Dollhouse heads find those vulnerable or desperate enough to give themselves up to the corporate entity to be hired out by the wealthy, and even "broken" people are put to constant use to keep the operation running. While Paul Ballard is repeatedly told that such "fantasy" is "[Rossum's] business, but not their purpose," in the final analysis, it hardly matters if they have a purpose beyond making money; they have perfected a system guaranteed to generate income to fuel either research or salaries ad infinitum; it is Michel Foucault's "biopower" ("an explosion of numerous and diverse techniques for achieving the subjugations of bodies and the control of populations" [Foucault 140]) taken to its logical extreme.

It is easy to view the Actives as mere (programmed) cogs in this particular capitalist/technological machines, but that obscures the ways in which the Rossum's employees are part of the same machine. As Andrew Zimmerman Jones argues, Rossum easily understood Topher's programming, just as Topher himself understood how to program the Actives. The technology is Topher's instrument, and he cannot help but play it to the best of his ability—even creating the "tech" that ushers in what he names the "thought-pocalypse"—his personal programming, Jones asserts, is "just as controlling as that uploaded into any Active" (Jones 89). Like the Actives, his abilities are used by the corporation in a similar sense to that of the Actives bodies. That Topher realizes that "everybody's programmed" ("Echo" 1.0) does not prevent his own blindness in seeing how this applies to himself.

In the penultimate episode of the series, in fact, this is made manifest when Adelle, Boyd, Echo, Paul, Mellie, and Topher travel to Rossum's headquarters in Tucson, Arizona, using Echo (who Rossum wants) as their way in. Echo, who has been drugged by Boyd, is mentally incapacitated, but Boyd's partner Clyde (Amy Acker), tells Adelle, "The mind doesn't matter; it's the body we want" ("The Hollow Men" 2.12). Like Rossum's tagline ("Your Minds Are Our Business"), this assertion is layered and (somewhat) contradictory. For all of the Actives, their individual (original) minds may not matter, but those uploaded for clients certainly do. Further, when it comes to Echo, both do in fact matter; it may be a physical process that allows her to "block imprints" (which makes her valuable to the corporation), but that physical process has a direct effect on her mental processes. Most importantly, it is the minds (the original Clyde [Adam Godley], Topher) that allowed this technology to be created and improved. The minds, then, matter a great deal to Rossum.

This concept is explored again in later series *Agents of S.H.I.E.L.D.*, with the aforementioned development of LMD Aida and the alternate reality Framework. The major feature of said Framework is that for all the minds inserted within it, their biggest regret has been fixed: a child who died at four days old lives, a son reunites with his father, a mission that led to massive loss of life ends with everyone saved. Aida, created by the technological prowess of Holden Radcliffe, and changed by the quasi-mystical text known as The Dark Hold, questions the "paradox" of her "parameters" to protect both the Framework and Radcliffe himself; if, as Radcliffe claims, "reality is just perception," what is the use of physical bodies at all, if the mind is engaged with a reality in which their greatest regret is ameliorated? Aida solves the paradox by inserting Radcliffe back into the Framework after slitting his wrists, thereby destroying the physical to keep the mental "framework" intact ("Self Control" 4.15). In this respect, technology has been used in a similar way to that seen in *Dollhouse*, with one important distinction. While in both instances, both Actives and those in the Framework live an existence in which regret, trauma, or other types of issues have been resolved or removed, *Agents of S.H.I.E.L.D.* comes to a different conclusion regarding the tension between mind and body. If for Rossum, the body is given primacy over the mind (all the Actives, both male and female, fit into Western standards of beauty), in *Agents of S.H.I.E.L.D.*, the body is merely an obstacle to living out what appears to be ("appears" being the operative word) a happy or fulfilled existence. In both cases, technology allows body and mind to be severed from one another, with *Agents of S.H.I.E.L.D.* replicating the Cartesian duality embodied in *Dollhouse* from the other side.

As Kate Rennebohm argues, however, within *Dollhouse*, "an individual's identity was grounded in his or her body; a person's identity existed in the interaction between, on one hand, the body, and on the other hand, the memories, beliefs, and feelings which arose from their time in the world" (Rennebohm 9), although Taylor Boulware argues that Rennebohm's assertion that the series is subverting a nihilistic reading of essentialism is flawed. For Boulware, it is queer theory that provides a better match, as a "radical and liberating intervention in ways we think about identity and the self" (Boulware para 9). Both Rennebohm and Boulware do not disagree that even absent their "minds," the physical self has a vital role to play in how an individual is viewed in the world, even with something as basic as gender (Boulware's analysis of an accidental personality switch, in which Victor is imprinted as a woman and Echo as a man is on point [para 1–2]). This may be why, the brief glimpse the viewer is given of the minds of *Agents of S.H.I.E.L.D.* protagonists within the Framework do not seem to jibe with what we know of their personalities and motivations up to that point in the narrative: for example, May (Ming-na Wen) working for antagonist Hydra, or Coulson (Clark Gregg) teaching about the danger of aliens ("Self Control" 4.15); indeed, the removal of only one individual's greatest regret—May had to kill a child whose power was inciting violence in others ("Melinda" 2.17)—had a ripple effect that allowed the antagonist Hydra to take over in the name of national security ("What If..." 4.16).[2] Both Rossum and Aida's potential failures clearly rest on the technological disinterring of the mind from the physical self.

For Topher, who initially seems to err on the side of prioritizing the mental over the physical, the task for him, as much as for Echo and the other Actives, is to find a way to integrate the two. This is embodied in the shift from amorality to Topher's eventual guilt-ridden and morally driven death as the second season of the series progresses, a process that begins near the end of the first season. Even as Topher dismisses Ballard's claim that the technology "steals the souls" of the Actives in the penultimate episode of season one, his own is starting to develop and grow. The episode "Omega" features one of the LA Dollhouse's "mistakes" coming back to haunt them in the form of former Active Alpha (Alan Tudyk). In the grand tradition of unregulated medical experimentation, Rossum first tested the technology on prisoners, in exchange for commuting their sentences. Alpha, formerly Carl William Croft, was a serial killer in the making, who delighted in cutting people. The fact that this predilection survived multiple wipes and imprints underscores Ballard's assertion that the technology cannot wipe away an individual's essence. When Alpha attacks Whiskey (Amy Acker), cutting her flesh in the same way he did when he was Croft, he is restrained and wiped; in the ensuing struggle, all of his imprints are downloaded into his brain. Following that, he goes on a rampage and escapes, returning only to kidnap Echo—whom he correctly surmises is biologically similar to him—and all her imprints; his goal is to make himself a companion in a not-so-subtle nod to Frankenstein.

While Alpha is successful in doing to Echo what was done to him (he uploads all of her imprints into her brain simultaneously), she uses this violation as a means to fight against both Alpha and his plans for her (that is, against both his body and mind), and is eventually returned to the Dollhouse and wiped. At the end of the episode, in a scene that resonates on multiple levels, she turns to Topher and rests her hand on his heart as Beck's cover of "Everybody's Got to Learn Sometime" plays. Not only was the song used in a film that could certainly have served as inspiration for the series (*Eternal Sunshine of the Spotless Mind*), but the lyrics "change your heart" are sung as Echo reaches out to a Topher who looks overwhelmed. In this respect, he directly parallels Echo, whose growing self-awareness takes an irreversible turn due to the events of this episode. While more subtle that Echo's transition, the spectre of Alpha, driven insane by the technology Topher venerates, and Dr. Saunders' realization that she is in fact an Active herself (designation: Whiskey)—in her words, a "series of excuses" ("Vows" 1.1) created by Topher—set the stage for the greater developments Topher undergoes in season two. J. Leavitt Pearl, using philosopher/theologian Michael Henry's work on the phenomenology of the soul, ties *Dollhouse*'s conception of the "soul" as the ability to "feel," that is, to have an affective response that is not necessarily programmed, but organic to Actives even in their "wiped" states (Pearl 123–137). While not a Doll, this development of an affective response against the wishes of the corporation for which he works is clear from that scene in "Omega," a moment that can be read as Topher's "soul" emerging despite corporate pressure.

*Dollhouse* merely represented the latest iteration in Whedon's oeuvre in terms of the existence or purpose of a soul. While my goal in this chapter is not to engage in a philosophical or theological analysis of the presence or absence of souls, I do want to touch on the interactions between technology and, for lack of a better word, soulfulness within the Whedonverse generally, and *Dollhouse* in particular. Whedon's first series, *Buffy*, as well as its spin-off *Angel*, constantly engaged in questions regarding souls, first through the ensouled vampire Angel—most vampires do not have souls in Whedon's canon—and later through both the vampire Spike and various human villains. Spike in particular is related to the concerns of this chapter; the aforementioned Initiative that created Adam also implanted a chip in Spike's brain that controlled his violent impulses and prevented him from feeding on humans. Jacob Grossman contends that while this technological addition does prevent Spike from harming humans, it does not provide any moral or ethical reasons for non-violence, as the presence of a soul would. The desire to hunt and kill still exists in Spike; he is only, like Alex DeLarge in *A Clockwork Orange*, prevented from acting on these impulses. "The chip removes the element of personal choice by forcibly preventing Spike from taking certain actions ... while the soul forces him to consider his actions, and their consequences" (Grossman 10). While Topher is human, and not a sociopath— the narrative makes this clear by having Topher compare his own brain scan to that of an incipient serial killer ("Belle Chose" 1.3)—his fascination with technology and its uses acts in a similar way to Spike's chip; he prevents himself from parsing the full implications of what the technology means—although he clearly does not want it used on himself ("Needs" 1.8).

Previous to the events of "Omega," however, Topher often serves as the embodiment of the corporation's psychopathic nature (Bakan 2004). He refers to the Actives as "bison" ("Grey Hour" 1.4); he has no compunctions about sending Echo into engagements with significant deficits, such as asthma ("Ghost" 1.1) and total blindness ("True Believer" 1.5) if it is what the client or the corporation has requested; and he has little desire to parse the consequences of either his actions or that of Rossum, as long as he gets what he wants. Nor is this a secret, from either the Actives or Rossum; after being sent to "The Attic," one of Echo's nightmare scenarios is Topher literally playing with brains in the imprinting room, in true mad scientist fashion ("The Attic" 1.10). Adelle also points out that "the cold reality is that everyone here was chosen because their morals had been compromised in some way. Everyone except you, Topher. You were chosen because you had no morals. You had always thought of people as playthings. This is not a judgment. You always take good care of your toys" ("Belonging" 2.4).

That this is no longer true of Topher by the time Adelle says this does not change its basic relevance; through both flashbacks and the majority of season one, Topher is the amoral child, complete with a work area filled with both technology and actual toys (indeed, in the episode "Epitaph One," the group that discovers the Dollhouse years after the events of the first season mistake Topher's work area for a day care). Further, when he is given permission to what he calls "run a diagnostic" on an Active, but in actuality is an excuse to make himself a companion with which to celebrate his birthday, he creates a personality that bears a startling resemblance to himself: full of pop culture knowledge, likes playing video games and laser tag, eats junk food, and wants to "play with the sleepies" (aka the Actives) ("Haunted" 1.10).

Yet, the more powerful the corporation wielding the technology grows—installing a Doll as a U.S. Senator, weaponizing the erasure and imprinting process—the more ethical and moral Topher gets. Much as Echo, as stated above, begins to develop a self created out of what the technology forced upon her, so to does Topher develop a conscience based on what he can see the technology being used for. While this technology is used to strip out the personalities and individuality of the Actives, these corporate-created technologies actually manage to, in essence, permanently imprint a moral compass in the least likely individual.

## *Conclusion*

While it is clear that any individual whose best known for his work in mediums such as film and television would not be a Luddite, Whedon and company nonetheless recognize the particular dangers such "progress" can represent. From Adam in *Buffy* to the "life model decoy" storyline on *Agents of S.H.I.E.L.D.*, it is clear that it is not the technology itself that is necessarily the problem, but the uses to which it is (or can be) put. Like

Echo and Topher, it is the development of an awareness of consequences—something that the Dollhouse (and the Framework) promises to rid us of—that should be at the forefront of the ways in which we develop and use technological advances. This allows the series to question, without necessarily pathologizing innovation, how such progress comes about, and who benefits the most.

CHAPTER SEVEN

# "We're pimps and killers, but in a philanthropic way"
## Interrogating Corporate and Governmental Politics[1]

The announcement of the cancellation of *Dollhouse* early in its second season meant that particular narrative arcs that would have spanned at least the season, if not several seasons, were by necessity compressed. An overarching story for season two was supposed to be that of Senator Daniel Perrin (Alexis Denisof), introduced briefly via a news conference, in the season's first episode ("Vows" 2.1). He was portrayed as a crusader against the corporation Rossum, which he believes withheld vital treatment that would have saved his mother from the ravages of Alzheimer's disease ("Instinct" 2.2). He later discovers reports of human trafficking—which the viewer already knew were true—as well as a former Active willing to come forward. In all respects, Perrin seems positioned as a protagonist with enough power to fight corporate malfeasance.

In a revelation that could have served as a climax of the season's arc—but instead is revealed in episode five ("The Public Eye" 2.5)—Perrin is revealed as an Active himself, positioned not to fight Rossum, but to offer the appearance of accountability and transparency and thereby inoculate the corporation against further scrutiny while simultaneously destroying its competition. It is a stunning revelation, even in its compressed form. Most importantly, it indicates a sophisticated understanding of the collusive interaction, in contemporary America, between the corporate and governmental sectors. As Boulware writes: "The government and the profit-driven corporation that actively oppresses and denies value to those without capital are one and the same; they are in alliance to perpetuate the biopolitical schema that preserves access to life to those already in power and uses that power to further oppress those without capital on whom their privilege depends" (Boulware para 7).

In this chapter, I will examine the ways in which *Dollhouse* explored the nature of the relationship between the corporate sector and the government, particularly the ways in which it literally embodied these struggles through the Actives in particular, but also though Rossum employees and unwitting individuals. I will extend the arguments Naomi Klein used in her analysis of Milton Friedman's economic policies—in theory and in practice—which she connects with a series of shock therapy experiments performed in Canada at the behest of the U.S. government in the 1950s and 1960s. Further, I will touch on the ways in which the fatalist response to the corporate-created apocalypse shown in the series shares numerous features with certain sects of legalistic Christianity's response to issues such as climate change, natural disasters, and war. Finally, I will conclude with an examination of the ways in which the character of Echo subverts expectation and corporate embodiment by forming a different kind of "corporate" entity within herself.

## *"It's embarrassing how naïve you are": The Unholy Corporate/Government Alliance*

In the 2016 election season, much was made of candidate Hillary Clinton's ties to Wall Street, including six-figure speeches she gave to Goldman-Sachs (Drezner 2016), with the argument that such ties rendered her fundamentally unfit to take seriously the concerns of the working class over that of corporations. That point-of-view, however, did not take into account that the majority of decision-makers (both Democrats and Republicans) within government have significant ties to corporate America. More than half of the Senate and a third of the House have received large donations from finance, insurance, and real estate corporations, among numerous other entities such as agribusiness, law, and energy (Gilson 2010). Indeed, the current administration's cabinet has, in essence, put the wolves in charge of the hen house: putting a pharmaceutical executive in charge of Health and Human Services (Tom Price), an oil company executive in charge of environmental protection (Scott Pruitt), and a Goldman Sachs executive in charge of the National Economic Council (Gary Cohn), among others (Weissman 2017).

This collusive relationship between the governmental and corporate sector is nothing new, although with the passage of the Citizens United decision (as will be addressed below), it has certainly accelerated. Lee Drutman pinpoints corporations' frustration with increased government regulation, spurred on by public interest groups, in the 1950s and 1960s, as instrumental in the shift from corporations merely wanting to be able to do what they want sans government interference, to corporations essentially becoming partners in the governance of the United States. While Drutman points to corporations increasing comfort with lobbying, as well as victories over governmental regulation in the 1980s and 1990s, one of their biggest success stories was, not surprisingly, within the pharmaceutical sector. The adoption of Medicare Part D by the Bush Administration, which offered a prescription drug benefit but did not allow bulk purchasing, saved drug companies approximately $205 billion a year. Corporations now spend approximately $2.6 billion a year across numerous sectors to influence corporate-friendly policies and politicians, which exceeds the amount spent by the government to fund Congress (Drutman 2015). This massive expenditure of both money and labor has born fruit with favorable court rulings, less regulation, and a voice that exceeds that of non-corporate citizens by a comfortable margin, transitioning a representative democracy such as the United States, into a corporatocracy: "a partnership of 'too-big-to-fail' corporations, the extremely wealthy elite, and corporate-collaborator government officials" (Levine 2011).

There are several instances within *Dollhouse* that reflect this reality. While I will discuss the ultimate corporate politician, Daniel Perrin, in greater depth below, it is the more subtle moments that speak to the collaborative relationship between the government and the corporation within *Dollhouse*, ones that require no technological wizardry to distance the series' reality from our own. In the first season, Echo is placed within a cult as an unwitting spy to assure government agencies that said cult poses no danger, at the behest of a U.S. senator who is also a Dollhouse client. Given the nature of the engagements, many romantic, some illegal, that are shown within the series, said senator has essentially put a great deal of power into the hands of a corporation. Adelle sums up their relationship quite succinctly: "I don't wish to be vulgar, but one of the many benefits of having you as a client is that you help us avoid entanglements with federal agencies," clearly prioritizing his relationship with Rossum over his responsibilities to his constituents. Even his arguments in favor of the Dollhouse providing assistance are entirely self-serving: it is an election year, with "the family values voters on the right, the women's issue constituency on the left, all coming after me if anything untoward is going on behind those compound walls." To complete this unnamed senator's position as a corporate tool, he affirms that the government cannot perform the task of infiltration nearly as well as the corporation ("True Believer" 1.5), a familiar argument of lobbyists and other corporate supporters across the corporate/political spectrum. In other words, clients, whether government employees or CEOs, can expect a level of service from Rossum that includes, as per example, buying off judges to avoid prison time for a wealthy benefactor's "wayward nephew" (for wayward, read: serial killer) ("Belle Chose" 2.3), in exchange for the corporate body being left to regulate itself.

The senator's prizing of corporate abilities over governmental ones is undermined four episodes later, when it is revealed that the LA Dollhouse's head of security Laurence Dominic (Reed Diamond) is a mole placed by the National Security Agency (NSA) to monitor Rossum. While the series is never explicit about how long Dominic held his position at the Dollhouse, it was certainly enough time for him to be a trusted advisor to Adelle. The senator's earlier contention that a "wet-behind-the-ears" Quantico graduate would merely bungle the job of infiltration shows he was clearly unaware of the fellow governmental employee who had managed not to break cover even when accidentally dosed with an de-inhibiting drug ("Echoes" 1.7). The conversation Dominic has with Adelle when he is unmasked is instructive for what it says about the corporate/governmental relationship:

> ADELLE: Why did you want to bring down the Dollhouse? What can the NSA do with it that we can't?
> DOMINIC: I wasn't sent to bring you down. I was sent to make sure you didn't bring yourself down. If it weren't for me, Paul Ballard would have found you. I never lied to you about my methods or my priorities.
> ADELLE: You lied about your intentions.
> DOMINIC: You know what the world will be like when Rossum lets the Dollhouse slip from its grasp? The technology needs to be reigned in and controlled.
> ADELLE: By a clandestine organization with little government oversight?
> DOMINIC: It's embarrassing how naive you are. ("A Spy in the House of Love" 1.9)

Putting aside the irony of a representative of the NSA having the moral high ground in an argument about governmental regulations and control, this conversation is particularly resonant both within the narrative and within the real world. In essence, Adelle is arguing for corporate self-regulation in the Friedman tradition, while Dominic's concerns speak directly to the disingenuousness of the entire concept that the corporate body would do anything beyond what benefits itself. The naiveté Dominic accuses Adelle is (at least) two-fold: the idea that the NSA's only interest in Rossum's technology is self-interest; i.e., "what can the NSA do with it that we can't," and the hypocrisy of her accusation of the NSA as "clandestine" and unregulated during a conversation occurring within a secretive corporate underground facility that clearly has been subjected to little (or no) oversight itself.

This lack of oversight and regulation from anything other than Rossum itself is one of the reasons why its technology, in Dominic's words, "spiraled out of control," taking the rest of the world with it. While earlier series *Firefly* referred to the government as a "body of people, usually notably ungoverned" ("War Stories" 1.8), in contemporary society there are particular checks and balances baked into the system that theoretically prevent governmental bodies from the kind of unencumbered power Rossum wields. Instead, in *Dollhouse* as in the real world, it is merely a revolving door (Levine 2011) of quid pro quo, where only the wants and needs of the wealthy and powerful are worth considering.

## *"It's about what you need": Economic Shock and the Dollhouse*

Dr. Ewan Cameron, a Scottish psychiatrist at Allen Memorial Institute in Montreal in the 1950s, believed the best way to treat his psychiatric patients was to regress them to an infantile state, a slate blank of personal history and neuroses. Once regressed, Cameron thought he could reprogram them into healthy individuals through repeated taped positive messages. To accomplish this, he subjected patients to massive doses of electroconvulsive therapy (ECT), hallucinogenic drugs, and isolation chambers. By many accounts (Klein 2007; Foreman 1998; Bindman 1992), Cameron didn't succeed in anything except fragmenting the memories and personalities of those subjected to the treatment, along with dooming them to a lifetime of physical and mental anguish (Klein 25–29). In using Cameron's experiments as a metaphor for untrammeled global capitalism, Naomi Klein argues that, following economist Milton Friedman's ideas, governments and corporations use wars, natural disasters, and political vacuums to attempt to create the kind of tabula rasa that Cameron sought with his patients. Once a society is reduced to its basic elements (free of regulation and government interference), it will blossom into a capitalist Eden, in which the resources of that country can thus be sold to the highest corporate bidder and create prosperity for all (Klein 50).

Despite the fact that Friedman's economic theory has been developed and taught for decades, it has only recently been applied within a real-world context: in Chile under Augusto Pinochet, in Russian under Boris Yeltsin, and in Iraq during the second Iraq War. Even, to an extent, in the United States following the events of September 11, 2001, or in places like the Katrina-ravaged New Orleans, where private corporations used the devastation to push through shifts like creating charter schools and breaking the teachers' union (Klein 5–6), or outsourcing body removal to private companies in no-bid contracts (Klein 406–413). As per example, Kenyon International, a Bush donor and large corporate mortuary service, was hired for body removal at a rate of $12,000 per day, freezing out local, primarily African American-owned mortuaries that volunteered their services. In addition to already having what CorpWatch called a "scandalous past" that included both dumping bodies and influence peddling, Kenyon botched the job, failing to collect identifying information on the bodies they found, not collecting bodies with expedience (some were discovered more than a year after the hurricane), and billing for expense such as "DVD players" and "beef jerky" (Briggs 12–13). It is the "shock" of disaster—whether human- or nature-made—that Klein asserts creates the best conditions for a Friedman-style economic rebuilding, as well as the abuses that seem built into such a system. It is the human cost of these economic policies and corporate control, however, that wreak the same type of damage as Cameron's experiments did on his patients, with the same (ultimately) disingenuous contention that such "treatments" will make things better.

In what I argue represents a subversive televisual narrative explicating the machinations and outcomes of such policies as argued by Klein, the series *Dollhouse* offers a thoroughgoing critique within its narrative of unregulated corporate power, making manifest, through its fictional lens, Klein's analysis of the dangers of these policies. As stated earlier, *Dollhouse* is a series about a pharmaceutical and biomedical corporation (Rossum) that funds its research and development with several underground establishments called "Dollhouses." The series indicates that these exist worldwide ("Man on the Street"). The fact that Rossum is funded and enriched by the work of literally depersonalized individuals trapped in a corporate subsidiary easily parallels the numerous companies who employ sweatshop labor in developing or struggling countries, where oversight is minimal to nonexistent (Klein 195–229, Fishman 2006). While Rossum, both through its above-board (Alzheimer's treatments, medical equipment) activities and the illegal Dollhouses, has made billions, there is little narrative indication that the Rossum Corporation, at its highest levels, was interested in creating prosperity and power for any other entity than itself, with tentacles stretching into the government and academia. This is despite avowals on the series-associated website that the "Rossum family" only has "your best interests at heart" as well as that of its shareholders. Such language mirrors similar real-world companies' websites; Astra-Zeneca's indicates they offer "real value" for patients as well as "a continued focus on innovation" for shareholders, because "health connects us all" (Astra-Zeneca), offering, in essence, an ersatz version of progressive or socially responsible capitalism. (It also recalls the ersatz "family" language used by Brian the manager in *Roseanne*'s "Chicken Hearts" episode, as discussed in chapter two; the corporate "family" is a point I will address in the following chapter.)

Friedman himself, as mentioned earlier, indicates that the only social responsibility a corporation should engage is to increase profits for its shareholders (Bakan 34). That being said, it is interesting to note that at a 2014 Apple shareholder meeting, members of the National Center for Public Policy Research (NCPPR), a conservative think tank, confronted Apple CEO Tim Cook, calling on him to disclose the cost of the sustainability programs Apple engages in, as they doubted that they did anything to improve share price or the bottom line, and to commit to focusing only on the company's profitability. Cook retorted that he didn't care about the "bloody ROI [return on investment]" and told NCPPR that "If you want me to do things only for ROI reasons, you should get out of this stock" (Chaffin 2014). The continuing revelations of Apple's labor practices (Rollman 2016) undermining Cook's contentions is worth noting, although a deeper examination of this particular hypocrisy is beyond the scope of this chapter.

Putting aside the implications of the idea that the profit motive is the highest good, there *is* a particular hypocrisy in many corporations "greening" of themselves or their products. Bakan explicated this years before the Deepwater Horizon spill in the Gulf Coast revealed the hollowness of British Petroleum's assertion that they were environmentally committed to cleaner fuel options, simply by pointing out that the "green" initiatives were "relatively inexpensive, designed to enhance performance and yield short- and long-term benefits that outweigh their costs" (Bakan 45). In other words, it offers the necessary public relations spin—particularly for companies whose reputation is damaged—but also can serve to increase profits. As Bakan points out, though, as a corporation beholden to shareholders, British Petroleum could not take steps that would damage their bottom line; thus, they may donate money to environmental causes, fund research into fuel alternatives, and still drill in protected areas that damage the environment.

## *"Marketing campaign that big? He's hiding something": What You See Isn't What You Get*

This disconnect between the public face and private actions of corporations is frequently explored throughout *Dollhouse*'s two seasons. The episode "Echoes" (1.7), which is told partly in flashback, features a pre-wiped Echo, when she still had her original identity as Caroline Farrell. Caroline is an idealistic, recent college graduate inspired both by reports of animal cruelty and a Rossum ad campaign to fight against the corporation. Caroline and her friends view the ad campaign, featuring a smiling Rossum executive, Clive Ambrose (Philip Casnoff), with his multiracial family, as evidence of the gulf between Rossum's image and their actual practices ("Echoes" 1.7). "I don't want to say evil..." Caroline says, to which her boyfriend Leo (Josh Cooke) responds with "Yeah, you really do."

In the episode "Echoes" (1.7), it is revealed that Caroline Farrell went to Freeman College (a fictional university), for which Rossum is the corporate sponsor of their science department. "I spent four years partying in the shadow of that building," Caroline says. "Someone has to stand up." Indeed, the plot of "Echoes" pivots around a graduate student at Freeman College who colludes with another to commit corporate espionage (that is, stealing a Rossum-created dementia treatment and selling it to Rossum's competition); unlike Rossum, however, Sam's (Mehcad Brooks) motivation is to save his mother's house from foreclosure. Sam's action in the present day—dosing his co-conspirator Owen (Josh Fadem) to avoid sharing the profits and Echo to escape, causing Owen to commit suicide and facilitating an outbreak when the drug becomes airborne—are paralleled with Caroline's actions against Rossum years earlier. She and her boyfriend Leo's plan to film animal abuse and post it on YouTube goes fatally awry, leading to Leo's death. While Sam (and Caroline's) motivations might have been noble (helping his mother, exposing corporate abuse), it is clearly impossible, as shown in previous chapters, to not be affected by the environment of the particular beast both were taking on. Like Caroline, Sam's potential consequences for criminal behavior (jail time at least, less legal measures by the corporation possible) are eliminated when Adelle offers him a contract to be an Active.

The gap between the marketing and practices pointed out in "Echoes" (1.7) gestures toward the larger issue within the corporate structure. The tension between profit motives and more altruistic works within a corporation was an ongoing thematic element within *Dollhouse*. Adelle DeWitt, to clients, employees, and Actives, initially universally puts both the work of Rossum's and of the Dollhouses themselves in altruistic terms, insisting across multiple episodes that "we're giving people what they need." While on one level, such an assertion is part of the sales pitch to both Actives and clients (that is, selling the Active on a contract that will make them wealthy and/or alleviate a difficult situation; selling a client on the "reality" of the experience they are paying for), DeWitt clearly believes that she is both providing a valuable service to both Actives and clients and that she provides a unique level of care to her employees and Actives, just as Sam and Caroline considered they were doing the right thing in taking care of family members or the environment. For DeWitt, that the clients pay an eight- or nine-figure sum to meet their needs is immaterial, although there is narrative evidence that DeWitt herself is not entirely convinced of this. In "A Spy in the House of Love," she confides to her lover Roger (actually an imprinted Active) that she used to "grow replacement organs out of stem cells" and could actually "tell people what I do for a living" instead of serving "pathetic, deluded souls" like the Dollhouse clients (1.9). As mentioned in the previous chapter, Dollhouse employees and Actives cannot speak about the Dollhouse to non-employees; the only reason Adelle could confide in "Roger" is because he would be "wiped" when the engagement was completed. Yet the fact that she has made herself the very client she dismisses as "pathetic" and "deluded" by using one of the Actives for this romantic getaway is evidence of a certain degree of self-hatred for what she does for Rossum.

This self-hatred may be a secondary motivation for, as Topher explains to fellow programmer, Ivy, why: "Everyone wants to be righteous when they can afford it," whether it is programming Echo to serve as counselor to an abused child ("Briar Rose" 2.11), working with federal law enforcement to bring down a cult ("True Believer" 1.5), or stopping the shipment of an international arms dealer ("Vows" 2.1). In these instances, such actions could theoretically serve to assuage the consciences of the individuals within the corporate structure—as well as for the indiscretions for which they are guilty—but the structure itself would remain conscienceless. Bakan's argument, through his analysis of the contemporary corporate structure, is that if the corporation were indeed more than a "legal" person, that individual would hold the clinical diagnosis of a psychopath. That is, the psychopathic corporation provides a convenient cover for any number of negative consequences, using what Robert Monks calls "the externalizing machine" (qtd in Bakan 70).

An externality is, as Friedman defines it, "the effect of a transaction ... on a third party who has not consented or played any role in carrying out that transaction" (qtd in Bakan 61); the corporation itself is structured to externalize the environmental, social, and human costs of doing business, with the profit motive as its only concern (Bakan 73). The concept of externalized consequences to corporate behavior is made manifest in the literal embodiment of the Rossum Corporation's malfeasance in the numerous Dollhouses they have created to fund their research. As Bakan writes: "The corporation ... is programmed to exploit others for profit. That is its only legitimate mandate" (Bakan 69); everyone else, from employees to adversely affected unaffiliated individuals are not, he argues, "human *beings*" but "human *resources* [italics in original]" (Bakan 69). Rossum, by funding its research through the exploitative use of the Dollhouses, manifests this semantic division perfectly; not only are individuals devalued as "resources," but they literally "program" others for profit. The Actives, whose real names have been replaced with military codes (i.e., Echo, Sierra, Victor, November), are throughout the series referred to as "bison" ("Gray Hour" 1.4), "veal" ("Getting Closer" 2.10), or "pets" ("Needs" 1.08), among other dehumanizing designations. This not only externalizes the consequences for the corporation itself, but it is arguable that such dehumanization of those being exploited makes it easier for the employees that must carry out the processes of exploitation. If the Actives are not really human, who are they really hurting?

This cognitive dissonance becomes blatantly manifest in the arc of the character Priya Tsetsang (designation: Sierra). Introduced in the first episode of the series as a new Active (indeed, it is through Sierra that we see the initial "wiping" process that removes the original personality to make room for new ones), it is later revealed that unlike the nominal "consent" required of most of the other Actives (nominal due to their policy of targeting vulnerable individuals), Priya was supposedly suffering from paranoid schizophrenia, which the wiping and imprinting process attempted to treat. Topher, in seeking her out at a mental institution affiliated with Rossum, considered his treatment of Priya to be one of the "righteous" acts that assuaged his conscience. In fact, her schizophrenic

## Seven. "We're pimps and killers, but in a philanthropic way" 137

behavior was induced by Nolan Kinnard (Vincent Ventresca), a neuroscientist working for Rossum who was enraged by Priya's rejection of his high-priced advances, including commissioning a painting and throwing lavish parties in Priya's honor that made use of several Actives. Since engaging Actives costs in the "low millions" (Mitovich 2009), Kinnard either paid out of pocket, or Rossum fronted the cost, since Kinnard was a "rising star" in the corporation. When Priya tells him, "Nothing in this world could make me love you," he sets in motion the process that will divest her of her personality and rebuild her into a Priya that is devoted to him ("Belonging" 2.4). As addressed in the previous chapter, Topher's belief in the technology is both significantly undermined by Nolan's actions, and elucidates the ways in which the corporation understands Topher's own "programming" that allows him to be used as well; Priya's schizophrenia is a problem Topher can feel good about solving, as well as self-confirmation of his own brilliance. Further, Angela Zhang points out that the abuse narrative around Priya and Nolan "demonstrates ... that the 'real life' institutions permit it to happen. Behind Nolan Kinnard's power is also the support of the medical institution and an incredibly rich and powerful corporation, not to mention the inequities inherent in Nolan's status as a wealthy, educated American ... and Priya's status as poor, struggling artist and undocumented worker from Australia" (Zhang 405). In other words, whether Topher or Adelle is aware of it, they are complicit in Kinnard's actions even if they had no real knowledge of them. While Kinnard is clearly, in DeWitt's words, "a raping scumbag one tick shy of a murderer" ("Belonging" 2.4)—a surprising, if unacknowledged, admission by Adelle that the process of wiping away an individual's personality is morally close to murder—it is the corporate structure that allows him to flourish with an environment with seemingly limited oversight, from Adelle and Topher's ignorance allowing them to be used, to Rossum executive Matthew Harding's nonchalance when Adelle tells him what Nolan has done. Indeed, Harding warns Adelle against accusing a valuable Rossum "asset" of rape, mentioning Adelle's own indiscretions, dismissing concern that they are "slave merchants," and reminding her that she "wouldn't like the early retirement plan" (that is, the Attic, where problematic Actives and employees are sent).

The abuse narrative Zhang indicates exists between Nolan and Priya is also operative, if more subtly, in the story arc around Senator Daniel Perrin. True to Friedman's contention that regulation and government interference pervert the market and are antithetical to pure capitalism, the Rossum Corporation works to remove regulation and government interference through the use of Perrin. As Klein writes of Friedman's economic policies, Friedman promises that "the market, left to its own devices, would create just the right number of products at just the right prices, produced by workers at just the right wages to buy those products—an Eden of plentiful employment, boundless creativity, and zero inflation" (50). While Perrin initially seems positioned to expose Rossum's misdeeds—indeed, he mentions the Dollhouse by name: "an innocent word … that will take on a new and grim meaning … that will become synonymous with human trafficking, prostitution, and unconscionable abuse of neural technology" ("The Public Eye" 2.05)—it is merely a long game by Rossum itself to simultaneously inoculate itself from criticism and regulation and destroy the competition by placing the blame for subsequent events (including the murder of Perrin's wife/handler Cindy [Stacey Scowley] ["The Left Hand" 2.06]) on other neurotechnology corporations. Perrin, having been created by the corporation, is thus positioned to write favorable legislation on its behalf. That Perrin only has a brief awareness, quickly and literally erased by Rossum, that he is being used, only underscores his tragedy, and ties his arc with that of Priya's.

Despite Friedman's policies in favor of "pure capitalism," even the most basic dictionary definition of the word indicates that capitalism itself indicates a competitive market. Although fictional, Rossum's actions recall the particular medium on which the series is presented—that is, television—and the concentration of media in general following the Telecommunications Act of 1996, which removed restrictions for media companies' concentration of ownership and was essentially written by the lobbyists for major telecommunications companies (McChesney 51–53). By eliminating competition from other biomedical companies, Rossum and its real-world counterparts are in fact acting in a way that is antithetical to capitalism, despite Friedman's contentions.

Furthermore, despite the efforts to remove regulation and other "perversions" within the context of the series, Rossum did not, in fact, create Friedman's envisioned Eden, but rather a wasteland of *dumbshows* (those with no personality or memory) and *butchers* (those wiped but trained to kill), leaving only a small group termed *actuals* who had avoided wiping and imprinting. Like corporations such as WorldCom or Enron in the early 2000s, Rossum was brought down by its own hubris and greed, but it took the rest of the world down with it, in what Topher Brink terms the "thought-pocalypse." (Topher, as addressed in the previous chapter, is responsible for both imprinting the Actives and for making the technology "mobile"; in essence, his work creates the "thought-pocalypse," a fact that will eventually drive him to madness ["Epitaph One" 1.13; "Epitaph Two" 2.13]). As Klein argues, the experiments of Friedman-style economics in places such as the southern cone of South America, Iraq, and New Orleans after Hurricane Katrina—that is, places "shocked" by political vacuums, war, or natural disasters—were testing grounds for economic "shock therapy," all of which found the majority of their citizens in worse straits due to these policies. In Chile, for example, Friedman himself was on hand to advise Augusto Pinochet after the U.S.-facilitated coup (Kornbluh 2003) that resulted in the death of the democratically elected Salvadore Allende on September 11, 1973, suggesting that Pinochet create a recession that would thus "shock" Chile's economy into health, mainly by privatizing both services and economics and selling off the country's resources to private companies. This "therapy" led to large spikes in unemployment and poverty for everyone except those in political or economic power (Klein 80–83), in addition to the brutal realities of living under a military dictatorship, including tens of thousand civilians who were jailed or tortured, and an estimated 3095 civilians killed or "disappeared" ("Former Chilean army chief..." 2016).

This "shock doctrine" (that is, creating blank mental and/or physical terrain in which new information can be written), is a useful lens through which to examine how such corporate behavior and its potential outcomes are made manifest in *Dollhouse*'s two-season arc, particularly the apocalyptic world of "Epitaph One" (1.13) and "Epitaph Two: Return" (2.13), which visually mirrors the ravages of places who have experienced natural, economic, or political disasters, as well as through the storylines around Daniel Perrin and Scytheon, Rossum's military division. *Dollhouse*'s narrative arc eventually reverses Rossum's well-oiled externalizing apparatus first by revealing what lies beneath the marketing Caroline points out, but more importantly, by embodying these actions and reactions of the corporate structure in both employees and Actives.

## *"They were supposed to fix us; instead they left us empty": On (Not) Escaping the Corporation*

Under Clinton's and both Bushs' administrations, large swathes of military operations were sold to private contractors, under the aegis that private industry could better perform many of the essential functions of the military than the government (Yeoman 2003), a contention, as elucidated above, that played out in *Dollhouse* as well. Private military companies such as Blackwater were hired to provide both equipment and personnel. Brown and Root, a subsidiary of Halliburton, was tasked with certain logistical operations that used to be the purview of the U.S. military itself: entertainment, laundry, meal services, and recreation, as well as setting up base camps in foreign countries and training foreign troops. They won the right to provide these services under a no-bid contract ("Blackwater's rich contracts" 2007) and with little in the way of pressure from the federal government in terms of corporate accountability. This was made horribly clear in 2007, when Blackwater employees shot and killed 17 Iraqi civilians and injured 40 others; a massacre that took nearly a decade to effectively prosecute (Roberts 2017).

This privatization of military services, as well as the quiet boom in security-based companies—that is, surveillance equipment, software to monitor video and audio transmissions, and data mining and analysis—represents what Klein calls an "unprecedented convergence of unchecked police powers and unchecked capitalism, a merger of the shopping mall and the secret prison" (306). The recent, and ongoing, revelations about the NSA's foreign and domestic surveillance (Gellman 2013) are indicative of the policies that followed after September 11, 2001.

Further, the physical space of the Dollhouse within the series functions as both a "shopping mall" and a "secret prison." As a shopping mall, not only are the Actives given access to unlimited clothing, equipment, and physical care (in exchange for their personalities and freedom), but more significantly, the wealthy clients that Dollhouse services can "shop" for the perfect personality and body to satisfy their desires, whether it is a professor who fantasizes seducing a student while reading Chaucer ("Belle Chose," 2.03), a wealthy young man who enjoys elaborate romantic comedy scenarios on his birthday ("Ghost" 1.1; "Echoes" 1.7), or a man recreating his first success that his wife's sudden death prevented him from sharing with her ("Man on the Street" 1.06). Yet, both Actives and clients, it can be argued, are also trapped in a "secret prison"; the Actives are more literally trapped within the Dollhouse, although they lack the awareness to realize it, yet its clients are also trapped by their own desires, motives, or immaturity, a point the series makes across numerous episodes ("Man on the Street" 1.6; "A Love Supreme" 2.8). That nearly all of Echo's romantic engagements—with the exception of Joel Mynor, who stops reliving his fantasy of his dead wife and moves on ("A Love Supreme")—end with the client's death or serious injury (the professor is stabbed in the neck in "Belle Chose" 2.3, Alpha targets and kills Matt Cargill [Brett Claywell] and others ["A Love Supreme"]) is a brutal but interesting take on the dangers of living primarily in corporate-created fantasies.

Bennett argues that the series itself engages in what she refers to as an "increasingly apparent and hostile critique" of the "Hollywood dream factory," as well as the corporate structure that supports it. While Bennett rightly indicates that real-world pharmaceutical companies generally do not dabble in the entertainment industry—although, as addressed in the previous chapter, their advertising is a significant source of funding for it—she argues that "by making the Dollhouses part of a larger, multi-faceted conglomerate, the series highlights the interconnection of the entertainment industry with other branches of the Western capitalist infrastructure" (Bennett para 11), including the ways in which pharmaceutical companies use celebrity endorsements and large-scale advertising campaigns. Both Tresca and Bennett see within the series a critique of the current media conglomeration climate, with Tresca offering a point-by-point comparison of both character and narrative to the series' creator, writers, and actors. Tresca's contention that Topher Brink is a stand-in for creator Joss Whedon (Tresca 412–413) adds a particular resonance to Topher's final decision to "broadcast" (Topher's words) a signal that would restore people's original selves but kill him, which dovetails with Whedon's contention that he was finished with television (Kushner 38–39). Along with Tresca, Bennett points out that it is relatively easy to read the Rossum Corporation as a stand-in for the Fox network, and by the second season, with the continued network interference and imminent cancellation of the series, Rossum/Fox were clearly portrayed as more unambiguously evil (Bennett para 34). In her analysis of the episode "The Attic" (2.12), in which three of the main characters are trapped in a nightmare landscape powered by their own fears as they are kept in a vegetative state, Bennett argues: "'The Attic' seems to suggest that for all Hollywood's image as a dream factory, it should really be viewed as a place of nightmares. The entertainment industry is fueled by the imaginations of the creative people who work within it, not to mention the imaginations of the audiences who consume their output" (Bennett para 39).

Bennett's analysis teases out the metaphor of the episode, which reveals that the Rossum mainframe is in fact powered by the minds and adrenaline of those who are emptied and sent there, recalling Bakan's contention that in the corporate mindset, humans are merely "resources" at the company's disposal, as is the audience's investment in the products the "dream factory" produces.

By making Rossum a biomedical company, the narrative of *Dollhouse* thus creates a corporation that literally reaches inside the human brain, a most intimate incursion. An "ad" (created by Fox/Mutant Enemy as paratext/publicity) for Rossum (November Ad, 2009) actually baldly states Rossum's company slogan: "Your Mind Is Our Business" (see chapter six for an in-depth analysis of this). As the narrative unfolds across the 26 episodes of the series, it becomes apparently this is not just marketing; Rossum has access to every brain scan taken by its equipment ("Omega" 2.12) and thus the ability to create or recreate the personalities of those individuals without consent, and, in essence, rent those personalities to anyone who can pay the price. Rossum touts itself as the world leader in MRI equipment manufacturing, as well as drug research and development, meaning its reach is truly global.

Season two reveals that they have also branched out into areas similar to the aforementioned Blackwater and Halliburton subsidiaries by providing soldiers for hire through their military division, Scytheon, something Boyd explicitly names as "Rossum's answer to Blackwater." As a fictional construct, Scytheon capabilities far exceed their real-world counterparts; they use former soldiers with Active architecture (that is, brains rewired to accept personality imprints) to create a "hive-mind army" out of former military personnel diagnosed with post-traumatic stress disorder who were treated by Rossum as part of military services privatization. The title of the episode in which this is introduced—"Stop-Loss" (2.9)—thus takes on extra resonance, as "stop-loss" is a military term for the extension of a tour of duty past the parameters of the original contract. Despite the fact these soldiers are supposedly no longer bound either by military or corporate contracts, they are, in essence, conscripted back into the Rossum corporate umbrella because, as one soldier refers to it: "The military was supposed to fix us ... but they left us empty"; so too did the corporation. Since the Active architecture is not reversed when an Active's contract is up, that corporation essentially remains with them permanently, or, as Ballard says, "No one ever really leaves here, do they?" ("The Public Eye" 2.05).

This is also made abundantly clear in the arc of the character Madeleine Costly (Miracle Laurie). She signs up to be an Active (designation: November) after the sudden death of her young daughter, with the promise (from Adelle) that they would take away her debilitating grief. When she is released from her contact and her original personality restored—sans grief—it seems to have worked; however, when asked if she was "happy," her only response is "I'm not sad" ("Instinct" 2.2). The obvious inference is that even the painful emotions define and create an individual,[2] and thus to remove those through technological (or pharmaceutical, as lowered affect and anhedonia are often side effects of antidepressants) means an individual is left empty and emotionless, a shell.

This type of emptiness is a familiar Whedon theme explored expertly in season five of *Angel*, in which, as discussed in chapter one, the character of Fred is emptied out, a "shell," to make room for a "god-king" ("A Hole in the World" 5.15; "Shells" 5.16). Such a fate is especially poignant in Fred's case; during a conversation between Fred and Gunn about their shared revenge killing of her mentor, Fred affirms she would rather feel the guilt and pain of their actions than live as a "heartless, uncaring shell" ("Sacrifice" 4.20). The vampires featured in both *Buffy* and *Angel*, whose souls depart upon being turned, provide an additional example, as well as the Reavers in *Firefly*. The Reavers, in many respects represent a close approximation of the Actives; a pharmaceutical intervention they did not consent to hyped their aggressive responses "beyond madness" (*Serenity*). Like the Actives, there is no reset; once exposed, they never reverted back, just as the "Active architecture" is never removed, and it is unclear whether they have any control over their murderous actions.

Thus, it is not only what the corporation puts in Madeleine's head (the Active architecture), but what they removed (her grief) that make her vulnerable to further abuse by Rossum. This is also true of the soldiers recruited into Scytheon. In both instances, there is the outward appearance of "helping" or "curing" these individuals (as Topher thought he was curing Priya; see chapter six), making the reality far more insidious. In Madeleine's case, the glimpses of her reintegration into her life make it clear she can no longer connect with either her friends or the memory of her daughter. In one scene, she holds her daughter's favorite stuffed animal, staring down at it with great concentration, as if she is attempting to access feelings that are no longer there, before putting it in a box marked for donation to Goodwill. While the shortened episode running time for the second season meant that most of these scenes with Madeleine were relegated to DVD extras, they add extra resonance to the idea that without the grief, she can experience none of the happiness.

For the soldiers, the "curing" of their PTSD left them with no real purpose, much as their battles fought in Iraq and Afghanistan seem to have been neither as productive nor as noble as they may have anticipated when they enlisted. The series underscores this through a brief and subtle point about the war in Afghanistan, mainly through the demeanor of the active Victor, when his original personality (Anthony Ceccoli) is returned, only to find out the war that traumatized him is not only still going on, but escalating ("Stop-Loss" 2.9). Later, his Attic-induced nightmare is a loop of a battle within Afghanistan, in which a fight with a suspected insurgent reveals that he himself is the insurgent, possibly suggesting that Anthony himself bore doubts about the ethics of that particular invasion. Rossum uses this emptiness to thus conscript both Madeleine and the soldiers into further service to the company—without even the earlier, if nominal, appearance of consent—to the former Actives' own detriment and the corporation's benefit.

Madeleine is also used as a pawn by Rossum. She agrees to testify about the Dollhouse, only to have her reputation and sanity impugned by it; they provide manufactured evidence to Perrin's Senate subcommittee that she was in a mental hospital in Canada being treated for delusions. Following this, she is taken to the Washington, D.C. Dollhouse (despite her contract being up), wiped, and abandoned ("The Public Eye" 2.6). The Scytheon soldiers, meanwhile, are tasked with seeking out fellow soldiers/Actives recently released from their contracts; even before Anthony is released, Scytheon had accessed his file, and he is not out of the Dollhouse an entire day before a group of soldiers invade his hotel room and kidnap him. Once they explain their purpose—"their Active architecture allows their minds to be linked via neural radio" (in other words, a hive-mind)—Anthony is happy to sign up. As one of the soldiers says, they are soldiers, they "need something to fight." That this fight is for the benefit of a corporation that not only left them "empty" but also clearly will not let them go is not a question they ask. Questions and individuality are not only not allowed, but the soldiers programmed to kill any of their number if said individual resists the programming. They represent an early version of the aforementioned "butchers" seen in the Epitaph episodes, whose only programming is to kill those not programmed to kill. For both Madeleine and the Scytheon soldiers—and eventually, the rest of the world—the corporation's desires and needs trump the autonomy, and even lives, of others.

As Naomi Klein writes of Dick Cheney (but could apply to numerous individuals in both the public and private sector), whose connections with Halliburton are well known, "he ... has ... built a fortune based on the profitable prospect of a grim future" (291); namely, an endless "war on terror." In *Dollhouse*, it becomes clear that the "hive mind" technology Scytheon uses is directly related to the eventual mass imprinting of individuals as the aforementioned "butchers." Both in the series *Dollhouse* and in contemporary America, there are billions to be made by the canny exploitation of the vulnerable, fearful, or angry.

Yet banking on a "grim future" is precisely what the end narrative of *Dollhouse* interrogates. In "Epitaph Two," despite the fact that the world is essentially destroyed, the last remaining Rossum executives—Clive Ambrose (Nate Dushku) and Matthew Harding (Noah Harpster)[3]—are still reaping the benefits of the technology by "upgrading" their bodies and, in the case of Harding, using them to indulge all of his appetites before discarding them for another "suit." That is, both Ambrose and Harding gather "dumbshows" within which they can upload their personalities; that Harding looks at these individuals as clothing further underscores their object status. The grim future Rossum created is thus for the benefit of a small amount of individuals, much as the security companies financially benefitted throughout the 2000s due to the events of September 11.

These same security companies have come under fire for allegations of using shell companies in the Cayman Islands (Stockman 2008); bribing foreign government officials (Department of Justice 2009); negligence in building and in protection of soldiers (Risen 2008); and sexual abuse (McGreal 2008) and human trafficking (Vogel 2009)[4]—the latter two also accusations frequently leveled (and proven to be true) at the Rossum-owned Dollhouses—while simultaneously claiming to make the world safer and more efficient. While others who work for Rossum, like Adelle DeWitt, insist that they are helping people—both clients and Actives—through the use of this technology, such a delusion is exposed as such most blatantly in the behavior of Harding in "Epitaph Two" (2.13). Heather M. Porter and Sherry Ginn, in their analysis of Dollhouse clients and in pursuit of the question as to why clients use the services of the Dollhouse, found that the Dollhouse's biggest and most frequent client (at least for the engagements seen or referenced in the series) was Rossum itself. "It pretends to be in the business of fulfilling fantasies and giving people what they need," they write. "However, when these engagements are examined, the majority of the time, Rossum is fulfilling its own needs" (Porter and Ginn 106). In that respect, Harding's actions, even past the end of the world, are still fully aligned with Rossum's. Harding's consumption of both food and bodies as the world falls apart around him bespeaks a corporate greed that will never be sated.

## *"Everyone's programmed, Boyd"*: *The Crusade for the End of the World*

This corporate self-interest is established throughout the narrative of *Dollhouse*. This is seen most particularly in their placement of an Active as a U.S. senator (and, according to the *Epitaphs* graphic novel series, eventual president), as well as through Boyd Langton, one of the original founders of Rossum, and his use of the Los Angeles Dollhouse employees and the Active Echo to shield himself from the effects of his own technology; an off-shore account, so to speak. Using the language of corporate branding—Adelle, Topher, and actives Echo are his "family"; he "loves" them—further underscores the hollowness of such assertions within the corporate sector and points to a particular fatalism with regard to the consequences of unchecked development and use of resources that is seen frequently in the overlaps of capitalism and certain evangelical Christian sects. In particular, it is seen in adherents to Hal Lindsey's book *The Late, Great Planet Earth* (and its many revisions) that environmental and social catastrophes are inevitable (and welcome) signs of "End Times" (Lindsey 1970). While neither Boyd nor the narrative itself makes explicitly mention of this particular strain of Christian thought, both his words and actions are congruent with it. Boyd claims that the technology exists, and thus will be used; the end of civilization is a given, and therefore one can choose to either be conquered or the conqueror. His hand-picked group of Adelle, Topher, and Echo can all be "saved" if they chose to side with him.

As Stephen Pfohl argues in his analysis of the popular apocalyptic *Left Behind* series, in which technological advances are both the tools of Satan and the tools of redemption, it is important to acknowledge "the complete of wisdom lodged in the flesh, rather than to honour fundamentalist dreams of rising above the body and paying homage to the Word alone" (Pfohl 362). To put this in the context of *Dollhouse*, both Boyd and Rossum, have invested themselves and looked for salvation in technology, which in *Dollhouse*, as well as in the *Left Behind* books, is both destructive and redeeming, as I discussed in the previous chapter. In essence, the "technology of the Word" (362) seeks to separate from and revenge itself on the flesh (363), a concept that Kate Rennebohm exposes as a hopeless endeavor; the body itself interacts in the world in a way that has an effect on the mind, even if the mind is unaware of it (14–16). In the post-apocalyptic "Epitaph" episodes, the aforementioned Actuals (who have retained their original personalities) assiduously avoid lengthy exposure to any "tech" (technology)—radios, walkie-talkies, phones—as they are the tools by which the mind is divorced from the flesh, in a kind of secular Rapture that takes the "soul" and leaves the body. The scare quotes around "soul" are indicative of Dollhouse employees' dismissal of the concept as fantastical and foolish; as Topher says to Paul, who refers to the wiping process as "stealing their souls": "Yes, and then we put 'em in a glass jar with our fireflies" ("Omega" 1.12). Yet it is the figure of Topher that in many ways is the primary encapsulation of this mind/body dichotomy within *Dollhouse*; it is his mind that sees the connections between disparate technologies and creates the device that is responsible for society's destruction, as well as the device that restores it, and his body he sacrifices to "fix everyone else" ("Epitaph 2: Return" 2.13), as was addressed in the previous chapter.

In her analysis of the rise of fundamentalism in Judaism, Christianity, and Islam, Karen Armstrong argues that between the mid–1920s (after the Scopes trial), and the 1960s, Christian fundamentalists expressed another contradiction, that is, seeing the end of the world in the shifts in modern society, and feeling "a sense of confidence and superiority" about their "privileged information" regarding what these shifts meant in Biblical terms (Armstrong 217). For fundamentalists, such catastrophes are inevitable, but would not touch them, as they would be "saved." The concomitant view of inevitable destruction and divine intervention that Armstrong argues represents moral nihilism is precisely the language and view Boyd and others espouse. When Ambrose, in the body of the Active Victor, informs Adelle and Topher that Rossum plans to sell all the Actives' bodies for "nine figures," allowing the wealthy immortality through an endless supply of flesh, he uses Biblical terms to sell the idea to Adelle and Topher: "You've both earned a place on the ark; Mr. Brink, you practically built it" ("Epitaph One" 1.13). Ambrose's offer to them comes from the same place that Armstrong explicated above; he radiates both the confidence and superiority of the fundamentalists, and considers that he (as well as those he chooses), hold a privileged place and special understanding of what life (and afterlife) holds. In essence, Ambrose offers a corporate view of an afterlife strikingly similar to the concept of the Rapture, in which believers are taken, flesh and soul, into Heaven, which he refers to as "complete anatomy upgrades": "Imagine what one man can do if he has no fear, and can live forever?" Boyd too expresses his ultimate plans in theological terms; he knows that the technological apocalypse is coming, and tells his chosen few that "Echo is going to save us all" ("The Hollow Men" 2.12), thereby positioning his protégé as a kind of messiah.[5]

The fatalism of this viewpoint—that such catastrophes will occur, cannot be stopped, and will not affect the chosen—is labeled "spectacularly insane" ("The Hollow Men" 2.12) by Adelle, and indeed none of the potential "saved" agrees to join Boyd or give into the despair or fear that such a viewpoint implicitly suggests. By shifting such a worldview from its religious origins into a socioeconomic construct allows it to be both interrogated and subverted without bringing in the particularly divisive subject of religion into the conversation. Not that capitalism and religion, at least in a Western context, operate in different spheres. The Reconstructionist movement envisions as society based on their interpretation of the Bible, including a "strictly capitalist economy [that] must be enforced; socialists ... are sinful" (Armstrong 361). The parallels to that type of Christian belief within *Dollhouse*, and Boyd, are inescapable.

Further, Boyd's claims of a paternal love for his chosen few thus not only exposes the patriarchal nature of such practices and beliefs, but represent an inversion of a Whedon trope—that of a "created" family of friends and associates, whose bonds are often stronger than those of blood relatives (Burr and Jarvis 269–283)—a point I will explore in greater detail in the next chapter.

To understand how this is made manifest in *Dollhouse*, it is important to return to the metaphor that Naomi Klein uses in her analysis of "disaster capitalism." She compares the exploitation by corporations and government of natural (such as hurricanes or tsunamis) and human-made (war, industrial accidents, terrorist attacks) disasters to Cameron's CIA-funded experiments with shock treatments in the 1950s. That is, the fear and sense of dislocation that disasters cause in a country's inhabitants (that is, the "shock") offers the savvy corporation a blank slate in which to impart new messages or ideas outside of the "distortions" of such things as workers' rights, minimum wage requirements, regulation, and state-funded education (Klein 53). On a governmental and corporate level, the "shock" of the September 11 attacks allowed the government to impose regulations on behavior (wire-tapping, suspension of habeas corpus) that an unshocked, less susceptible population may not have agreed to, using repeated messages like "terror," "axis of evil," and "radical Islam" to program the population to accept these new rules. Such thinking seems to also be on offer in the recently elected Trump administration and GOP-lead congress, with large cuts in services that primarily help the economically disenfranchised in favor of tax cuts that primarily aid the wealthiest (Levey 2017) under the auspices that such cuts would create economic growth without such regulatory "distortions."

In a similar vein, the Actives in *Dollhouse* are controlled by a series of coded messages; certain words or phrases can create a trust bond between handler (i.e., those responsible for Actives on assignment) and Active ("Ghosts" 1.1; "The Target" 1.2; "Omega" 1.12) or even program an Active to fight or kill ("Man on the Street" 1.6; "The Left Hand" 2.6; "A Love Supreme" 2.8; "The Hollow Men" 2.12), a process whose technology, as well as the Active's reactions to these "treatments," is visually similar to ECT. Yet the series also makes a larger point about the coded messages of everyday life; the episode "Man on the Street," in which the narrative is interspersed with several vox pop interviews, even features one man claiming: "You think it's not happening? You think they're *not* controlling you? Don't worry about it. Just sit back and wait for them to tell you what to buy." While this is just one of numerous perspectives offered within the interviews, it does gesture toward the use of the media to make the previously undesired thing or untenable practice more acceptable. Robert McChesney contends that profit competition within commercial media allows companies to "give the people what they want," a point Whedon explicitly addressed in an early interview, stating that narratives should *not* "give people what they want" but rather "give people what they need" (Robinson 2001); that, not the "happy path" or "easy resolution" but what feels narratively correct. Of course, the blurred line between "want" and "need" is precisely what *Dollhouse* interrogates.

For media companies, McChesney concludes that they inevitably determine that "the only policy option is to unleash the market" and eliminate the government regulations on media as "undemocratic" (9); this is one of the structuring myths that prop up a media system that falls far short of democratic discourse (see also McChesney 2000). Media and the advertising that support it, he further argues, "accentuate ... class bias," since both the programming and the media itself have a vested interest in attracting only affluent viewers. Thus, neither in *Dollhouse* nor the real world, do corporations have any true incentive to be democratic in either their policies or in the distribution of resources, despite public avowals to the contrary.

Both Cameron's and DeWitt's assertions that they were helping people are also revealed as hollow. Cameron's research was funded by the CIA and is currently used as "advanced interrogation" techniques; in *Dollhouse*, employees like DeWitt are either willing participants or unwitting pawns in a greater scheme. The mind-wiping technique leaves the Actives vulnerable to the corporation, as their brains are permanently rewired, even after their contracts are up, and to any abuse of the technology. Cameron's patients, as well, were cured of nothing by his treatment; instead, they suffered lifelong memory loss, seizures, and bone fractures from the intensity of the shocks they received (Klein 25–48).

The character of Senator Daniel Perrin within *Dollhouse* also closely aligns with the erase and rewrite objectives of both Cameron and Rossum, as well as the inherent vulnerabilities such a "treatment" causes. This is not the first time that a Whedon series has referenced to contemporary politics or policies. Whedon's first series, *Buffy the Vampire Slayer*, had the Initiative, a government-sponsored military operation supposedly dedicated to eradicating supernatural threats, but in reality using human and demonic individuals to create powerful cyborg soldiers. Spin-off series *Angel* added another facet to the Initiative; in a World War II flashback episode ("Why We Fight" 5.12), the Initiative (then known as the Demon Research Initiative) approaches Angel for help with a submarine overrun by demons; the plot makes clear that the technology seen on *Buffy* was appropriated by the Initiative from Nazi scientists, paralleling the real-world actions of Operation Paperclip following World War II (Interagency Working Group). As Rhonda Wilcox points out, and as addressed in chapter two of this work, the sixth season narrative arc, in which Buffy gets a subsistence level job at the fictional fast food chain Doublemeat Palace, does allow the series to examine the larger corporate structure, particularly the "disadvantages for workers at the bottom rung" (Wilcox 93). While the episode where the chain is introduced ("Doublemeat Palace" 6.13) has Buffy convinced that there is a corporate conspiracy that turns the workers into zombies, only to reveal that it is a lone demon drugging and consuming workers, it is also the case that the hopeless of the positions themselves contributes to the dead-eyed and empty staff. Wilcox points out: "[T]he fact that Doublemeat is not involved in a conspiracy makes it clear that there is a problem in the system—which, in the real world, does not have to be conspiratorial to be problematic" (Wilcox 93). It is the series *Angel* and *Firefly*, however, that are the true antecedents to *Dollhouse*'s narrative regarding corporate America. As Zhang points out, *Buffy* focused more on fighting the patriarchy, as represented by villains such as the ancient vampire known as The Master (Mark Metcalf), the male-dominated Watcher's Council that was supposed to train and guide slayers, or Sunnydale's demonic mayor's corrupt local government, which Zhang argues were "framed as 'supernatural' and separate from … 'normal life'" (404).

That being said, Zhang's contention that the "real-world' institutions … portrayed in Buffy are typically benign and unproblematic" (Zhang 404) does not take certain things into account, particularly two significant "real world" institutions featured in the series. The portrayal of the Sunnydale police, for example, ranges from ineptitude ("Ted" 2.14) and complicity ("School Hard" 2.03; "Empty Places" 7.19) in their repeated attempts to ignore or downplay evidence of the supernatural, to downright hostility ("Empty Places"). The high school administration, primarily represented

*Seven. "We're pimps and killers, but in a philanthropic way"* 151

by Principal Snyder (Armin Shimerman), condone locker searches and censor books ("Gingerbread" 3.14); expel Buffy ("Becoming, Part 1" 2.21); or stand idly by while a demon attacks students ("Graduation Day, Part 2" 3.22). It is important to note that the Doublemeat Palace arc works as a corporate critique precisely because it is one of the few examples of a diagetic establishment in the series that is at least a national corporation, as most of the establishments on Buffy—the Espresso Pump, the Magic Box,[6] and the Bronze being the most noticeable—are, if not locally owned, are at least not recognizable franchises.

Addressed in chapter two, *Buffy*'s small town setting necessarily limits both character and narrative interaction with the corporate structure. *Angel*, the *Buffy* spin-off set in Los Angeles, is better positioned to incorporate such critiques within its narrative. Wolfram and Hart combines legal maneuvering with the supernatural to undermine Angel and his team's stated mission to "help the helpless." It is only when they offer the firm and all its resources to Team Angel that Wolfram and Hart does the most damage to the characters. By placing them in a position where profit margins trump everything, they successful keep the heroes from changing the system. Their liaison to the "Senior Partners" (a group of powerful demons who exist on a different plane of existence) continually reminds them, a la Friedman's dismissal of corporate greening, that any "good" they do cannot jeopardize profitability, or they will lose the resources they have ("Conviction" 5.1; "Hellbound" 5.4, "Time Bomb" 5.19). *Firefly*, of course, featured the megacorporation Blue Sun, with enormous power and resources and the same appalling lack of accountability as *Dollhouse*'s Rossum.

Within *Dollhouse*, however, corporate malfeasance is a more thoroughgoing part of the storyline with a real-world resonance. That is, the "rewriting" of the partying scion of a wealthy political family cannot help but call to mind former president George W. Bush and his claims to have stopped drinking and partying after being "born again" (Borger 2005). Daniel Perrin is indeed "born again" in a technological sense; while he ostensibly remains Daniel Perrin (unlike Actives such as Victor, Sierra, or Whiskey [Amy Acker], who are un-imprinted until hired), those parts of his personality that were untenable to a political career were removed and replaced with ambition and political savvy. He thus represents the ultimate corporate-sponsored politician, with a similar representation of technology as religion displayed in Boyd and the other Rossum executives, as discussed above.

While the series offers numerous examples (as elucidated above) of the sociopathic nature of Rossum, their action toward Daniel Perrin bespeak of an even more insidious lack of regard for others. As mentioned at the start of the chapter, Perrin is initially presented as antagonistic toward Rossum, with a personal motivation—he believes they withheld research and medication that could have helped his Alzheimer's-afflicted mother—that adds gravitas to his crusade. When it is revealed to both Perrin and the viewer simultaneously that not only is he a programmed creation of the very corporation he is fighting, but also one that is primarily programmed to help rather than harm Rossum, he is fractured to a greater degree than other Actives seen within the narrative. He first cannot accept the reality of their interference in his mind and his body, and when he does, his first instinct is to return to his family's home, despite the fact that, as Echo points out to him, it would be the first place they would look ("The Left Hand" 2.6).

Further, while Perrin agrees with Echo that Rossum needed to be taken down for the numerous crimes they perpetrated, he is particularly vulnerable due to the interweaving of his own personality with the "enhancements" wired into him—ambition, intelligence—making it more difficult for him to discern what about him is real and what is manufactured by the corporation. This is mirrored in the resolution of the Perrin storyline, when Rossum rewrites the unexpected consequences of his awakening and escape—including Perrin being given a "sleeper protocol" that led him to kill his handler/wife—to their own advantage, continuing to twist what was there to benefit themselves. The relationships developed between Rossum and the government, discussed above, were clearly not enough influence to give the corporation's best client—itself—what it needed.

What is curious about Perrin is that there is no indication that he was given a choice or consented to being thus rewritten. A flashback indicates that he remembers his partying past, but only in the context of something his political opponents could potentially use against him ("The Left Hand"). While most of the Actives we see at least nominally consented, Perrin seemingly has more in common with Priya (Sierra), who was an Active only because of the machinations of psychiatrist Nolan Kinnard as revenge for her rejection of him. One of the problematic aspects of the Perrin arc ties him even more closely with Priya's story. In order to discover Rossum's plans for the senator, DeWitt authorizes a plan in which Perrin is drugged and Echo programmed as a prostitute that would make an incriminating sex video while he was under the influence ("The Public Eye" 2.5). In essence, given that Perrin is unable to consent, DeWitt essen-

Seven. "We're pimps and killers, but in a philanthropic way" 153

tially orders Perrin raped, something that is not acknowledged by DeWitt, Perrin, Bree (the personality with which Echo is programmed), or the narrative itself. This continues a problematic pattern in Whedon series that seem uncomfortable addressing non-consensual sex inflicted on men as rape, including Riley Finn (Marc Blucas) in *Buffy* ("Who Are You" 4.16; rogue Slayer Faith [Eliza Dushku] switches bodies with Buffy and goes after boyfriend Riley) and Grant Ward (Brett Dalton) in *Agents of S.H.I.E.L.D.* while under mind control ("Yes Men" 1.15; the perpetrator is a powerful female alien who can control humans with her voice). Both Riley and Ward's "feeling and emotional well-being are ignored after they are victimized, furthering the myth that men should be strong enough to cope with being raped" (Lenk and Lynch para 30). Indeed, in both instances, they are blamed by their partners for what happened, and are not allowed to express feelings of trauma (Lenk and Lynch para 32).

This abuse of Perrin goes even further, however, given that Perrin has no idea he is an Active until a remote wiping device is used on him. The choice of Perrin by Rossum (and presumably with the consent of his family) seems motivated by the resonance of the Perrin family name. While the series does not go into detail with regards to his history, one can assume from the context that in the Dollverse, the name "Perrin" could be equivalent to "Bush" or "Kennedy" in terms of a long-term association with politics and government. It is the power of this name that allows the "real" Daniel Perrin to be thus hollowed out and replaced with a more "brand-friendly" version of himself. While I discussed in chapter three the way in which Marvel branded the series *Agents of S.H.I.E.L.D.* as a Joss Whedon series despite his minimal involvement, and related it to the ironic exhaustion Whedon had expressed years earlier in his song "Heart, Broken," this idea of making an individual a brand, as are both Whedon and Perrin, is both applicable and closer in time in this context. For both Whedon and Perrin, it is the name that matters more than the actions, at least to the corporation.

Indeed, Rossum seems particularly gifted in the area of brand management. While the Dollhouse (and potential uses of their technology) is clearly illegal, they have made the necessary connections that allow them to be left to regulate themselves. With the creation of the new Daniel Perrin, Rossum thus controls the outcome by using Perrin to initiate an investigation into their business practices that will inevitably reflect favorably on Rossum and destroy its competition; in essence, using a real investigation to provide a false corporate transparency. Yet the ultimate outcome of Rossum's technology destroys the world, turning people either into blanks (dumbshows) or weapons (butchers), which seemingly negates their efforts to destroy their competition and become a world-leader in neuro-technology. Rossum's power and the inevitable consequence of marrying political, medical, and social power with a single-minded focus on profit is initially pointed recalls the aforementioned conversation between Adelle and Dominic ("A Spy in the House of Love" 1.9). This particular argument takes on a greater resonance in the current political climate, with the aforementioned corporate interests in positions of authority within the governmental agencies that would normally be tasked with policing their activities and a budget proposal that further guts governmental funding and ability to call such corporate actors to any kind of accountability (Soffen and Lu 2017). Dominic's prediction is accurate in that Rossum does let the technology "slip from its grasp" in its quest for more power and control, which begs the question: If there is little world left to rule over, what then becomes the point?

For the answer to this question, one need only look at contemporary corporate culture. When companies like Enron collapsed, leaving thousand of employees out of work and pension-less, or the housing bubble burst and led to thousands being rendered effectively homeless, many of those in charge retained their fortunes. Indeed, despite their key role in causing the current recession, Goldman Sachs and Merrill Lynch executives still received multi-million dollar bonuses the year after the bailout (Coster 2009). Thus, despite any economic, environmental, or social damage a corporation causes, there are the privileged few who are cushioned from the effects of their own errors, which, as discussed earlier, was precisely what Boyd attempted to do in using Echo.

## *"We're not anybody, we're everybody": Echo as Corporate Body*

In 2009, the Supreme Court, in its Citizens United decision (Kennedy 2010), ruled that a corporation has the same right to free speech as a human, thus extending previous rulings dating back to the 19th century that introduced the concept of corporate personhood. (The recent Hobby Lobby [Alito 2014] ruling also apparently granted corporations freedom of religion as well.) At the basic level, Actives within *Dollhouse* represent a parallel to the real-world implications of the Citizens United Supreme Court decision. Rossum, as revealed in "The Attic" and discussed in the previous chapter, not only literally uses the minds and bodies of humans to power itself,[7] it also imprints its goals on to Actives to either distract or, in the case of Daniel Perrin or Scytheon, run the world. As both Echo and November tell Ballard as he is investigating the Dollhouse: "Fantasy is their business, it is not their purpose" ("Man on the Street" 1.06; "Haunted" 1.10). The fact that Ballard neglects to heed this message, wrapped in his own fantasy of playing white knight for a woman he had not met shows how effective this distraction could be, even if the target, in his instance, was not a client. The use of T.S. Eliot's "The Hollow Men" as the title of the penultimate episode of the series is telling: "this is the way the world ends/not with a bang but a whimper." *Dollhouse*'s narrative thus literalizes the dangers of corporate personhood; in its focus on profit and power, it has the ability to drown out individual voices with the sheer volume of its money-fueled "free speech." Rossum infantilizes the Actives so that they become whomever is desired by those who pay the greatest amount for them, robbing them of their voice; when the technology gets out of hand, it robs most of the rest of the world of theirs as well.

It makes sense, in terms of the narrative arc, that the one individual who has the ability to counteract Rossum's technology represents an inverted version of corporate personhood. Right before being wiped of her original personality and becoming the active Echo, Caroline Farrell said: "You ever try to clean an actual slate? You always see what was on it before" ("Ghost" 1.1). By naturally retaining all of her imprints despite the absence of her original personality, Echo, in essence, is a human who becomes a corporation, that is, Echo *is* actually a "body formed and authorized ... to act as a single person" (Webster's Ninth). While Echo indicates in numerous episodes ("Meet Jane Doe" 2.6, "Stop-Loss" 2.9), that "there's a lot of noise from the chorus girls" (2.6), she is the entity that arranges and manages these various personalities in order to locate friends in danger ("Stop-Loss" 2.9), aid an undocumented woman who ended up in prison due to helping a helpless Echo, in escaping detention and building a new life ("Meet Jane Doe" 2.7), and eventually bring down the corporation responsible for inflicting these personalities on her ("The Hollow Men" 2.12; "Epitaph 2: Return" 2.13) rather than using them to undermine competition, make a profit, or manipulate others. As Klein writes: "Unlike the fantasy of the Rapture, the apocalyptic erasure that allows the ethereal escape of true believers," hope can be found in "local ... renewal movements" that "begin from the premise that there is no escape from the substantial messes we have created and that there has already been enough erasure of history, of culture, of memory" (466). In essence, Echo represents one of those who, as Klein asserts, "do not seek to start from scratch but rather from scrap, from the rubble that is all around" (466). (Indeed, in the final episode of the series, Echo indicates that they actually set up what is referred to as "Safe Haven" near to the remains of Rossum's headquarters in Arizona, poaching Rossum's resources in order to create a technological barrier against imprinting technology ["Epitaph 2: Return" 2.13].) The word "apocalypse" is a Greek derivation of the phrase "lift the veil." Through its use of the Rossum corporation, the narrative of *Dollhouse* lifts this veil to reveal a damning picture of the modern corporation and its consequences.

CHAPTER EIGHT

# "Call us what you want, just not family"
## Undermining Whedon Tropes in the Dollhouse[1]

In the previous chapter, I discussed the ways that the narrative of *Dollhouse* interrogates contemporary corporate culture, with the series drawing a germane and indicting parallel between corporate America and its relationship to the U.S. government, particularly its dehumanizing effects. Building on that, in this chapter I'll explore how the deforming effects of corporate culture, both on a narrative and an industrial level—that is, textually and extratextually—subvert certain tropes associated with Whedon's work. In particular, it is the "created family" trope present in both earlier Whedon series—*Buffy the Vampire Slayer, Angel,* and *Firefly*—and in the Marvel Studios co-production *Agents of S.H.I.E.L.D.*—that *Dollhouse* subverts in order to highlight the inability to make lasting and trusting connections within a corporate environment. In that regard, I will touch on the other series in Whedon's oeuvre to elucidate the ways in which *Dollhouse* either differs (particularly in the case of *Buffy*) or extends this particular subversion hinted at in both *Firefly* and *Angel*. That the narrative does this at all speaks to a larger point regarding the toxicity of the corporate environment, in which a corporation can be legally considered a person, and people, in the words of Joel Bakan, are reduced to "resources" whose only use is the ways in which they serve the company (Bakan 69).

In the episode "Echoes" (1.7), the viewer gets their first full-length introduction to Caroline Farrell, later to be known as the Active Echo. Previous to this episode, she had appeared in a yearbook video, claiming that she wanted to "do everything," in a "be careful what you wish for" moment ("Ghost" 1.1). We saw her intake interview with Adelle DeWitt, looking haggard and cornered ("Echo" 1.0). These moments revealed facets of Caroline—outspoken, idealistic—but "Echoes," as discussed in the pervious chapter, broadens the picture. She is an animal rights activist and an anti-war protestor, who has targeted a corporation called Rossum for their potential animal testing and abuse. While the audience doesn't get the full story of where Caroline Farrell's personality and preferences for fighting against oppression came from, "Echoes" gives a hint of what inspired her fight against Rossum: the advertisement featuring Rossum executive Clive Ambrose and his children, with the tagline, "Because Minds Matter." As one of Caroline's friends remarks: "Marketing campaign that big? He's hiding something." While it is clear that neither Caroline nor her friends realize exactly how much Rossum is hiding, Caroline's objection to the situational ethics hidden beneath the marketing ("Whatever they say in those ads, the ends don't justify the means") has a deeper resonance throughout the narrative of the series.

It is a small moment, but it points directly to the main concerns of the narrative: the corporate environment. As Madeleine Muntersbjorn said in her examination of *Dollhouse*, "The show is about a place, not a person or a crew, and a nasty place at that" (para 5). Unlike the Scoobies on *Buffy*, the Fang Gang on *Angel*, or the passengers and crew of Serenity in *Firefly*, the Actives and employees of the Dollhouse may look like family—Adelle DeWitt espouses an ethic of care for her charges, Boyd Langton comes off as supportive of Echo's intellectual development, almost fatherly—but all of these elements are in service of and able to be subordinated to the needs of the corporation. The "family" of *Dollhouse* is no more real than Clive Ambrose's posing with his children means he is a good father or a good corporate steward.

There is a reason why the ad campaign that inspires Caroline Farrell to take on the Rossum Corporation is a picture of a family. This ad, which Caroline and her friends correctly surmise means that Rossum is "hiding something big," offers a moment to question what has become a trope in the Whedonverse: the notion of the created family of friends and relatives as preferable to "kin." This trope was first made explicit in season 5 of *Buffy*. Tara Maclay is introduced in season four ("Hush" 4.10) as a shy but powerful witch who catches fellow witch Willow's eye. The two of them embark on a relationship that spans two seasons, but little is known of her background—beyond the fact that her mother was also a witch who had died—until the episode "Family" (5.06). In "Family," Tara's relatives arrive in Sunnydale to bring her home. The Maclay men had convinced the women in their family that they were demons whose demonic sides would manifest on their 20th birthdays,[2] claiming that Tara's magical abilities were the direct result of the demonic evil inside her. As Willow and Tara's relationship was originally coded as "witchcraft" to appease American broadcast censors hesitant over a portrayal of a long-term same-sex relationship, there is a clear inference that the "evil" her family wishes to purge from her is Tara's sexuality. When they try to take her away, claiming "we are her blood kin," Buffy succinctly trumps that concept by telling him, "We're family."

In this instance, family is clearly defined as those who support and love you because of who you are, rather than due to biological links. Xander's parents are violent alcoholics ("Amends" 3.10; "Restless" 4.22; "The Replacement" 5.03; "Hells Bells" 6.16), Willow's are absent (with one notable exception, when her mother tries to burn her at the stake ["Gingerbread" 3.11]); and Anya (Emma Caulfield) is a 1000-year-old ex-demon whose human family was clearly long dead. Buffy's father is also absent (he does not even attend his ex-wife's funeral ["Forever" 5.17]), and her sister Dawn (Michelle Trachtenberg) was constructed by magic ("No Place Like Home" 5.04). Buffy's only blood relation is her mother Joyce (Kristine Sutherland), who also serves as de facto parent for Buffy's friends, with Buffy's watcher/trainer Giles (Anthony Stewart Head) as father figure. This created family is strong enough to fight both personal and actual demons because of their avowed commitment to one another.

As a spin-off of *Buffy*, the series *Angel*, featuring a 240-year-old vampire atoning for a century of evil, also constructs a family of friends to battle against the forces of darkness. With one exception, each member of the team has either no or absent "kin": Angel killed his parents and sister when he became a vampire ("The Prodigal" 1.15); Gunn had to kill his sister when she was also turned into a vampire ("War Zone" 1.20); Cordelia's parents were indicted for tax evasion and disappeared ("The Prom" 3.20); Wesley's father is cold and distant, with the series offering occasionally instances of him trying to connect with a father who belittles him ("Belonging" 2.19; "Lineage" 5.07); and Lorne, an empathic demon who grew up in a hell dimension focused on battles of good and evil; he is the only one who can hear music and hates fighting, and his family is ashamed of him for this difference ("Through the Looking Glass" 2.21). Fred holds the distinction of being the only character in the Whedonverse to have two normal, supportive, and loving parents ("Fredless" 3.05; "Shells" 5.15; "The Girl in Question" 5.20). While the series had no such rousing declaration as *Buffy*—although Angel refers to himself and Wesley as Cordelia's family in "Expecting" (1.12)—the idea that Angel, Cordelia, Wesley, Gunn, Lorne, and Fred were family undergirded much of the series, starting with Wesley's first appearance in "Parting Gifts," when Angel serves Cordelia and Wes breakfast (1.10). Significantly, it is the birth of Angel's son Connor that represented the beginning of the end for Angel's created family ("Lullaby" 3.09); Angel's single-minded focus on protecting, providing, avenging, and then merely trying to control his son's rage undermines his connection with his "family" across the two seasons that featured Connor, a job finished off when they transition to a corporate environment ("Home" 4.22).

If one substitutes the word "family" for "crew" in both *Firefly* and *Serenity*, this trope also existed within *Firefly*. While crew and passengers consist of both a brother and sister (Simon and River Tam) and a married couple (Zoe and Hoban Washburne), Zoe and Mal are bonded by being war veterans and serve as de facto parental, or at least authority, figures within the home/work space that the ship Serenity represents. The relatively brief glimpses the viewer gets of Simon and River's family of origin shows a comfortable and wealthy existence—they live on a large estate and have access to the latest technology—that is nonetheless overly concerned with status. When Simon is arrested trying to rescue his sister, his father Gabriel (William Converse-Roberts) disowns and abandons him; this is contrasted with the crew of Serenity, who take considerable risks in both hiding the fugitive siblings and rescuing them when they are kidnapped ("Safe" 1.5).

That being said, Samira Nadkarni argues that the society of Serenity often replicates that patriarchal structure of contemporary culture, despite being set in the future, writing that "Mal exhibits numerous characteristics by which he establishes himself as a patriarch, and that racial, political and gendered aspects play into the means by which a pyramid structure within the crew is simultaneously produced and reinforced by a certain degree of invisibility and consent" (Nadkarni 75–76), rather than subverting said patriarchal characteristics through the looser familial structures of Whedon's other series. The fact that the ship Serenity operates as both a home and a work space adds resonance to Nadkarni's argument, and foreshadows the complete subversion of the created family trope in *Dollhouse*, a point I'll address in greater depth below. The film *Serenity* also attempted to establish the created family structure, with mechanic Kaylee Frye explicitly arguing with Mal about a departing Simon and River: "You could have made them family" (*Serenity* 2005).

*Agents of S.H.I.E.L.D.*, despite Whedon's minimal involvement, at least gestures in the direction of making the individuals working with Phil Coulson and Melinda May—orphan/hacker Skye, scientists Leo Fitz and Jemma Simmons (Elizabeth Henstridge), and Agent Grant Ward—into a loose collective, with Coulson and May as the parental figures, and each individual bringing their own particular skill to the fight. Skye, known as Daisy from mid-season two onwards, also develops a brotherly relationship with Mack (Henry Simmons), a S.H.I.E.L.D. member added in season two; they support and look out for one another, as well as enjoying each other's company ("A Wanted (In)Human" 3.03). Despite its formulaic structure, the series does subvert expectations and suggests the levels of betrayal of the chosen family concept that so informed *Dollhouse* when it revealed Ward was a double agent working for S.H.I.E.L.D.'s longstanding nemesis Hydra, mentored by quasi-father figure John Garrett ("Turn, Turn, Turn" 1.17). Further, when Skye does locate her parents in season two, she finds a father with chemically induced rage issues, and her mother, Jiaying (Dichen Lachman) tries to kill her ("S.O.S. Part 2" 2.22). Both father Cal (Kyle McLachlan) and mother Jiaying offer resonances to both Whedon and Marvel's works, with Cal's transformations resembling that of Marvel's Hulk, and Jiaying not only requiring the lives of others to survive ("Scars" 2.20)—recalling the vampires of *Buffy* and *Angel*—but also played by *Dollhouse* alumnae Lachman. That Cal must kill Jiaying to save his daughter, and then has his memory erased as both gift and punishment (he had committed several murders of his own) only reinforces the concept that prizes Daisy's fellow S.H.I.E.L.D. agents as a more supportive and nurturing family than her biological one.

More in keeping with *Dollhouse* and less with Whedon's earlier works, however, these familial bonds are tested in *Agents of S.H.I.E.L.D.* more than once, revealing the tenuousness of such connections when they are in a work (even if not a corporate) setting. Daisy's transformation midway through the second season ("Aftershocks" 2.11) into what becomes known as an "Inhuman"—that is, those with alien DNA who, when exposed to a substance called Terrigen will develop physical or mental powers—elicits fear and mistrust between Daisy and her coworkers, particularly Jemma and Mack. Garrett's mentoring relationship with Ward recalls Boyd's self-serving manipulations of Echo and others within *Dollhouse*, under the rubric of a created family bond; Garrett nurtures Ward's resentment and potential sociopathy to his own ends. (That Ward eventually massacres most of his biological family for the sake of "closure" indicates he may have been a lost cause either way ["The Things We Bury" 2.10]). Jiaying's stated desire is to keep her Inhuman "family" safe is a goal for which she will go to any lengths to achieve ("Scars" 2.20). For Daisy, her upbringing as a foster child and the search for, and eventual loss of, her biological family leaves her vulnerable; when the Inhuman Hive (Brett Dalton) appears on earth to create an army of willing followers, Daisy is not only targeted but, once under his sway, willing to give her life if needed ("Failed Experiments" 3.19). When Hive's control over her is broken, so too is Daisy; she begs him to re-establish the connection that filled the empty spaces left by said losses ("Ascension" 3.22). This particular arc seems to indicate that even the closeness she feels to her "chosen" family cannot quite compensate for the loss of her family of origin.

This increasingly darker turn to Whedon's work may have been due to the production difficulties that beset his output following *Buffy*. As discussed previously, *Firefly* was mistreated, with a promotional campaign that focused primarily on special effects and humor as the series' selling point; this was made manifest in the aired episode order, which focused on episodes heavy on action and humor to the detriment of character development and continuity, a clear instance of network scheduling "re-authoring" the television text. Further, the 2007–2008 writer's strike did not end in favor of the writers, and *Dollhouse* itself was plagued with many of the production-side issues that *Firefly* was—last-minute pilot replacement, poor scheduling, and a promotional campaign that, like *Firefly*, at the very least showed a misunderstanding of the series premise by focusing primarily on Dushku's scantily-clad body, and at worst, was in collusion with the concepts the series was trying to interrogate (most particularly, exploitation of vulnerable individuals)—all of which may have played a part in the subversion of many of the elements associated with Whedon's previous works, while extending other narrative elements explored in series such as *Angel* and *Firefly*. Or, as Whedon himself put it: "More and more we're interested in dealing with the abuse of power and the various ways people can do that and what it will do with our characters when they're pushed to the edge" (Comic Con Panel).

In season five of *Angel*, the remaining members of the Fang Gang—Angel, Fred, Wesley, Lorne, and Gunn, take over the corporate law firm Wolfram and Hart, given to them in supposed gratitude for "ending world peace" ("Peace Out" 4.21; "Home" 4.22). While the events of the previous seasons—sexual jealousy ("Waiting in the Wings" 3.13), the birth ("Lullaby" 3.9) and subsequent kidnapping of Angel's son ("Sleep Tight" 3.16), a rogue power-that-was enslaving humanity ("Shiny Happy People" 4.18; "The Magic Bullet" 4.19; "Sacrifice" 4.20; "Peace Out" 4.21), and a trusted friend going to the dark side ("Inside Out" 4.17)—had already splintered the group, it was their move into a corporate environment, where the focus was, by necessity, on profits over people, that went the furthest in terminating their connections to one another. Episode after episode reminded the Fang Gang that regardless of what they wanted to do with the resources at their command (i.e., help the helpless), this could not happen at the expense of profitability. As the liaison to the Senior Partners, in the form of Eve (Sarah Thompson) and later Marcus (Adam Baldwin), kept reminding the Fang Gang, the bottom line was the only line that mattered ("Conviction" 5.1; "Hell Bound" 5.4; "Time Bomb" 5.19). Much as *Buffy* used the metaphor of the hellmouth to explicate the different ways that high school was indeed hell, *Angel*, in its fifth season, manifested the toxic environment of the corporation through those who worked there. By the time they left Wolfram and Hart for their last battle in the alleyway behind the hotel where they'd lived for three out of the five seasons of the show, Wesley was dead, Fred had turned into the vessel for an ancient god ("A Hole in the World" 5.15), Lorne had left, and Gunn had minutes to live ("Not Fade Away" 5.22). This chosen family, built carefully over the seasons of the show, despite demons, rogue gods, and betrayal, was not able to maintain itself in a corporate environment.

Much as Eve Bennett argues for *Dollhouse* as a metaphor/critique of the entertainment industry (Bennett 2011), season five of *Angel* also addressed similar concerns. The wholesale slaughter of the majority of the characters was a seemingly apt metaphor by Whedon and company for the way the WB network treated the series. After *Buffy* and *Angel* were severed in 2000, due to a battle between Fox and the WB over licensing fees, *Buffy* moved to a different network, and the WB moved *Angel* all over the schedule. By the time it was cancelled in 2004, it had aired on Tuesdays, Wednesdays, Thursdays, and Sundays, without ever quite finding another series that matched its tone and subject matter within the WB schedules.

Although the created family trope had its genesis with the series *Buffy*, even within that series, it was never shown to be an entirely unproblematic structure. In season four, the half-human/half-demon cyborg Adam (George Hertzberg), created by Maggie Walsh and the government-funded Initiative as a super-soldier, refers to his creator as "Mother" and the other Initiative soldiers who have been (unknowingly) pharmaceutically modified as his "brothers." Jeffrey Bussolini refers to this as a surprising iteration of the "chosen family" trope in the Whedonverse (331), particularly the way that Adam returns "home" (that is, the Initiative laboratories) for answers about why he exists, identifying it and his "mother" as "the source of answers to his most fundamental questions" (Bussolini 330). Yet because Adam does not have a soul in the way its been understood within the series, and is "a being of such power and possible destruction who is without ethical awareness" (Bussolini 330), not only do his "brothers" reject this definition of family, but the narrative in fact posits its opposite in the way in which the "real" chosen family of Buffy, Xander, Willow, and Giles literally (and magically) combine their strengths within Buffy to defeat him. In this respect, the "Combo Buffy" is a mirror of Adam, in that she is made up of the heart (Xander), mind (Giles), spirit (Willow), and strength (Buffy) of her chosen family; the difference is one of consent, as seen in *Dollhouse*. Adam, whose human identity before experimentation "not a man among us can remember" ("Restless" 4.22), is as likely to have consented to the monstrous modifications Walsh inflicts on him as the Actives have in *Dollhouse*, is clearly no match for the combined strength and support that Buffy and her friends provide for one another, despite the season-long issues that plagued the group as they moved from a high school to a college environment ("The Yoko Factor" 4.20).

That being said, it is interesting to note that this created family breaks apart to a large degree in the sixth season, with the loss of both "parents": Joyce to a brain tumor ("The Body" 5.16) and Giles' return to England ("Tabula Rasa" 6.8), as well as the earlier introduction of sister Dawn in season five ("Buffy vs. Dracula" 5.1). Without the influence of parents both real and chosen, the group not only drifts into ethical and moral grey areas (and beyond; Willow murders the man who murdered her girlfriend ["Villains" 6.20]) but away from one another. Indeed, it is not until the final episode of the series that the group arrives again at the closeness and understanding that underpinned their earlier dynamic. In this respect, the series seems to be indicating, as does *Agents of S.H.I.E.L.D.*, that even a created family doesn't truly subvert or substitute for the nuclear family dynamic.

In a similar vein, the two Whedon-directed *Avengers* films touch on both of these dynamics: coworkers as family, and the effects of said work on biological ties. The first *Avengers* film is tasked with taking a disparate group of high-powered individuals who "don't work well with others" and turning them into a family that can fight off those that threaten a world they are tasked with protecting. Whedon's facility in working with ensembles, as discussed in chapter three, was one reason why he was an excellent choice as director (Hurd 447–454). Indeed, the fact that the threat itself, Loki (Tom Hiddleston), an alien demi-god, was in fact the half-brother

### Eight. "Call us what you want, just not family"

of Avenger Thor (Chris Hemsworth), seemed to point in the direction that the Avengers family was superior to that of the aforementioned "kin." (Indeed, Thor dismisses him with an off-handed "he's adopted.") While the group spends much of their time fighting one another, allowing Loki to get a foothold, when they finally come together, they are able to stop the alien incursion.

There are two particular elements, in both *The Avengers* and *The Avengers: Age of Ultron*, that complicate the reification of this particular created family. The first, and possibly most vital, is the fact that the particular event that made them put aside their differences and work together, was the death of Phil Coulson. Nick Fury excoriates their petty infighting by pointing out how Coulson himself viewed them as heroes, showing them the trading cards of Captain America, Iron Man, and others that Coulson always carried with him, now stained with Coulson's blood. This is enough motivation for the group to come together, and yet it is almost immediately revealed that Fury stage-managed the entire scenario: the cards were in Coulson's locker, and Fury dipped them in Coulson's blood to make his point. In essence, he manipulated Coulson's death to his own ends. Even if those ends included saving the world, it remains a problematic situation, and the group continues to struggle to form a coherent bond in subsequent films.

Further, in *Avengers: Age of Ultron*, the group seeks shelter from the mess Stark has created with Cliff Barton's/Hawkeye (Jeremy Renner) family, who lives on a farm in the country. The reveal that he has an entire life away from his work with the Avengers, including a wife and two children (with another on the way), is a surprise to almost all of the Avengers (except Natasha Romanoff/Black Widow [Scarlett Johansson], whom his children refer to as "Aunt Nat") and presumably, to the audience. Yet this is purposeful: Barton had specifically asked Fury to help him "hide" his family, not wanting to expose them to the dangerous work that he did. Rather than placing the "created family" above biological ties, *Age of Ultron* suggests that it is the created family itself that poses the greatest threat to the home life Barton has built. This is perhaps not a surprising development, given the ways, as I will discuss below, earlier series *Dollhouse* had complicated this particular Whedon dynamic.

As addressed in chapter one, the ongoing machinations of corporate antagonist in *Firefly*—the Blue Sun Corporation—seem to suggest that in order to preserve the family/crew structure, one must to absent oneself from any and all places where the corporation exists. In the case of *Firefly*, this was the so-called central planets that were seemingly both urban and prosperous—as well as full of advertisements for the ubiquitous corporation—but the reach of the corporation extended further than Serenity could fly. As examined in chapter one, the character of River Tam was being hunted down by agents of Blue Sun, who would go to any lengths to retrieve her, but beyond that, even the food and drinks the crew consumed had all been manufactured by that corporation (see Giannini 2015).

*Dollhouse*, not unlike *Angel*, descends into the belly of the corporate beast in an attempt to both elucidate its toxicity and bring it down. It is interesting to note that Caroline Farrell has, at best, limited success when trying to bring down Rossum from the outside. Her plan to film animal abuse goes awry: the taped evidence is lost, her boyfriend is shot and killed, and Caroline is forced to go on the run ("Echoes" 1.7). Her next major attack—befriending Rossum rising star Bennett Halverson—ends with test subjects killed and Bennett trapped under rubble with a destroyed arm and a lifelong vendetta against the woman she felt abandoned her ("Getting Closer" 2.11).

Instead, it is the risk of emptying herself, of becoming a part of the corporate structure, which allows Caroline to have even a marginal amount of success in destroying the corporation. While this is not initially part of her plan—she faces federal prison, if not the death penalty for terroristic acts due to her bombing of Rossum's headquarters ("Getting Closer" 2.11)—she is able to use this descent to better understand herself and the corporate machinations that her earlier perspective would not have given her. Yet, in keeping with the darker tone of the series, Echo/Caroline's second—and more successful—attempt at destroying Rossum has the unintended consequence of bringing about the very future she and the others feared: it unleashed the technology worldwide ("Epitaph 2: Return" 2.13).

So what of family? All of the elements that existed in Whedon's other series seem to exist in *Dollhouse*. Boyd, with his "trustworthy brow" ("A Love Supreme" 2.08) mentors Echo throughout the series, even risking his life to try and save her from a psychotic client (Matt Keesler) bent on re-enacting Richard Connell's short story, *The Most Dangerous Game* ("The Target" 1.2), something that should have been obvious to the employees of the Dollhouse, as said client used Connell as an alias. While the series established in the first episode that the Actives are imprinted to trust their handlers, "The Target" implies that the handler can imprint on the Active as well. When Boyd is shot by Connell, Echo offers to help him, using the same language used on her, asking Boyd the standard Handler question, "Do you trust me?" to which Boyd offers the standard Active response, "With my life." The fact that this happens absent of any neural technology implies that it is sincere, that the bond between this Active and this Handler is genuine.³

This concept is not limited to one episode. In both small ways—Boyd worries about Echo's performance as a back-up singer ("Stage Fright" 1.03), leading Topher to jokingly call him "Mama Rose"—and more significant ones. In "Man on the Street," Boyd uncovers and (violently) stops Sierra's continued rape by her Handler (1.06) due to Echo's sense that there is something wrong with Sierra. In the first season, he teams up with Paul to rescue Echo from Alpha, and again in season two, to hide Echo from Rossum ("Meet Jane Doe" 2.6), against the express wishes of Adelle, who is his boss (or so the viewer thinks at that time). When Echo is "wiped" during an engagement (a theft of a piece of the Pantheon on behalf of the Greek government), Boyd goes to extraordinary lengths to make sure she is safely extracted, including maiming one of the thieves who had betrayed the group. In a moment that seems it later subverted when it is revealed Boyd is actually the head of Rossum, he slips Echo a keycard that allows her unfettered access to numerous areas of the Dollhouse ("A Love Supreme").

If Boyd is positioned throughout most of the series as the fatherly Giles to Echo's Buffy, that makes Adelle the mother, and indeed, she both claims and frequently acts out a maternal role to the Actives. She equates the Actives to children "in [her] care" ("Belonging" 2.4), making sure they are fed, healthy, and undisturbed by harsh reality. Her pitch to potential Actives offers comfort on multiple levels; over herbal tea, she claims that their physical needs will be met (food, shelter), their lifetime financial security will be assured, and any emotional, legal, or psychiatric issues will be resolved ("Ghost" 1.1; "Echoes" 1.7; "Briar Rose" 1.12). She is adept at reading the child-like Actives; in a discussion with Echo, who had painted a simplistic watercolor of a house with a male and a female stick figure, Adelle correctly surmises that Echo wishes to finish an interrupted romantic engagement ("Man on the Street" 1.6).

She is also as capable as Boyd in condoning vengeance against those she perceives as violating the boundaries of her "children." The aforementioned handler who raped his Active—Joe Hearn (Kevin Kilner)—was executed by November on Adelle's orders, in what some would construe—Adelle certainly does—as poetic justice ("Man on the Street" 1.6).

This "mothering" is not limited to the Actives, however; Adelle repeatedly claims that despite its illegality, the services of the Dollhouse also help its clients, by meeting the needs said clients could not meet in conventional ways, whether romantic, legal, or psychological. While this could be read as merely good marketing, Adelle seems to believe that there is "good" in what the corporation provides Actives and clients: security, closure, love, to name a few. Further, by the post-apocalyptic end of the series, it is clear Adelle also mothers/nurtures a psychologically damaged Topher, as well as caring for the assorted group gathered at Safe Haven, a protected farm outside Phoenix. This Adelle, in contrast to the head of the LA Dollhouse with her tailored clothes and coiffed hair, had a softer look of casual, loose-fitting sweaters and indifferently styled hair. She still reacts, however, to even perceived slights to those in her care; when the Actual Zone (Zack Ward) mocks the now mentally-unbalanced Topher, Adelle lashes out, telling him: "You will keep a civil tongue in this house or we will put it in the stew" ("Epitaph 2: Return" 2.13).

As for Paul Ballard, he is harder to position within the "family" structure once he becomes part of the Dollhouse staff ("Omega" 1.12). Like Caroline, Ballard's attempts to bring down the Dollhouse remain fruitless and unsuccessful while he remains outside of the corporate structure, but even once inside, his primary goal remains "rescuing" Caroline; Echo is the one of the only ones with whom he seems to connect. Yet, even as he becomes Echo's handler (and friend), he struggles to view Echo as a person in the way as Caroline, that is, the way Echo integrated the multiple imprints inflicted on her to create a new identity separate from, if still related to, that of Caroline (Rennebohm 9–14). Indeed, it is only after an attack by Alpha that leaves Ballard brain dead, when Topher installs Active architecture into Paul's brain to repair the damage, that Paul begins to accept the idea of that these modified and modifiable people that Actives such as Echo and November represent, are individuals in their own right. Despite that, he still remains somewhat separate, first by his focus on Echo/Caroline and then his connection with Mellie/November, and Boyd's "chosen family" explicitly does not include him. "There's always one relative you can live without," Boyd says.

That leaves the Actives the viewer knows best to round out this family structure—Echo, Sierra, and Victor. Like Paul, the Active November does not quite fit in this dynamic, as the viewer knows her primarily as Mellie, Paul's neighbor. Topher, similar in age to the Actives, is more aligned with the "adults"—Boyd, Adelle, and the corporate world of Rossum—for the majority of the series. The dynamic of friends as family, watching out for one another, is relatively stable in the interactions between Victor, Sierra, and Echo. What Topher initially reads as manifesting a herd mentality is clearly, from the third episode on, the three of them "watch[ing] out for each other" ("Stage Fright" 1.3), in as far as they are capable in their Active state. It is Echo, rather than Topher, Adelle, or any of the other staff, who notices Sierra is unhappy and abused ("Man on the Street" 1.6; "Belonging" 2.4), and is more adept at pinpointing the cause than those supposedly entrusted with the Actives' care. (Dr. Saunders, for instance, views Topher as the cause of Sierra's unhappiness; he's "the bad man" Sierra's work is pointing to. This, however, is clearly driven by Saunder's own dislike of him than anything Sierra's behavior displays.) While the Actives are seemingly unaware that the environment, and the corporation itself, is less interested in their needs beyond how they benefit the bottom line, their instinctive ability to develop care and friendship for one another ties them the created families of *Buffy*, *Angel*, and *Firefly* more closely than the rest of the characters. By the end of the series, and despite Echo's assertion that she needs Sierra and Victor to help fight her war against Rossum, she lets them go to spend the night with each other, telling them: "If you somehow forget the way back here, that's OK too" ("Getting Closer" 2.11).

Topher, as stated earlier, complicates this dynamic. He is responsible for the technology that empties and rewrites the Actives; in one of Echo's nightmare sequences in the episode "The Attic" (2.09), she sees Topher as a mad scientist, who is literally playing with peoples' brains. Topher is dismissive of the Actives for most of the first season, placing himself both mentally (genius) and physically (his office overlooks their living and sleep quarters) above the child-like Actives. Yet, his connection to them in the created family structure is suggested by the games and toys that surround him in what he considers his space—the imprinting room—and, as discussed in chapter six, he too develops an awareness that the Actives are not "toys" with which he plays. This shift from "grown-up" and "programmer" to part of the Active family is complete by the post-apocalyptic future of the "Epitaphs" episodes: Topher and the Actives have switched places—Sierra, Victor, and Echo have either returned to their original personalities (Priya and Tony) or integrated imprints to create a new one (Echo/Caroline), while Topher, finally feeling his responsibility for his part in the destruction around them, buries himself in the Actives' sleeping pods, his mind fractured. (That these pods, which are featured in the opening credits of all the episodes [barring the two "Epitaphs" episodes], strongly resemble that of Wal-Mart, a corporation known for its exploitative practices, is surely not accidental [Osterndorf 2015].) Between the fascinated, amoral genius of the first season and the broken man at the end of the series, however, Topher develops a greater awareness of consequences and a sense of empathy that allows him to be more integrated into the friends as family structure Sierra, Victor, and Echo develop.

On the surface, the main characters of *Dollhouse* do resemble the other "chosen families" of the Whedonverse. One could argue that *Dollhouse* is the apotheosis of this trope, as there is no indication of any "blood kin"[4] for any character for most of the series. Yet there are several ways in which the series subverts the trope. While the word "choice" is used several times by Adelle in her pitch to potential Actives, the narrative makes it clear that the choice is pyrrhic at best. Anthony suffered from debilitating post-traumatic stress disorder from his tour in Afghanistan ("Stop-Loss" 2.09), Caroline was facing federal terrorism charges for her bombing of Rossum's labs ("Getting Closer" 2.11), and Madeleine was broken by grief over her daughter's death ("Instinct" 2.2). Priya, as discussed in the previous chapter, was given no choice at all ("Belonging" 2.4). (This is not counting the Actives or potential Actives we only see once, such as the paranoid Mike [Teddy Sears] in "Needs" [1.8] or Sam, who stole Rossum's drug formula in "Echoes" [1.7]).

One does not to probe deeply beneath the surface of the narrative to understand that these roles—particularly those of Adelle and Boyd—are just that: roles. Boyd represents the most clear-cut subversion. As Christopher Souza argues, Boyd's fatherly actions misdirect the viewer; anything he does that seems either self-interested or passive is read as Boyd being pressured by his environment to act (or not act). Helping Paul hide Echo, as per example, seems noble at the time, but once he reveals that every time Echo blocks an imprint, her body creates the necessary chemical for a vaccine against imprinting ("The Hollow Men" 2.12), it is clear he allowed this development to hone a valuable resource. As Souza argues, every seemingly "good" action Boyd takes was rooted in an attempt to play both sides: the corporate interest and the anti-corporate coalition. He cites Boyd's failure to step in to stop Priya from being sold off to her rapist, preferring to use the opportunity to see how Topher would react ("Belonging" 2.4) (Souza 209–210) as one example. That this leads to the death of Nolan with Priya as his murderer, and Topher required to undertake the task of literally disintegrating Nolan (Boyd instructs him to dismember the body and soak it in acid) because of Boyd's inaction, is a clear indication that he has little in common with the supportive Whedonverse father figures, such as Giles or Coulson; rather, he is more in line with the more absent or toxic ones, such as the vengeance-filled Holtz or the absent Hank Summers (Dean Butler).

The reveal of Boyd as the unknown head of the Rossum Corporation makes even the good actions he took entirely self- and corporate-motivated. If, as Adelle implies, the Actives are akin to children in their non-imprinted state, it makes sense that an Active's handler would assume a parental role, for the Active at least. Boyd, however, embodies what the ad campaign with Clive Ambrose implied: families matter only as far as they provide a service to the corporate body. His original partner and best friend, Clyde Randolph, who invented the technology, is wiped and sent to Attic so that Boyd can claim both the technology and the cash. Despite Echo's clear love for them, Boyd is quick to exclude Paul Ballard, as well as Priya and Anthony, from this particular "chosen family"; he triggers Mellie to kill Paul, and sends assassins to take care of Priya and Anthony ("The Hollow Men" 2.12). The fact that he allowed Priya to be potentially sold to her rapist when he had the power to stop it only underscores this fact. Clearly, he does not consider them to be as useful as Adelle (who provided leadership), Topher (technological know-how), or Echo (a biological agent against imprinting), regardless of the rest of his avowed family's thoughts or feeling on the matter.

It is instructive to look at the aforementioned green initiatives that Friedman dismissed. As I touched on in the previous chapter, British Petroleum, in the late 1990s/early 2000s, announced it was dedicating itself to alternative energy and cleaner petroleum, yet the months-long Deepwater Horizon spill and then-CEO Tony Hayward's blasé reaction ("I'd like my life back" [Lubin 2010]; never mind the death of marine life or the fates of those who depended upon it) revealed the hollow, public relations spin of the earlier stance. Boyd's actions, even risking his life, are similarly empty of actual concern for anything but himself and his corporation. It is significant, beyond the reference to T.S. Eliot, that the episode in which Boyd's true loyalties are revealed to all is called "The Hollow Men." His argument to Adelle, Echo, and Topher, is that they are his "family": "I love you guys" (2.12) is his claim. His actions, however, make him less of a father and more of a patriarch—the leader and prime mover of those he considers in his care. In this instance, Boyd's claim of family is akin to that of Vivian Burr and Christine Jarvis' analysis of "vampire" families, which offer a "feudal" structure "in its emphasis upon obedience and servitude" in which "[r]elations are anything but democratic; individuals exist principally to benefit their parents/sires, not themselves" (273). His assertions of love are revealed as empty, mirroring his ultimate fate: wiped by Topher and turned into a human bomb by Echo. That is, not only is Boyd hollowed out of what makes him "Boyd," as the Actives are, but Caroline/Echo's second bombing of Rossum to stop the apocalypse, ends up bringing it about more quickly. There are no real victories or heroes in the Dollhouse, or *Dollhouse.*

While Adelle eventually recognizes the illusions she had held with regard to Rossum's real purpose, her position as a maternal figure is nearly as problematic as Boyd's. Nadkarni makes a cogent case for viewing Adelle as a "transgressive mother," defined as "a gender neutral portrayal of maternal work that, while outwardly displayed as socially acceptable, often transgresses these boundaries in way that could connote an abuse of the authority granted by the act of mothering itself" (82). That is, while Adelle claims to care for the Actives, it is, as Nadkarni argues, "simply another fantasy" (84); the Actives are never—either in doll state or imprinted—able to actually consent to the uses to which the corporation puts their bodies (84).

There are two particular transgressions, however, that illuminate this. First, there is Adelle's imprinting Victor as "Roger," to serve as her lover, putting her morally closer to Hearn's rape of Sierra than she suspects or the narrative implies (Nadkarni 85). The fact that "roger" is British slang for sex—as Adelle actually makes reference to within the series ("I want you to roger me, Roger")—lends credence to Nadkarni's contention; she has named him for what he does, not who he is. Further, when "Roger" rejects her, citing Victor's love for Sierra as the cause, Adelle assumes it is a trick directed at her by Topher, rather than an expression of Victor's autonomous feelings, indicating that even this late in the series' narrative, she struggles to view the Actives as fully human ("Stop-Loss" 2.9).

Further, her position as head/mother figure in the LA Dollhouse is threatened after Echo's disappearance; another Rossum executive (Matthew Harding) has taken her place, and Adelle is reduced to fetching coffee and completing paperwork for the men who have taken over her office to smoke cigars and drink scotch like throwbacks to the *Mad Men*-era ("Meet Jane Doe" 2.7). She has no control over the uses to which the Actives are put, and even is subjected to an in-earshot commentary on her attractiveness as if she could not hear or understand, placing her on the commodified level of those same Actives. Adelle thus resorts to any means necessary to regain her position. In this instance, it is passing along to Harding the blueprints of the very technology, created by Topher, that causes the "though-pocalypse." While it is later revealed that Adelle was playing a long game—gaining control to bring Rossum down—it is difficult to argue that her reduction in status and resulting objectification by the male executives did not play a part in her actions.

The fact that these same men were clearly not considering the health, safety, or needs of the Actives was clear, including Harding's command that Topher separate the clearly connected Sierra and Victor ("she'd be perfect for the Dubai house" ["Meet Jane Doe" 2.7]); as Echo says, "their bad guys" were clearly worse that "our bad guys" ("The Public Eye" 2.5). That being said, Adelle's actions still violate her espoused ethic of care; to help and care for the few, she risked the many who would be harmed by putting that information into Rossum's hands. While a similar decision in season five of *Buffy*, in which the titular heroine refuses to consider sacrificing her sister for the greater good—putting her desire for family and avoidance of additional loss above the massive suffering in store for the world if they do not succeed—this can be attributed both to Buffy's youth and the losses she had suffered, and is redeemed by Buffy sacrificing herself in Dawn's stead ("The Gift" 5.22). Adelle enacts no such selfless sacrifice. Indeed, in this instance, Adelle occupies the same ethic she labels "spectacularly insane" ("The Hollow Men" 2.12) in Boyd; she has put her own needs and the needs of her chosen family above that of the rest of the world in order to regain her position. Despite her assertions that she could do more good by directing the LA Dollhouse as a focal point of the resistance, the fact remained that she put "the most dangerous technology" ("Meet Jane Doe" 2.7) in the hands of those with the know-how and economic resources to implement was clearly too high a cost. For both Boyd and Adelle, they have not subverted, but been subverted by the corporate structure.

By making Rossum a corporation that funds itself on the manufacture of fantasy fulfillment, the series makes a point that subverts one of the most significant aspects of Whedon's previous work: it is perhaps only the Whedon trope itself that leads a viewer to seek that family dynamic between Boyd and Echo (echoes of Giles and Buffy), between Topher and Adelle, between Echo and Tony and Priya. The notion that one can create one's family may be just as much of a fantasy as Joel Mynor resurrecting his dead wife once a year ("Man on the Street" 1.6), or Matt Cargill's romantic comedy birthday scenarios ("Ghost" 1.1; "Echoes" 1.7; "A Love Supreme" 2.8). In essence, this subversion asks the viewer not only to see the tenuous of these types of bonds on *Dollhouse*, but could in fact reverberate into viewer's analyses of the relationships seen on *Buffy*, *Angel*, and *Firefly*.

It is instructive, in this regard, to look at the episode "Belle Chose" (2.3); in particular, at the sociopathic Terry Karrens (Joseph Sikorra), who kidnaps women close to the age of his aunt, mother, and sister, doses them with animal tranquilizer so they cannot escape, and recreates his fantasy of being included in his family: an afternoon of croquet and conversation. As Cynthea Masson argues in her analysis of "Belle Chose," Karrens is "both a glossator and an author; he glosses the original women in his life by replacing them with his interpretations; but he also manipulates the gloss to create a new story" (Masson para 5), pointing out that glossing means both to interpret and to misinterpret something. Karrens not only overwrites the reality of his actual family with one he has created, but he also is seemingly blind to the reasons for his exclusion from it. As Topher points out, when examining Karren's brain scan: "'See these dark areas? How they extend all the way out to here? Do you know why that looks like that? That's because Terry Karrens doesn't use that part of his brain. And that's where you would find stored such things as empathy, compassion, an aversion to disemboweling puppies'" ("Belle Chose" 2.4).

Yet, as Martha Stout writes in *The Sociopath Next Door*: "Sociopaths are infamous for their refusal to acknowledge responsibility for the decisions they make, or for the outcomes of their decisions. In fact, a refusal to see the results of one's bad behavior as having anything to do with oneself— 'consistent irresponsibility' in the language of the American Psychiatric Association—is a cornerstone of the antisocial personality diagnosis" (50).

The episode itself is quite obviously paralleling Karrens' behavior of kidnapping and rewriting these women to be whom he wants with the work of the Dollhouse itself. Yet, I argue that this episode exists in a direct line to Boyd's assertion that Echo, Adelle, and Topher are his "family" in the penultimate episode "The Hollow Men." Like Karrens, who turns women into mannequins, endlessly playing croquet in an Astroturf garden, Boyd too has positioned his supposed family members into a scenario of his devising. Topher realizes that Boyd is just as trapped in his fantasy as is Karrens; his reference to *The Wizard of Oz* (which includes, of course, a fake wizard trying to manipulate others) is on point: "I'm the tin man, she's the lion, and you're the head of the lollipop guild who's a traitor." Building on the work of Robert Hare, an expert in personality disorders, Bakan directly asserts that if a corporation was actually a person, that person would be a sociopath on the level of a Terry Karrens. As Bakan writes: "Unlike the human beings who inhabit it, the corporation is *singularly* self-interested and unable to feel genuine concern for others in any context. The corporation is *irresponsible*, ... tr[ies] to '*manipulate* everything, including public opinion,' ... *grandiose*, always insisting 'that we're number one, we're the best.' ... [displays] [a] *lack of empathy* and *asocial tendencies* ... and ... often refuse to accept responsibility for their own actions and are unable to feel remorse" (Bakan 57).

Boyd never comes across as the typical media-infused view of a sociopath; as Topher says, he has a "trustworthy brow" ("A Love Supreme" 2.8). Yet as an avatar for Rossum, he embodies the psychopathy of the corporate structure quite well; he is "self-interested" and attempts to "manipulate everything," from consigning his partner Clyde to the Attic, to aiding Echo's increased self-awareness simply for the biochemical reactions it produces in her body. Indeed, Echo's biochemistry is, in essence, a way for Boyd to not accept responsibility for the technology he facilitated. Despite Echo's ability to overcome and integrate multiple imprints, Souza asserts: "Boyd represented the last 'program' Echo had to overcome in order to complete her journey from naïve doll to self-aware heroine" (213), and one she could only overcome once she had integrated her original personality.

In this way, Echo comes full circle, from the idealistic activist to apocalyptic warrior, by making a corporate self, as addressed in the previous chapter. That is, it is clear from the narrative that Caroline could see through Rossum's marketing enough to know something bad was going on. Yet, she had to bodily experience Rossum's corporate malfeasance in order to make any headway in bringing the corporation down. Caroline's attempts to bring down Rossum—with her boyfriend Leo, and later with Bennett—using at first bad public relations (i.e., posting Rossum's animal abuse on YouTube), and then violence, only brought death and destruction to Caroline and her friends. Echo, however, by risking her mind AND body within the Dollhouse, and later the Attic, by merging 39-plus personalities into one like a media merger gone nuts, was able to understand what lay beneath the façade in a way Caroline could not grasp. Boyd's claim of family ties, when connected with the ad campaign featuring Clive Ambrose, is in the context of a corporate setting just one more, as Souza argues, "program." Echo, both implicitly through the merging of her disparate personalities, and explicitly, in her words to Priya and Tony in "The Hollow Men" ("Call us what you want, just not family") understands that when dealing with an overarching, sociopathic corporation that appropriates what it wants without regarding for the humans that exist both in- and outside it, a new definition is needed. When Caroline first decided to take on Rossum, she was convinced that if she and her friends could get evidence of Rossum's abuses: "They'll be shamed into policy changes." Echo understood that one cannot shame a person, corporate or human, that has no guilt. If the "created family" has been taken over and commodified, the best one can hope for is a safe haven.

# Conclusion
## Whedon as Corporate Critique, or Can TV Change the World?

In 2011, as he finished filming *The Avengers*, Whedon also filmed an adaptation of *Much Ado About Nothing* at his home in California. It was shot in black and white, and featured many of the actors that were associated with Whedon's previous work, including Amy Acker and Alexis Denisof (*Angel/Dollhouse*), Sean Maher and Nathan Fillion (*Firefly*), Tom Lenk (*Buffy the Vampire Slayer/The Cabin in the Woods*), Reed Diamond (*Dollhouse/Agents of S.H.I.E.L.D.*), Fran Kranz (*Dollhouse/The Cabin in the Woods*), and Clark Gregg (*The Avengers/Agents of S.H.I.E.L.D.*). While Whedon made no substantive changes to the text, he did set in contemporary times, and featured such accoutrements as luxury cars and music played through iPhones.

*Much Ado* starts with a group of gentleman, lead by Don Pedro (Reed Diamond), returning from a successful campaign. What type of "campaign" is not addressed within the adaptation, only that Don Pedro arrives at Leonato's (Clark Gregg) house with his illegitimate brother Don John (Sean Maher) in handcuffs. Ensley F. Guffey has suggested that these "campaigners" are akin to Blackwater executives (Guffey 2013), a concept leant some credence through Whedon's shifting of the character of Antonio (Pedro's older brother in the text) to an executive assistant who references spreadsheets when discussing said campaign with Leonato's daughter Hero (Jillian Morgese) and niece Beatrice (Amy Acker), in addition to the aforementioned luxury cars and expensive suits. Whedon also, in the commentary accompanying the film, refers to Leonato as a "politician" ("Much Ado" commentary track), a resonant updating of the original; this may be one of the few remaining contexts in which Leonato's reaction to the accusations of his daughter's infidelity (he blames her with scant evidence) rings true; it is easy to imagine a politician being more concerned about the "optics" rather than the reality.

Thus, even when adapting a 500-year-old play, Whedon can still manage to offer sly commentary on contemporary corporate U.S. society. Throughout this work, I have strived to provide an overview of the ways in which the bulk of Whedon's oeuvre either directly or indirectly engages with the overwhelming presence of corporatism in contemporary U.S. society. Whether it is the homogenizing and dehumanizing effects of producing and consuming fast food in *Buffy* and *Roseanne*, the bodily incursions of such corporations as Blue Sun, Wolfram and Hart, and Rossum that threaten the mental, physical, and moral integrity of both those caught within the beast as well as those attempting to escape it, or even the conglomerated media/studio system in which all of these works are produced, Whedon has offered in-depth and frequently nuanced portrayals of those both in and outside the corporate structure.

The last series that Whedon claimed at least partial involvement in shaping was *Dollhouse*, which ended its run in 2010. Since then, he has been in the belly of another beast—Marvel Studios as a writer and director—as well writing and producing microbudget films through his own studio, Bellwether Pictures. Neither *Much Ado About Nothing* nor *In Your Eyes* (2014) address corporatism and its effects to any great degree, and it is uncertain whether Whedon plans to return to the television medium that has allowed him to tell these stories in greater depth (and length) than film often allows. During the 2016 election, however, he created the "Save the Day" SuperPac, to encourage viewers and fans to vote, and to reject messages of division and hate, enlisting many of the actors from across Whedon's entire oeuvre, from Tom Lenk to Robert Downey, Jr. (*The Avengers*) ("Save the Day").

While he may not return to television, it was vital that Whedon's narratives existed when they did, and that they still continue to resonate. Robert Thirkell, formerly of the BBC, believes that what is produced on television, both in the states and abroad, has the power to be a "catalyst for change" ("Can TV Change the World?") by shining a light on what often is dismissed as just the way things are. While Thirkell was speaking primarily of documentaries, I would argue that the character and narrative of dramas and comedies, of science fiction and fantasy, has the capacity to address the more troubling aspects of contemporary culture, particularly through creating compelling stories and characters, rather than mouthpieces or propagandists for particular points of view.

It is instructive to examine the narrative of the film *Serenity* for one answer to this question. As discussed in chapter one, *Serenity*'s plot turned on a buried government secret, in which a pharmaceutical intervention on the planet Miranda killed 99.9 percent of its population, and turned the remaining inhabitants into the cannibalistic Reavers. The film starts with a video, watched by a government official known only as The Operative (Chiwetel Ejiofor), that features River Tam's escape, aided by her brother Simon, from the facility that tortured her to create a psychic assassin. The physician who lead many of the experiments on River (and others like her), brags to Simon (who is in disguise) that "top members of Parliament" have viewed River's abilities and were duly impressed. This video tells the Operative precisely what he needed to know: both the love between the siblings, and the arrogance of the physician: "The minds behind every military, diplomatic and covert operation in the galaxy, and you put them in a room with a psychic" (*Serenity*).

The film climaxes with another video, one that reveals precisely what happened on Miranda, what Mal refers to as "the truth that burned out River Tam's brain." In trying to create a peaceful world, they, like Jasmine on *Angel*, removed the inhabitants' free will. As the sole surviving member of the search and rescue team explains, the airborne drug mixed into the planet's environment sapped the population's will to live; even basic activities such as eating were deemed too much effort, and they let themselves die. As Jacob Clifton writes: "*Serenity* is a story about media, about the abuses of media that are possible, and more than probable in the current day, and the way those media can be used to subvert and question the very ways in which they are used to control the population, both within the story and without" (Clifton 204).

This extends not only to the opening and (near) closing videos discussed above, but as Clifton points out, also a character introduced at the mid-point of the film, Mr. Universe. Mr. Universe is a media junkie/hacker adept at seeing the difference between the "puppet theater" (a concept recalled in *The Cabin in the Woods*) the Alliance/corporate media "foists on a somnambulant public" and what he calls "the truth of the signal," that is, what the media seeks to hide under layers of propaganda and entertainment. When the crew discovers the aforementioned video, it is to Mr. Universe they turn in order to broadcast this video to the rest of the galaxy. While the battle to broadcast said video ends with Mr. Universe dead and many of the Serenity crew members dead or injured, the crew succeeds in their goal. The video is broadcast, and the Alliance's power is weakened. In essence, media did in fact change the world (of Serenity). As Clifton concludes, the film also offers the opportunity for its audience to change the world: "By keeping our eyes open to propaganda and manipulation in all its forms, by taking in the transmission and telling it anew, we perform our part of the alchemy: we join in the signal, and ensure it never stops" (Clifton 215).

Whedon once said that he would never write a "very special episode" of *Buffy* (Rochlin 19), that is, the trope of 1980s dramas and sitcoms that addressed social problems such as drug use, drunk driving, or sexual assault, in which everyone learns a (frequently didactic) lesson and goes on the next week as if nothing untoward had happened. Not only do Whedon's critiques exist organically to the characters and narratives, but the characters themselves are changed by these experiences, perhaps no more so, as the case study elucidates, than those in the series *Dollhouse*. For Angel, taking over the corporate entity that had caused the team so much suffering was the best way of teaching them how impossible it is to take down such entities: "We are legion, we are forever" ("Not Fade Away" 5.22), Marcus Hamilton, the Senior Partners liaison, tells Angel in the final episode of series. While on the surface, it is a depressing message, on a subtextual level, the lesson seems to be the same as the "epiphany" Angel experienced in the second season: "If nothing we do matters, then all that matters is what we do" ("Epiphany" 2.16).

This is reiterated when Gunn goes to visit Anne, the young woman who runs the homeless shelter Wolfram and Hart attempted to use to launder money, just as the shelter is preparing to move to a new location. As he helps her load up a truck, he asks her: "What if I told you it doesn't help? What would you do if you found out that none of it matters? That it's all controlled by forces more powerful and uncaring than we can conceive and they will never let it get better down here? What would you do?" Anne's response encapsulates the reasons why it is not about "winning" the fight against these corporate actors: "I'd get this truck packed before the new stuff gets here" ("Not Fade Away" 5.22). In essence, there will always be injustice, and disadvantage; the best thing to do is try to and make it better.

In *Firefly* and *Serenity*, the antagonists are not as easy to pinpoint as a demonic law firm; Blue Sun is an entity that provides goods and services, and creates a degree of prosperity for some. As with many such corporations in the real world, it is what happens below the line that is often hidden beneath the brand's face. To use a contemporary example, in 2007, the Chiquita brand was required to pay a $25 million fine for its funding of the United Self-Defense Forces of Columbia, which had been labeled a terrorist organization by the United States. The $1.7 million paid to the group was to protect Chiquita's corporate interests in the region, rather than merely leaving (as they had been advised to do by their own legal team). Neither the initial payment nor the $25 million fine levied against the corporation, however, had any real affect on either the corporate bottom line or the company's share prices (O'Carroll 2007). Nor do any of the events of *Firefly* or *Serenity*—including the multi-global release of a video implicating the government in a massive cover-up—make the kind of difference to the corporation that they do to the Alliance government. This may be an even darker outcome than that of *Angel*, as one cannot fight against an antagonist one does not perceive as an enemy. Whether this would have been a part of additional seasons of the series (the agents of Blue Sun do make an appearance in the comic books that bridged the narrative gap between series and film) will likely remain unknown.

For *Buffy* and *Roseanne*, even their relatively small towns were not safe from corporate incursion. While both series are different in terms of tone, genre, and era—among other things—it is significant that these two disparate women, one with great physical strength (Buffy) and one with a sharp mind and sharper tongue (Roseanne)—are as ground down as the food they serve merely by the environment of the fast food industry. Here too is a corporation that so frequently hides its darker side (environmental damage, poor worker treatment) under a smiling, often child-friendly brand ambassador.

Like Ronald McDonald, Whedon's relationship with Marvel seem to, at times, relegate his position to that of brand ambassador, particularly with regards to the series *Agents of S.H.I.E.L.D.*, something I argued he preemptively addresses in the web series *Dr. Horrible's Sing-Along Blog*, in which protagonist Billy both decries his nemesis as a "corporate tool" while seeking to become one himself. Even when individuals within corporations have good intentions, as Stark does in *Age of Ultron* argues— an argument continued in *Agents of S.H.I.E.L.D.*—these intentions have the effect of making things worse. This is something that *Dollhouse* also makes abundantly clear, as addressed in the previous chapter.

This focus on corporate malfeasance was directly addressed by Whedon himself, particularly with regards to the less-hopeful narratives of *Dollhouse* or horror film *The Cabin in the Woods*. "[S]o much of our society is more and more in the hands of a few very rich, very corrupt people, or very well-meaning people who have no business controlling the lives of others" (Whedon and Goddard 19). The senior partners, Boyd and Clyde at Rossum, the employees at the Facility, all represent those who, at the very best, think they are giving people "what they need" and at worst, show little compunction at sacrificing others to further themselves.

At the start of this book, I listed the numerous genre-crossing series in which the antagonists were corporations and those within them. Many of these contemporary series offer nuanced portrayals of both, addressing Philip Lapote's complaint in 2000 that the anti-corporate films essentially set up corporate villains as "empty suits," undermining these films ability to be really subversive (Lapote 2000). As per example, the series *Veronica Mars* (of which Whedon was a big enough fan to merit a cameo ["Rat Saw God" 2.5]) offered the corporate villain Kane Industries. While Jake Kane (Kyle Secor) either did or countenanced numerous bad acts—including interfering in a police investigation and employing a "fixer" who did not stint at executing Kane family enemies—much of this was protect his son, whom he erroneously assumed killed his sister during a seizure ("Leave It to Beaver" 1.22). While his reasoning does not excuse his actions, it is a far cry from the "empty suit" antagonists that Lapote decried.

Even a series such as *Gilmore Girls*, which takes place in a small town (like *Roseanne* and *Buffy*), not only includes corporate antagonists (particularly media magnate Mitchum Hunztberger [Gregg Henry] and a subplot that includes the Wal-Mart corporation ["Keg! Max!" 3.19]), but even involves ethically questionable behavior from one who is a main character: protagonist Lorelai's (Lauren Graham) father Richard (Edward Herrmann). Richard's job as an insurance executive is a subplot to many of the seasons of the series, from being "aged out" of his position in the second season ("Introducing Lorelai Gilmore" 2.6) to his Machiavellian maneuvers to get said job back ("Afterboom" 4.19). That his actions result in his daughter being humiliated and the end of Lorelai's relationship with her current boyfriend (he was the collateral damage) is nothing Richard seems to feel the need or desire to apologize for. It is implied, in fact, that this is merely the cost of doing business.

The goal of this work has not been to imply that the critiques against corporatism are the only political or social messages within Whedon's work, or that they represent polemics in televised form. Whedon's work has been examined through the lens of race (Iatropoulous and Woodall 2016), philosophy (South and Irwin 2003), literary theory (Comeford and Burnett 2010), and religion (Mills et al. 2014), to name a very few elements of the large Whedon studies corpus. My hope is to add to the existing scholarship around Whedon's oeuvre, by highlighting the sociopolitical necessity of critiquing the overwhelming corporate socioeconomic structure, both nationally and globally, that undergirds contemporary culture.

# Chapter Notes

## Introduction

1. See, however, Samira Nadkarni's analysis of Whedon's series *Firefly* and the way it recapitulates patriarchal/kyriarchial structures despite the character's "outsider" statuses (Nadkarni 69–84).

2. It should be noted that the follow-up film, *Serenity*, reversed this somewhat, it suggested that school was training genius children at the behest of the government; however, the graphic novels that filled in the narrative gaps between series and film posited an alliance between the corporation and the government.

3. Given the focus on media properties, as well as the daunting corpus of available background material, I will not be examining the canonical comics that continue the story arcs of *Buffy*, *Angel*, and *Firefly*, or his comics for Dark Horse or Marvel. Also absent from this analysis is Whedon's adaptation of *Much Ado About Nothing* (although I will touch on it briefly) or the film *In Your Eyes*, written by Whedon and released by his production company Bellwether Films. *In Your Eyes*, as a romantic fantasy film, does not engage in or feature any corporate structures of note.

## Chapter One

1. That being said, Andy Hallett is not added to the opening credits of the series until midway through the fourth season ("Release" 4.14).

2. Gwyn Symonds points out that even if Connor had not been kidnapped, he still would have been rebellious and challenged Angel's adult-oriented noir perspective on the world—although perhaps not to the near-patricidal degree to which he did in the series—in order to differentiate and discover himself in contrast to those around him (Symonds 155–165).

3. Amusingly, one of these "futures" is a deal with ABC Disney as a series showrunner, a metafictional reference to *Angel* co-creator David Greenwalt's recent exit from the series to head up the similar show *Miracles*.

4. The MTV series *Daria* tackled this type of school corporate sponsorship more than a year before *Firefly* aired; the episode "Fizz Ed" (5.1) shows the principal of Daria's high school forced to go to insane lengths to please sponsor Ultra Cola when they threaten to withdraw their funding.

## Chapter Two

1. Lear's series include *All in the Family* (1971–1979), centered around the working class Bunker family in Queens, New York; *Sanford and Son* (1972–1977), about a father and son and their salvage business in Watts, Los Angeles; *One Day at a Time* (1975–1984), about a single mom struggling to raise her two daughters in Indianapolis; and *Good Times* (1974–1979), which focused on an African-American family living in the Cabrini-Green housing projects in Chicago (never stated explicitly, but visually in the credits). Both *All in the Family* and *Sanford and Son* were remakes of BBC series *'Till Death Us Do Part* and *Steptoe and Son*.

2. In an interview, Whedon mentions that the original concept for that episode was that Jackie had gotten an abortion and was afraid to tell her sister. As the first episode he was chosen to write, Whedon was thrilled that the series would be tackling such an important issue; however, the network executives nixed that storyline, which Whedon referred to as his "first heartbreak" in his television writing career (Pascale 2014).

3. Not unlike many of the aforementioned Lear working-class series, *Roseanne* is set in the Midwest, while *Buffy* takes place in California.

## Chapter Three

1. See also Deborah Jaramillo, who argued that HBO's marketing of its original series as distinct and better than broadcast television (made manifest in its branded tagline "It's Not TV, It's HBO") as if it was in competition with broadcast series obscures the fact that only a small number of media conglomerates provide programming across broadcast, cable, and satellite, thus limiting actual competition (Jaramillo 2002:59–60).
2. While Whedon's involvement in the series is minimal, I am including it in this volume because it is partly created under his Mutant Enemy production company, he wrote the pilot episode, and its showrunners are both former collaborators and family members (Jed Whedon and Maurissa Tanchareon).

## Chapter Four

1. At one point, *Angel*, which blended noir and horror, was paired with Aaron Spelling's long-running series *Seventh Heaven*, a series about a preacher's family and the important life lessons they learn.

## Chapter Five

1. Parts of this chapter were presented as "'The Status is Not Quo': *Dr. Horrible*, *Dollhouse*, and the Shifting Boundaries of American Television" at the 31st Annual Southwest/Texas PCA/ACA Conference, Albuquerque, NM, 10–13 February 2010.
2. For an in-depth analysis of the series' connection to *RUR*, see both Koontz (2010) and Noone (2011).
3. See the special double issue of the journal *Slayage* and Buckman et al. (2014).
4. The Remote-Free TV initiative did not generate the kind of income that Fox had hoped, and was scrapped at the end of the 2008/2009 television season ("Fox Scraps").
5. One of the clues that Echo has evolved is when Boyd catches her reading something that is not a picture book ("Belonging," 2.4).

6. Nearly every season of *Supernatural* has featured a story with that type of narrative, including "Hollywood Babylon" (2.18), which referenced actor Jared Padelecki's previous role on another WB series, *Gilmore Girls*, as well as showrunner Eric Kripke's panned debut film "Boogeyman," "The Monster at the End of This Book" (4.18)—itself a metafictional children's book—about a series of books that chronicled the brother's adventures, "Changing Channels" (5.8), which takes place in "TV Land"; "The Real Ghostbusters" (5.9), set at a *Supernatural* fan convention; "The French Mistake" (6.15), in which Dean and Sam Winchester are transported to an alternate universe in which they are actors named Jensen Ackles and Jared Padalecki; "Meta Fiction" (9.18), which is framed as a story by self-appointed scribe and ersatz deity Metatron (Curtis Armstrong), who in the *Supernatural* universe is an archangel who wrote the word of God; "Fan Fiction" (10.5), which features a high school musical based on the *Supernatural* books and stalked by the muse of theater; and "Baby" (11.4), told from the point of view of the brother's 1967 Chevy Impala.

## Chapter Six

1. Given the controversies, particularly around pricing, within the pharmaceutical industry, it seems less than surprising that the Heinz dilemma Lawrence Kohlberg used to assess the stages of moral development focuses on a chemist overcharging for a life-saving drug.
2. As of this writing, this storyline is still in process.

## Chapter Seven

1. An early version of this chapter was presented as "'Not with a Bang but a Whimper': *Dollhouse*'s 'Thought-pocalypse' as Cautionary Capitalist Tale," at the 33rd Annual Southwest/Texas PCA/ACA Conference, Albuquerque, NM, 8–11 February 2012.
2. This, obviously, is not a theme limited to Whedon's television oeuvre. An episode of the rebooted *Doctor Who*, "School Reunion" (2.3), makes a similar point. A former "companion" of the Doctor, Sarah Jane Smith (Elisabeth Sladen), says to an alien bent on rewriting the universe (played by *Buffy* alum Anthony Head), "The universe has to move

forward. Pain and loss, they define us as much as happiness or love."

3. Clive Ambrose and Matthew Harding were originally played by Philip Casnoff and Keith Carradine, respectively.

4. Nor are they the only ones; AstraZeneca, as per example, was accused of sexual harassment of employees (Maremont 1997) and was required to pay a multi-million dollar settlement.

5. In the final episode of the series, Zone (Zack Ward) actually refers to a version of Caroline (imprinted on a young girl), as "tiny messiah."

6. From seasons five through seven, the Magic Box is actually owned by the characters of Rupert Giles, Buffy's watcher, and Anya Jenkins.

7. As stated earlier, this is literalized within *Dollhouse* by making Rossum's mainframe computer human-powered; the electrical energy from human brains and bodies are the main power source of the corporation ("The Attic" [2.10]).

## Chapter Eight

1. An early version of this chapter was presented as "'Call Us What You Want, Just Not Family': Corporate Culture and the Subversion of the Created Family Whedonverse Trope in *Dollhouse*" at SCW6: Much Ado About Whedon: The 6th Biennial Slayage Conference on the Whedonverses, California State University–Sacramento, Sacramento, CA, 19–22 June 2014.

2. This concept, of delayed demonic heritage manifesting in adolescence or early adulthood, was originally introduced in the *Buffy* spin-off *Angel* ("City Of," 1.01).

3. See Padden 2011 for an analysis of the dystopian nature of language in *Dollhouse*.

4. The final episode of the series does reveal that Tony and Priya have a son ("Epitaph 2: Return," 2.13). There is also an ambiguous scene in the first episode of a naked, blood-covered man (later revealed to be former Active Alpha [Alan Tudyk]) watching a video of Caroline, with two dead bodies in the background. In theory, the two bodies could be Caroline's parents, but that is never made clear.

# Bibliography

Abbott, Stacey. 2008. Angel: *TV Milestones Series*. Detroit: Wayne University Press.

Abbott, Stacey. 2014. "Angel Remembered 10 Years On." *CST Online*. April 24. Available at: http://cstonline.tv/angel-remembered-10-years-on.

Abbott, Stacey, Bronwen Calvert, and Lorna Jowett. 2015. "A Part of Something Bigger: A Roundtable Discussion of *Marvel's Agents of S.H.I.E.L.D.*, Transmedia Television, and the Joss Whedon Brand." In: Money, Mary Alice, ed. *Joss Whedon: The Complete Collection, The TV Series, the Movies, the Comic Books, and More* (2nd revised and updated edition); 421–423.

Adalain, Josef. 2001. "Frog Net's Drama 'Angel' Folds Wings." *Variety*. February 13. Available at: http://variety.com/2004/tv/news/frog-net-s-drama-angel-folds-wings-1117900126.

Adams, Michael. 2003. *Slayer Slang: A Buffy the Vampire Slayer Lexicon*. New York: Oxford University Press.

Alito, Samuel. "Burwell v. Hobby Lobby Inc." Docket 13-354. SCOTUSblog.com. www.scotusblog.com/case-fules/cases/sebelius-v-hobby-lobby-inc/. Web.

Alvi, Zalina. 2011. "Goliath Is People: How Dollhouse Took Distrust to a Whole New Level." In: Espenson, Jane, ed. *Inside Joss' Dollhouse: From Alpha to Rossum*. Dallas: Ben Bella Books; 35–45.

"America's Worst Charities." 2015. *Tampa Bay Times* and the Center for Investigative Reporting. Available at: http://www.tampabay.com/americas-worst-charities/.

Anders, Charlie Jane. 2010. "We Need More Vampire Slayers—Just Not More Buffy." *io9*. November 29. Available at: http://io9.gizmodo.com/5700871/we-need-more-vampire-slayers—just-not-more-buffy.

Anderson, Devon. 2016. "Echoes of Frankenstein: Shelley's Masterpiece in Joss Whedon's *Dollhouse* and Our Relationship with Technology." *Slayage: The Journal of Whedon Studies* 14.1, no. 43, n. pag. Available at: http://www.whedonstudies.tv/uploads/2/6/2/8/26288593/anderson_slayage_14.1.pdf

Anderson, Tami. 2011. "Whose Story Is This Anyway?" In: Espenson, Jane, ed. *Inside Joss' Dollhouse: From Alpha to Rossum*. Dallas: Ben Bella Books; 161–173.

Armstrong, Karen. 2000. *The Battle for God*. New York: Alfred A. Knopf.

Arvidsson, Adam. 2006. *Brands: Meaning and Value in Media Culture*. London: Routledge.

Astra-Zeneca. "What We Do." Available at: http://www.astrazeneca.com/About-Us/What-we-do.

Bakan, Joel. 2004. *The Corporation: The Pathological Pursuit of Profit and Power*. New York: Free Press.

Barr, Roseanne. 2011. "And I Should Know." *New York Magazine*. May 15. Available at: http://nymag.com/arts/tv/upfronts/2011/roseanne-barr-2011-5/

Barraclough, Simon. 2009. "Chronic Diseases and Global Health Governance: The Contrasting Cases of Food and Tobacco." In: Kay, Adrian, and Owain David Williams, eds. *Global Health Governance: Crisis, Institutions and Political Economy*. London: Palgrave Macmillan; 102–128.

Barringer, Felicity. 1991. "After Layoffs, St. Louis Rethinks Future, Again." *New York Times*. January 14. Available at: http://www.nytimes.com/1991/01/14/us/after-layoffs-st-louis-rethinks-future-again.html.

Battis, Jess. 2005. *Blood Relations: Chosen Families in* Buffy the Vampire Slayer *and* Angel. Jefferson, NC: McFarland.

Bedell, Sally. 1981. *Up the Tube: Primetime TV in the Silverman Years*. New York: Viking.

Beeler, Stan. 2005. "Outing Lorne: Performance for the Performers." In: Abbott, Stacey, ed. *Reading* Angel: *The TV Spin-off With a Soul.* London: I.B. Tauris; 88–100.

Bennett, Eve. 2011. "Deconstructing the Dream Factory: Personal Fantasy and Corporate Manipulation in Joss Whedon's Dollhouse." *Slayage: The Journal of Whedon Studies* 9.1, n. pag. Available at: http://www.whedonstudies.tv/uploads/2/6/2/8/26288593/bennett_slayage_9.1.pdf

Bercovici, Jeff. 2012. "'Avengers' Director Joss Whedon on Trying to Be More Like Buffy." *Forbes.* May 3. Available at: http://www.forbes.com/sites/jeffbercovici/2012/05/03/avengers-director-joss-whedon-on-trying-to-be-more-like-buffy/#42190fbd6227.

Bernhardt, Amy M., Cara Wilking, Anna M. Adachi-Meija, Elaina Bergamini, Jill Marijnissen, and James D. Sargent. 2013. "How Television Fast Food Marketing Aimed at Children Compares with Adult Advertisements." *PLoS One* 8.8 (August): 1–6. Available at: http://journals.plos.org/plosone/article?id=10.1371/journal.pone.0072479.

Bianculli, David. 2016. *The Platinum Age of Television: From* I Love Lucy *to* The Walking Dead, *How TV Became Terrific.* New York: Doubleday.

Billson, Anne. 2005. Buffy the Vampire Slayer *(BFI TV Classics).* London: British Film Institute.

Bindman Stephen. 1992. "Brainwashing Victims to Get $100,000." *Gazette* (Montreal). November 18.

Birkner, Christine. 2016. "With the Threat of an Ad Ban Looming, Pharma Is Fighting to Repair Its Reputation: Under Fire from Washington, Again." *Ad Week.* March 27. Available at: http://www.adweek.com/brandmarketing/threat-ad-ban-looming-pharma-fighting-repair-its-reputation-170409/.

"Blackwater's Rich Contracts." 2007. *New York Times.* October 3. Available at: http://www.nytimes.com/2007/10/03/opinion/03ihtedblack.1.7733227.html?_r=1 Web.

Borger, Julian. 2005. "How Born-again George Became a Man on a Mission." *The Guardian.* October 6. Available at: http://www.theguardian.com/world/2005/oct/07/usa.georgebush.

Boulware, Taylor. 2013. "'I Made Me': Queer Theory, Subjection, and Identity in the *Dollhouse.*" *Slayage: The Journal of Whedon Studies* 10.1 (Winter), n. pag. Available at: http://www.whedonstudies.tv/uploads/2/6/2/8/26288593/boulware_slayage_10.1.pdf

Briggs, Brook Shelby. 2006. "Collecting Louisiana's Dead." In: King, R.J. *Big, Easy Money: Disaster Profiteering on the American Gulf Coast.* August: 12–13.

Brown, Todd. 2011. "Marvel in the 90's: The Death of the Incredible Hulk." *Screen Anarchy.* November 7. Available at: http://screenanarchy.com/2011/11/marvel-in-the-90s-the-death-of-the-incredible-hulk.html.

Buchanan, Ginger. 2004. "Who Killed *Firefly?*" In: Espenson, Jane, ed. *Finding Serenity: Antiheroes, Lost Shepharrds, and Space Hookers in Joss Whedon's "Firefly."* Dallas: Ben Bella Books; 47–54.

Buckman, Alyson. 2008. "'Much Madness Is Divinest Sense': *Firefly's* Big Damn Heroes and Little Witches." In: Wilcox, Rhonda, and Tanya R. Cochran, eds. *Investigating* Firefly *and* Serenity: *Science Fiction on the Frontier.* London: I.B. Tauris; 41–46. Print.

Buckman, Alyson. 2010. "'Go Ahead! Run Away! Say It Was Horrible!' *Dr. Horrible's Sing-Along Blog* as Resistant Text." *Slayage: The Journal of Whedon Studies* 8.1, n. pag. Available at: http://www.whedonstudies.tv/uploads/2/6/2/8/26288593/buckman_slayage_8.1.pdf.

Burr, Vivian, and Christine Jarvis. 2005. "'Friends Are the Family We Choose for Ourselves': Young People and Families in the TV Series *Buffy the Vampire Slayer.*" *Young: Nordic Journal of Youth Research* 13.3: 269–283.

Bussolini, Jeffrey. 2008. "A Geopolitical Interpretation of Serenity." In: Wilcox, Rhonda, and Tanya R. Cochran, eds. *Investigating* Firefly *and* Serenity: *Science Fiction on the Frontier.* London: I.B. Tauris; 139–152.

Bussolini, Jeffrey. 2014. "Technology and Magic: Joss Whedon's Explorations of the Mind." In: Wilcox, Rhonda, Tanya R. Cochran, Cynthea Masson and David Lavery, eds. *Reading Joss Whedon.* Syracuse: Syracuse University Press; 325–340.

Caldwell, John Thornton. 2006. "Critical Industrial Practice: Branding, Repurposing, and the Migratory Patterns of Industrial Texts." *Television and New Media* 7, no. 2: 99–134.

"Can TV Change the World?" 2013. Copenhagen TV Festival. Available at: http://cphtvfestival.dk/eng/program/sessions/session/?sesid=75.

# Bibliography

Canavan, Gerry. 2012. "Zombies, Reavers, Butchers, and Actuals in Joss Whedon's Work." In: Money, Mary Alice, ed. *Joss Whedon: The Complete Collection, The TV Series, the Movies, the Comic Books, and More*. London: Titan Books; 285–297.

Carbado, Devon W. 2005. "Blue-on-Black Violence: A Provisional Model of Some of the Causes." *The Georgetown Law Journal* 104: 1479–1529.

Cardona, Mercedes M., and John Fine. 2003. "The Next DTC: DVD Explodes: AD category Grows 56% in First Half to $400 Million." *Advertising Age* 74.36 (1 September), 1, 22.

Chaffin, Bryan. 2014. "Tim Cook Soundly Rejects Politics of the NCPPR, Suggests Group Sell Apple Stock." *Mac Observer*. February 28. Available at: https://www.macobserver.com/tmo/article/tim-cook-soundly-rejects-politics-of-the-ncppr-suggests-group-sell-apples-s.

Chambliss, Andrew, Maurissa Tancharoen, and Jed Whedon. 2011. *Dollhouse Epitaphs: Issues 1–5*. Dark Horse Comics; July 13.

Chandler, Holly. 2003. "Slaying the Patriarchy: Transfusions of the Vampire Metaphor in *Buffy the Vampire Slayer*." *Slayage: The Journal of Whedon Studies* 3.1, n. pag. Available at: http://www.whedonstudies.tv/uploads/2/6/2/8/26288593/chandler_slayage_3.1.pdf.

Chow, Lesley. 2010. "A Thousand Blooms: Inside Joss Whedon's Dollhouse." *Bright Lights Film Journal*. 10 May. Available at: http://brightlightsfilm.com/68/68dollhouse.php#.U3U-UC_SSgR.

Cieply, Michael, David Carr, and Brooke Barnes. 2007. "Screenwriters on Strike Over Stake in New Media." *New York Times*. November 6. Available at: http://www.nytimes.com/2007/11/06/business/media/06strike.html.

Cieply, Michael. 2008. "Writer's Vote to End Strike." *New York Times*. February 12. Available at: http://www.nytimes.com/2008/02/12/business/media/12cnd-strike.html.

Clifton, Jacob. 2007. "Signal to Noise: Media and Subversion in *Serenity*." In: Espenson, Jane, and Leah Wilson, eds. *Serenity Found: More Unauthorized Essays on Joss Whedon's Firefly Universe*. Dallas: Ben Bella Books; 203–215.

Colvin, Phil. 2005. "*Angel*: Redefinition and Justification Through Faith." In: Abbott, Stacey, ed. *Reading* Angel: *The TV Spin-off With a Soul*. London: I.B. Tauris; 17–30.

Comeford, AmiJo, and Tamy Burnett, eds. 2010. *The Literary Angel: Essays on Influences and Traditions Reflected in the Joss Whedon Series*. Jefferson, NC: McFarland.

"Comic-Con 2009 Entire *Dollhouse* Panel." 2009. Watching *Dollhouse*: Fansite & Forum for Joss Whedon's *Dollhouse* Fox TV Series. July 26. Available at: http://watchingdollhouse.com/comic-con-2009-entire-dollhouse-panel/#more-2026.

Confessior, Nicholas, and Karen Yourish. 2016. "$2 Billion Worth of Free Media for Donald Trump." *New York Times*. March 15. Available at: https://www.nytimes.com/2016/03/16/upshot/measuring-donald-trumps-mammoth-advantage-in-free-media.html?_r=0.

Consoli, John. 2007. "Strike Has Cash-back Clock Ticking." *Mediaweek*. November 19.

Coontz, Stephanie. 1993. *The Way We Never Were: American Families and the Nostalgia Trap*. New York: Basic Books.

Cooper, L. Andrew. 2013/2014. "The Cabin in the Woods and the End of American Exceptionalism." *Slayage: The Journal of Whedon Studies*. Special Issue: *"We Are Not Who We Are": Critical Reflections on* The Cabin in the Woods. Eds. Kristopher Woofter and Jasie Stokes. 10.2 & 11.1 (Fall/Winter), n. pag. Available at: http://www.whedonstudies.tv/uploads/2/6/2/8/26288593/cooper_slayage_10.2-11.1.pdf.

"Corporatism." *Merriam-Webster*. Available at: https://www.merriam-webster.com/dictionary/corporatism.

"Corporatocracy." *Oxford Living Dictionary*. Available at: https://en.oxforddictionaries.com/definition/us/corporatocracy.

Coster, Helen. 2009. "The Biggest CEO Outrages of 2009: This Year's C-Suite Hall of Shame." *Forbes*. November 25. Available at: http://www.forbes.com/2009/11/25/ceo-outrages-shame-leadership-ceonetwork-governance.html.

Curtin, Michael, and Jane Shuttac. 2009. *The American Television Industry*. New York: Palgrave Macmillian.

Day, Deanna. 2013. "Toward a Zombie Epistemology: What It Means to Live and Die in Cabin in the Woods." *ADA: A Journal of Gender, New Media, and Technology* 3, n.pag. Available at: http://adanewmedia.org/2013/11/issue3-day/.

Department of Justice. 2009. "Kellogg Brown and Root LLC Pleads Guilty to Foreign Bribery Charges and Agrees to Pay $402

Million Criminal Fine: Enforcement Actions by DOJ and SEC Result in Penalties of $579 Million for KBR's Participation in a Scheme to Bribe Nigerian Government Officials to Obtain Contracts" [press release]. February 11. Available at: http://www.justice.gov/opa/pr/2009/February/09-crm-112.html.

Dickey, Josh F. 2013. "$2 million for 'Veronica Mars' Breaks Kickstarter Records, Gets Greenlight." *Variety.* March 13. Available at: http://www.variety.com/2013/more/news/veronica-mars-kickstarter-reaches-1-million-in-funds-1200194274/.

DiMasi, Joseph. 2014. "Innovation in the Pharmaceutical Industry: New Estimates of R & D Costs." Tufts Center for the Study of Drug Development. November 18. Available at: http://csdd.tufts.edu/files/uploads/Tufts_CSDD_briefing_on_RD_cost_study_-_Nov_18,_2014..pdf.

Donaton, Scott. 2005. "The Marketing Revolution Will Be Televised, Online and on Demand." *Advertising Age* 76.11 (March 14), 26.

Drezner, Daniel W. 2016. "I Read Hillary Clinton's Speeches to Goldman-Sachs: Here's What Surprised Me the Most." *Washington Post.* October 17. Available at: https://www.washingtonpost.com/posteverything/wp/2016/10/17/i-read-hillary-clintons-speeches-to-goldman-sachs-heres-what-surprised-me-the-most/?utm_term=.66913ca23cc7.

Drutman, Lee. 2015. "How Corporate Lobbyists Conquered America: Businesses Didn't Always Have So Much Power in Washington." *The Atlantic.* April 20. Available at: https://www.theatlantic.com/business/archive/2015/04/how-corporate-lobbyists-conquered-american-democracy/390822/.

Durand, Kevin. 2009. "'Are You Ready to Finish This': The Battle Against the Patriarchal Forces of Darkness." *Slayage: The Journal of Whedon Studies* 7.4, n. pag. Available at: http://www.whedonstudies.tv/uploads/2/6/2/8/26288593/durand_slayage_7.4.pdf

Ehrenreich, Barbara. 2001. *Nickel and Dimed: On (Not) Getting By in America.* New York: Picador.

Erickson, Gregory T. 2014. "From Old Heresies to Future Paradigms: Joss Whedon on Body and Soul." In: Wilcox, Rhonda, Tanya R. Cochran, Cynthea Masson, and David Lavery, eds. *Reading Joss Whedon.* Syracuse: Syracuse University Press; 341–355.

Fahrenthold, David A. 2016. "Trump Recorded Having Extremely Lewd Conversation About Women in 2005." *Washington Post.* October 8. Available at: https://www.washingtonpost.com/politics/trump-recorded-having-extremely-lewd-conversation-about-women-in-2005/2016/10/07/3b9ce776-8cb4-11e6-bf8a-3d26847eeed4_story.html?utm_term=.40f786594835.

Fahri, Paul. 2004. "Network TV, Ensconced in a Blue Period." *Washington Post.* November 28. Available at: https://www.washingtonpost.com/archive/lifestyle/style/2004/11/28/network-tv-ensconced-in-a-blue-period/50cf681e-1dc3-4e30-98a3-4a6b7b3fb4b3/.

Fienberg, Daniel. 2009. "Fox Execs Talk 'Dollhouse' Renewal, 'Terminator' cancellation." Hitfix. May 18. Available at: http://uproxx.com/hitfix/fox-execs-talk-dollhouse-renewal-terminator-cancellation.

Fishman, Charles. 2006. *The Wal-Mart Effect: How the World's Most Powerful Company Really Works—and How It's Transforming the American Economy.* New York: Penguin Press.

Fleming, Mike, Jr. 2011. "Joss Whedon's 'Cabin in the Woods' with 'Thor's Chris Hemsworth Going to Lionsgate." *Deadline.* April 28. Available at: http://deadline.com/2011/04/joss-whedons-cabin-in-the-woods-with-thors-chris-hemsworth-going-to-lionsgate-126778/.

Flint, Joe, and Rebecca Ballhaus. 2015. "Cable TV Binges on Trump Coverage: CNN, More Than Rivals, Focuses on Candidates; All Get a Ratings Boost." *The Wall Street Journal.* September 15. Available at: https://www.wsj.com/articles/cable-tv-news-binges-on-trump-coverage-1442360415.

"Fluoxetine Hydrochloride." Drugs.com. Available at: https://www.drugs.com/monograph/fluoxetine-hydrochloride.html.

Foreman, Judy. 1998. "How CIA Stole Their Minds." *Boston Globe.* October 30.

"Former Chilean Army Chief Charged Over 1973 Killing of Activists: Retired General Juan Emilio Cheyre Denies Involvement in Deaths of 15 Left-Wing Militants During Pinochet Dictatorship." 2016. *The Guardian.* July 8. Available at: https://www.theguardian.com/world/2016/jul/08/former-chilean-army-chief-juan-emilio-cheyre-charged-1973-activists-killing.

Foster, Thomas Lalli. 2017. "The Reluctant Superhero: Marvel in the '70s." *PopMatters.* March 2. Available at: http://www.pop

matters.com/feature/the-reluctant-super hero-marvel-tv-in-the-70s/.

Foucault, Michel. 1990. *The History of Sexuality: Volume 1, An Introduction*. New York: Vintage Books.

"Fox Scraps Remote-Free TV." 2009. *New York Times*. May 14. Available at: http://mediadecoder.blogs.nytimes.com//2009/05/14/fox-scraps-remote-free-tv/.

"Friday Night Death Slot." TV Tropes. Available at: http://tvtropes.org/pmwiki/pmwiki.php/Main/FridayNightDeathSlot.

Frum, David. 2013. "Norquist: Romney Will Do As He's Told: Is Mitt Romney So Weak He Won't Be Able to Stand Up to Congress?" *The Daily Beast*. Daily Beast Company LLC. February 13. Available at: http://www.thedailybeast.com/articles/2012/02/13/grover-norquist-speech-cpac.html.

Frutkin, Alan James. 2002. "Fox Trying to Spark 'Firefly.'" *Mediaweek*. September 2.

Gellman, Barton. 2013. "Edward Snowden, After Months of NSA Revelations, Says His Mission's Accomplished." *Washington Post*. December 23. Available at: https://www.washingtonpost.com/world/national-security/edward-snowden-after-months-of-nsa-revelations-says-his-missions-accomplished/2013/12/23/49fc36de-6c1c-11e3-a523-fe73f0ff6b8d_story.html?utm_term=.3edb9eb6b9f0.

Giannini, Erin. 2013/2014. "'Charybdis Tested Well with Teens': *The Cabin in the Woods* as Metafictional Critique of Corporate Media Producers and Audiences." *Slayage: The Journal of Whedon Studies*. Special Issue: *"We Are Not Who We Are": Critical Reflections on* The Cabin in the Woods. Eds. Kristopher Woofter and Jasie Stokes. 10.2 & 11.1 (Fall/Winter), n. pag. Available at: http://www.whedonstudies.tv/uploads/2/6/2/8/26288593/giannini_slayage_10.2-11.1.pdf.

Giannini, Erin. 2014. "'This Isn't Wall Street, This Is Hell!' Corporate America as the Biggest *Supernatural* Bad of All." In: Hansen, Regina and Susan A. George, eds. Supernatural, *Humanity, and the Soul: On the Highway to Hell and Back*. New York: Palgrave Macmillan; 83–96.

Giannini, Erin. 2015. "'It Doesn't Mean What You Think': River Tam as Embodied Culture Jam." *Slayage: The Journal of Whedon Studies* 13.2. Special Issue: *"Lightin' Out for the Library: A* Firefly/Serenity *Special Issue."* Eds. Michael Goodrum and Philip Smith. Available at: http://www.whedonstudies.tv/uploads/2/6/2/8/26288593/giannini.pdf.

Giannini, Erin. 2015. "'Something Nightmares are From': Corporate Culture and Externalized Consequences." In: Frankel, Valerie, ed. *After the Avengers: From Joss Whedon's Hottest, Newest Franchises to the Future of the Whedonverse*. Chicago: PopMatters Media.

Giannini, Erin. 2017. "'They Brought It on Themselves!' Adapting and Reflecting Cultural Fears, from the Shop to Rossum." *Science Fiction Film and Television* 10, no. 2: 231–249.

Gibson, William. 1984. *Neuromancer*. New York: Ace.

Gilson, Dave. 2010. "Who Owns Congress? A Campaign Cash Seating Chart." *Mother Jones*. September/October. Available at: http://www.motherjones.com/politics/2010/09/congress-corporate-sponsors.

"GlaxoSmithKline to Plead Guilty and Pay $3 Billion to Resolve Fraud Allegations and Failure to Report Safety Data: Largest Health Care Fraud Settlement in U. S. History" [press release]. 2012. US Department of Justice. July 2. Available at: https://www.justice.gov/opa/pr/glaxosmithkline-plead-guilty-and-pay-3-billion-resolve-fraud-allegations-and-failure-report.

Goldberg, Lindsey. 2013. "Cobie Smolders Comic-Con Reveal: Secret 'Agents of S.H.I.E.L.D.' Role." *Hollywood Reporter*. July 19. Available at: http://www.hollywoodreport.com/livefeed/cobie-smolders-comic-con-shield-583195.

Goldman, Eric. 2008. "Big New Deal for Family Guy's Seth McFarlane Sticking with Stewie, Cleveland for Years to Come." *IGN*. May 5. Available at: http://www.ign.com/articles/2008/05/05/big-new-deal-for-family-guys-seth-macfarlane.

Goldman, Eric. 2014. "Marvel's Agents of SHIELD: Season 1 Review." *IGN*. May 21. Available at: http://www.ign.com/articles/2014/05/22/marvels-agents-of-shield-season-1-review.

Goldsmith, P. Gardner. 2007. "Freedom in an Unfree World." In: Espenson, Jane, and Leah Wilson, eds. *Serenity Found: More Unauthorized Essays on Joss Whedon's Firefly Universe*. Dallas: Ben Bella; 55–65.

Goodland, Robert, and Jeff Anhang. 2009. "Livestock and Climate Change: What If the Key Actors in Climate Change Are … Cows, Pigs, and Chickens?" *World Watch*. November/December: 10–19. Available at:

http://www.worldwatch.org/files/pdf/Livestock%20and%20Climate%20Change.pdf.

Goodman, Tim. 2009. "TV Review: 'Dollhouse' Is a Big Disappointment." SFGate. February 11. Available at: http://www.sfgate.com/news/TV-review-Dollhouse-15-9-big-disappointment-3172810.php.

Goodwin, Jennifer. 2009. "Will Fox Air Dollhouse's Final Episode or Not?" EOnline. April 9. Available at: http://www.eonline.com/news/117929/will-fox-air-dollhouses-final-episode-or-not.

Grainge, Paul. 2007. *Brand Hollywood: Selling Entertainment in a Global Media Culture*. London: Routledge.

Grossman, Jacob. 2004. "Spike, the Initiative and the Substitution of the Technological for the Metaphysical." Paper presented at the Slayage Conference on *Buffy the Vampire Slayer*, Nashville, TN, May 27–30. Available at: http://www.whedonstudies.tv/uploads/2/6/2/8/26288593/grossman.pdf.

Guffey, Ensley. 2013. *Joss in June* Conference discussion. Cleveland Community College. Shelby, NC, June 29.

Gullapalli, Diya, and Shefali Anand. 2008. "Bailout of Money Funds Seems to Staunch Outflow: Fear That Had Gripped $3.4 Trillion Market Abates, Ending the Reluctance of Funds to Buy Vital Commercial Paper." *The Wall Street Journal*. September 20. Available at: https://www.wsj.com/articles/SB122186683086958875

Hadas, Leora. 2014. "Authorship and Authenticity in the Transmedia Brand: The Case of *Marvel's Agents of S.H.I.E.L.D.*" *Networking Knowledge: Journal of the MeCCSA Postgraduate Network*. April 7, no. 1. Available at: http://ojs.meccsa.org.uk/index.php/netknow/article/view/332.

Hadyk-Delodder, Gareth and Laura Chilcoat. 2015. "'See What's Inside': Understanding the Reavers' Posthuman Identity and Role in *Firefly* and *Serenity*." In: Goodrum, Michael, and Philip Smith, eds. *Firefly Revisited: Essays on Joss Whedon's Classic Series*. Lanham, MD: Rowman and Littlefield; 37–52.

Hahn, Kelsie. 2013. "Lady Killer: Death of the Feminized Body in the Whedonverse." *Slayage: The Journal of Whedon Studies* 10.1, no. 35, n. pag. Available at: http://www.whedonstudies.tv/uploads/2/6/2/8/26288593/hahn_slayage_10.1.pdf.

Harrison, Janine R. 2005. "Gender Politics in Angel: Traditional vs. Non-Traditional Corporate Climates." In: Abbott, Stacey, ed. *Reading Angel: The TV Spin-Off With a Soul*. London: I.B. Tauris; 117–131.

Hettrick, Scott. 2005. "So They Just Discovered DVD? Studio Data Suggest No Clear Consumer Switch." *Variety* (special section: DVD Exclusive). July: 1.

Hibberd, James. 2007. "Joss Whedon Returns to Fox with New Series 'Dollhouse.'" *TV Week*. October 31. Available at: http://www.tvweek.com/blogs/james-hibberd/2007/10/joss_whedon_returns_to_fox_wit.php.

Hibberd, James. 2008. "On 'Dollhouse' Set: Whedon Talks Pilot Reshoot." *The Hollywood Reporter*. July 22. Available at: http://www.thrfeed.com/blogs/live-feed/dollhouse-set-whedon-talks-pilot-50558.

Hilmes, Michele. 2011. *Only Connect: A Cultural History of Broadcasting in the United States, Third Edition*. Boston: Wadsworth Cengage Learning.

Holmes, Linda. 2009. "Very Bad Ideas: Making a Whedon-free 'Buffy' Reboot." *NPR*. May 26. Available at: http://www.npr.org/sections/monkeysee/2009/05/very_bad_ideas_making_a_whedon.html.

"How Much Money Did Jonas Salk Potentially Forfeit By Not Patenting the Polio Vaccine?" 2012. *Forbes*. August 9. Available at: https://www.forbes.com/sites/quora/2012/08/09/how-much-money-did-jonas-salk-potentially-forfeit-by-not-patenting-the-polio-vaccine/#32a5cb5969b8.

Howard, K Shannon. 2010. "Charles Gunn, Wolfram & Hart, and Baudrillard's Theory of the Simulcram." In: Comeford, AmiJo, and Tamy Burnett, eds. *The Literary Angel: Essays on Influence and Traditions Reflected in the Joss Whedon Series*. Jefferson, NC: McFarland; 147–158.

Hoyt, Edward O'N. 2004. "TV's 'Rural Purge.'" *Washington Post*. December 2. Available at: https://www.washingtonpost.com/archive/opinions/2004/12/02/tvs-rural-purge/2516ce4b-9140-4f92-b30f-6bb3a9582ca1/?utm_term=.2167f8f06443.

Hurd, Matthew. 2012. "Six Reasons Why Joss Whedon Is the Perfect Director for *The Avengers*." In: Money, Mary Alice, ed. *Joss Whedon: The Complete Collection, The TV Series, the Movies, the Comic Books, and More*. London: Titan Books; 447–454.

Iatropoulos, Mary Ellen. 2015. "Of Whedonverse Canon and 'Someone Else's Sandbox': Marvel, *Much Ado*, and the Great Auteur

Debate." In: Frankel, Valerie, ed. *After the Avengers: From Joss Whedon's Hottest, Newest Franchises to the Future of the Whedonverse*. Chicago: PopMatters Media.

Iatropoulous, Mary Ellen, and Lowery A. Woodall III, eds. 2016. *Joss Whedon and Race: Critical Essays*. Jefferson, NC: McFarland.

Interagency Working Group. "Joint National Intelligence Agency." U.S. National Archives and Records Administration. Available at: https://www.archives.gov/iwg/declassified-records/rg-330-defense-secretary.

Interrante, Scott. 2015. "'I'm Every Bit the S.H.I.E.L.D. Agent You Are': Exploring Opposing Masculinities." In: Frankel, Valerie, ed. *After the Avengers: From Joss Whedon's Hottest, Newest Franchises to the Future of the Whedonverse*. Chicago: PopMatters Media.

"Interview: Amber Benson." 2003. BBC. December 10. Available at: http://www.bbc.co.uk/cult/buffy/interviews/benson2003/printpage.html.

Jaramillio, Deborah. 2002. "The Family Racket: AOL Time Warner, HBO, *The Sopranos*, and the Construction of a Quality Brand." *Journal of Communication Inquiry* 26, no. 1: 59–75.

Jarvis, Christine. 2016. "Battle of the Blockbusters: Joss Whedon as Public Pedagogue." *Slayage: The Journal of Whedon Studies* 14.1, no. 43, n. pag. Available at: http://www.whedonstudies.tv/uploads/2/6/2/8/26288593/jarvis_slayage_14.1.pdf.

Johnson, Catherine. 2007. "Tele-Branding in TVIII: The Network as Brand and the Programme as Brand." *New Review of Film and Television Studies* 5 no. 1: 5–24.

Jones, Andrew Zimmerman. 2011. "The Redemption of Topher Brink." In: Espenson, Jane, ed. *Inside Joss' Dollhouse: From Alpha to Rossum*. Dallas: Ben Bella Books; 79–92.

Kahm, Howard. 2015. "'They Couldn't Let Us Profit—It Wouldn't Be Civilized': Economic Modalities and Core-Periphery Relationships in the Political Economy of *Firefly-Serenity*." In: Goodrum, Michael, and Philip Smith, eds. Firefly *Revisited: Essays on Joss Whedon's Classic Series*. Lanham, MD: Rowman & Littlefield; 155–170.

Kelland, Kate. 2014. "Study Finds Deregulation Fuelling Obesity Epidemic." *Reuters*. February 2. Available at: http://www.reuters.com/article/health-obesity-deregulation-idUSL5N0L70PZ20140202.

Kennedy, Anthony. "Citizens United v. Federal Election Commission." Docket 08–205. SCOTUSblog.com. Available at: http://www.scotusblog.com/case-files/cases/citizens-united-v-federal-election-commission/.

Kessel, Mark. 2014. "Restoring the Pharmaceutical Industry's Reputation." *Nature Biotechnology* 32: 983–990.

Keyes, Rob. 2011. "Creative Differences Are Knocking Directors Out of Marvel Movies." Screenrant. December 9. Available at: http://screenrant.com/marvel-thor-2-directors-patty-jenkins-branagh-rob-142991/.

Keyes, Rob. 2014. "Edgar Wright Officially Drops Out of Marvel's 'Ant-Man.'" Screenrant. May 23. Available at: http://screenrant.com/ant-man-director-edgar-wright-exits/.

Keyes, Rob. 2015. "Why Joss Whedon Is Done Directing 'Avengers' Movies for Marvel." Screenrant. April 22. Available at: http://screenrant.com/why-joss-whedon-not-directing-avengers-3-4/.

King, Stephen. 1990. *The Stand*. New York: Anchor Books.

King, Stephen. 1991. *Danse Macabre*. London: Hodder and Stoughton.

King, Stephen. 2001. *On Writing: A Memoir of the Craft*. New York: Pocket Books.

Kirchner, Jesse Saba. 2006. "And in Some Language That's English? Slayer Slang and Artificial Computer Generation." *Slayage: The Journal of Whedon Studies* 5.4 (May), n. pag. Available at: http://www.whedonstudies.tv/uploads/2/6/2/8/26288593/kirchner_slayage_5.4.pdf

Kit, Borys. 2009. "'Buffy the Vampire Slayer' Returning to the Big Screen." *Reuters*. May 25. Available at: http://www.reuters.com/article/us-buffy-idUSTRE54P0KG20090526.

Klein, Naomi. 2002. *No Logo*. New York: Picador.

Klein, Naomi. 2007. *The Shock Doctrine*. London: Penguin Books.

Kompare, Derek. 2006. "Publishing Flow: DVD Box Sets and the Reconception of Television." *Television and New Media*. 7, no. 4: 335–60.

Koontz, K. Dale. 2010. "Czech Mate: Whedon, Capek, and the Foundations of the Dollhouse." *Slayage: The Journal of Whedon Studies* 8.2 and 8.3, n. pag. Available at: http://www.whedonstudies.tv/uploads/2/6/2/8/26288593/koontz_slayage_8.2-3.pdf

Kornbluh, Peter. 2003. *The Pinochet File: A Declassified Dossier on Atrocity and Accountability*. New York: The New Press.

Kushner, David. 2009. "Revolt of a T.V. Genius." *Rolling Stone*. February 19: 38–39.

Lapote, Phillip. 2000. "The Corporation as Fantasy Villain." *New York Times*. April 9. Available at: http://www.nytimes.com/2000/04/09/movies/the-corporation-as-fantasy-villain.html?pagewanted=all.

Lasn, Kalle. 2000. *Culture Jam: How to Reverse America's Suicidal Consumer Binge—And Why We Must*. New York: William Morrow Paperbacks.

Lavery, David. 2014. *Joss Whedon, A Creative Portrait: From Buffy the Vampire Slayer to Marvel's The Avengers*. London: I.B. Tauris.

Lenk, Leah and Denise Lynch. 2015. "'Yes Men'? Rape Myth and Gender Stereotypes in *Buffy the Vampire Slayer* and Marvel's *Agents of S.H.I.E.L.D.*" *Watcher Junior* 8, no. 2. Available at: http://www.whedonstudies.tv/uploads/2/6/2/8/26288593/lenk_and_lynch_watcherjunior_8.2.pdf.

Levey, Noam N. 2017. "Trump Budget Envisions Big Cuts for Health and Human Services." *Los Angeles Times*. March 16. Available at: http://www.latimes.com/politics/washington/la-na-essential-washington-updates-trump-budget-envisions-big-cuts-for-1489664310-htmlstory.html.

Levine, Bruce. 2011. " The Myth of U. S. Democracy and the Reality of U. S. Corporatocracy." *Huffington Post*. March 16. Available at: http://www.huffingtonpost.com/bruce-e-levine/the-myth-of-us-democracy-corporatocracy_b_836573.html.

Lewinski, John Scott. 2008. "Final Cost of WGA Strike Less Than Estimated." *Wired*. February 20. Available at: https://www.wired.com/2008/02/final-cost-of-w/.

Lindsey, Hal. 1970. *The Late Great Planet Earth*. Grand Rapids: Zondervan.

Little, Tracy. 2003. "High School Is Hell: Metaphor Made Literal." In: South, James B., ed. *Buffy the Vampire Slayer and Philosophy: Fear and Trembling in Sunnydale*. Chicago: Open Court Press; 282–293.

Littleton, Cynthia. 2008. "TV's Class Struggle: Working Stiffs Absent in Fall Fare." *Variety*. September 22, 1, 81.

Littleton, Cynthia. 2015. "Joss Whedon Says He Made More Money from Dr. Horrible Than the First Avengers Movie." *Variety*. October 15. Available at: http://variety.com/2015/tv/news/dr-horribles-sing-along-blog-joss-whedon-avengers-paleyfest-1201615455/.

Longworth, James. 2011. "Joss Whedon, Feminist" [reprint]. In: Lavery, David and Cynthia Burkhead, eds. *Joss Whedon Conversations*. Jackson: University Press of Mississippi; 42–63. Print.

Lotz, Amanda. 2007. "The Promotional Role of the Network Upfront Presentations in the Production of Culture." *Television and New Media* 8, no. 3: 3–24.

Lowry, Brian. 2005. "Nets Give Life to Mini Mania: Webs Again Bullish as Limited Series Gain Traction with Viewers, DVD Buyers." *Variety*. June 20–26: 15.

Lowry, Brian. 2009. "Review: 'Dollhouse.'" *Variety*. 8 February. Available at: http://variety.com/2009/tv/reviews/dollhouse-3-1200473773/.

Lubin, Gus. 2010. "BP CEO Tony Hayward Apologizes for His Idiotic Statement: 'I'd Like My Life Back.'" *Business Insider*. June 2. Available at: http://www.businessinsider.com/bp-ceo-tony-hayward-apologizes-for-saying-id-like-my-life-back-2010–6.

Lury, Celia. 2004. *Brands: The Logos of a Global Economy*. London: Routledge.

Maremont, Mark. 1996. "Aftershocks Are Rumbling Through Astra." *Business Week*. May 20. Available at: http://www.businessweek.com/1996/21/b347654.htm.

Masson, Cynthea. 2010. "Who Painted the Lion?—A Gloss on *Dollhouse*'s 'Belle Chose.'" *Slayage: The Online Journal of Whedon Studies* 8.2–8.3: Special Issue on *Dollhouse*. Ed. Cynthea Masson and Rhonda Wilcox. Available at: http://www.whedonstudies.tv/uploads/2/6/2/8/26288593/masson_slayage_8.2-3.pdf.

Masson, Cynthea, and Rhonda Wilcox. 2010. "Fantasy Is Their purpose: Joss Whedon's Dollhouse." *Slayage: The Online Journal of Whedon Studies* 8.2–3, no. 30–31, n. pag. Available at: http://www.whedonstudies.tv/uploads/2/6/2/8/26288593/dollhouse_intro.pdf

Masson, Cynthea. 2013. "'Break Out the Champagne, Pinocchio': *Angel* and the Puppet Paradox." *Studies in Popular Culture* 35, no. 2: 43–67.

Masters, Kim and Borys Kit. 2014. "Why 'Ant-Man' Director Edgar Wright Exited Marvel's Superhero Movie." *Hollywood Reporter*. May 28. Available at: http://www.hollywoodreporter.com/news/why-ant-man-director-edgar-707374.

McChesney, Robert W. 2000. *Rich Media, Poor Democracy: Communication Politics in Dubious Times*. New York: New Press.

McChesney, Robert. 2004. *The Problem of the Media: U.S. Communication Politics in the 21st Century*. New York: Monthly Review Press.

McClellan, Steve. 2003. "Will TiVo Kill Television, or Are Viewers Too Lazy to Zap?" *Broadcasting & Cable*. September 29: 19.

McClelland, Edward. 2013. *Nothin' But Blue Skies: The Heyday, Hard Times, and Hopes of America's Industrial Heartland*. London: Bloomsbury Press.

McCoy, Paul Brian. 2011. "Marvel in the '90s: The Death of the Incredible Hulk." *Screen Anarchy*. November 7. Available at: http://screenanarchy.com/2011/11/marvel-in-the-90s-the-death-of-the-incredible-hulk.html.

McGreal, Chris. 2009. "Rape Case to Force US Defence Firms into the Open: Senate Passes Measures Prompted by Women Prevented from Suing Over Alleged Rape by Halliburton/KBR colleagues." *The Guardian*. October 15. Available at: http://www.guardian.co.uk/world/2009/oct/15/defence-contractors-rape-claim-block.

McKinlay, John B., Felicia Trachtenberg, Lisa D. Marceau, Jeffrey N. Katz, and Michael A. Fischer. 2014. "Effects of Patient Medication Requests on Physician Prescribing Behavior: Results of a Factorial Experiment." *Medical Care* 52 no. 4: 294–299.

McLean, Bethany and Joe Nocera. 2011. *All the Devils Are Here: The Hidden History of the Financial Crisis*. New York: Portfolio.

"Medication Guide: PAXIL (PAX-il) (paroxetine hydrocholoride), Tablets and Oral Suppression." 2014. Food and Drug Administration; June. Available at: http://www.fda.gov/downloads/drugs/drugsafety/ucm088676.pdf.

Mills, Anthony R., John W. Morehead, and J. Ryan Parker. 2013. *Joss Whedon and Religion: Essays on an Angry Atheist's Explorations of the Sacred*. Jefferson, NC: McFarland.

Mitovich, Matt. 2009. "Joss Spills More *Dollhouse* Secrets! Plus, Is He Done with TV?" *TV Guide*. February 20. Available at: http://www.tvguide.com/news/whedon-dollhouse-secrets-1003097.

Moore, Robert. 2012. "How Buffy Changed Television." In: Money, Mary Alice, ed. *Joss Whedon, The Complete Companion: The TV Series, The Movies, The Comic Books, and More*. London: Titan Books; 140–153.

"More Joss Strike Talk." 2007. Whedonesque.com. Available at: http://whedonesque.com/comments/14650.

Morris, Wesley. 2016. "TV's Dwindling Middle Class." *New York Times Magazine*. April 27. Available at: http://www.nytimes.com/2016/05/01/magazine/tvs-dwindling-middle-class.html?_r=0.

MPAA Inc. 2007. "DVD and VCR." In: *Entertainment Industry Marketing Statistics 2007*. Motion Picture Association of America Inc.

Muntersbjorn, Madeleine. 2010. "Disgust, Difference, and Displacement in the Dollhouse." *Slayage: The Online Journal of Whedon Studies* 8.2–8.3, n. pag. Special Issue on *Dollhouse*. Ed. Cynthea Masson and Rhonda Wilcox. Available at: http://www.whedonstudies.tv/uploads/2/6/2/8/26288593/muntersbjorn_slayage_8.2-3.pdf

Murray, Simone. 2005. "Brand Loyalties: Rethinking Content Within a Global Media." *Media, Culture and Society* 27, no. 3: 415–435.

Nadkarni, Samira. 2014. "'In My House and Therefore in My Care': Transgressive Mothering, Abuse, and Embodiment." In: Ginn, Sherry, Alyson R. Buckman, and Heather M. Porter, eds. *Joss Whedon's Dollhouse: Confounding Purpose, Confusing Identity*. Lanham, MD: Rowman & Littlefield; 81–95.

Nadkarni, Samira. 2015. "This Is Where I Am.... Ain't a Place of Wishes": Kyriarchy and the Preservation of Power in *Better Days*. In: Goodrum, Michael, and Philip Smith, eds. Firefly *Revisited: Essays on Joss Whedon's Classic Series*. Lanham, MD: Rowman & Littlefield; 69–84.

Nadkarni, Samira. 2018. "In a World This Vulnerable": Tony Stark's In/visible Corporate Militarism and Drone Warfare." In: Nadkarni, Samira and Ensley F. Guffey, eds. *War and the Whedonverses*. Jefferson, NC: McFarland; Forthcoming.

Noone, Kristin. 2011. "Rossum's Universal Robots: Karel Capek Meets Joss Whedon in the Dollhouse." In: Espenson, Jane, ed. *Inside Joss' Dollhouse: From Alpha to Rossum*. Dallas: Ben Bella Books; 21–32.

O'Carroll, Eoin. 2007. "Columbia Seeks Eight in Chiquita Terrorist Scandal." *Christian Science Monitor*. March 22. Available at: http://www.csmonitor.com/2007/0322/p99s01-duts.html.

O'Connor, John J. 1988. "TV Weekend; Incredible Hulk Meets Mighty Thor." *New

York Times. May 20. Available at: http://www.nytimes.com/1988/05/20/arts/tv-weekend-incredible-hulk-meets-mighty-thor.html?scp=10&sq=bill%20bixby&st=cse.

Osterndorf, Chris. 2015. "10 Reasons Why Wal-Mart Is the Worst Company in America." May 25. *Salon.* Available at: http://www.salon.com/2015/05/25/10_reasons_wal_mart_is_the_worst_company_in_america_partner/.

Padden, Elizabeth. 2011. "The Word-pocalypse: Joss Whedon's Dollhouse and Dystopian Language." *Inquiries Journal* 3, no 1: 1–2. Available at: http://www.inquiriesjournal.com/articles/591/the-word-pocalypse-joss-whedons-dollhouse-and-dystopian-language.

Parker, J. Ryan. 2013. "As It Ever Was … So Shall It Never Be: Penal Substitutionary Atonement Theory and Violence in *The Cabin in the Woods.*" In: Mills, Anthony R., John W. Morehead, and J. Ryan Parker, eds. *Joss Whedon and Religions: Essays on an Angry Atheist's Exploration of the Sacred.* Jefferson, NC: McFarland; 196–212.

Pascale, Amy. 2014. "Joss and Roseanne: The Early Career of Joss Whedon." *Newsweek.* August 19. Available at: http://www.newsweek.com/joss-whedon-265403.

Pasley, Jeffrey L. 2003. "Old Familiar Vampires: Radicalism and Literalism in the Politics of the Buffyverse." In: South, James B., ed. *Buffy the Vampire Slayer and Philosophy: Fear and Trembling in Sunnydale.* Chicago: Open Court Press; 254–267.

Pateman, Matthew. 2014. *Firefly:* Of Formats, Franchises, and Fox." In: Wilcox, Rhonda, Tanya R. Cochran, Cynthea Masson, and David Lavery, eds. *Reading Joss Whedon.* Syracuse: Syracuse University Press; 153–168.

Pearl, J. Leavitt. 2013. "Actives, Affectivity, and the Soul: Interpreting *Dollhouse* Through the Phenomenology of Michel Henry." In: Mills, Anthony R., John W. Morehead, and J. Ryan Parker, eds. *Joss Whedon and Religions: Essays on an Angry Atheist's Exploration of the Sacred.* Jefferson, NC: McFarland; 123–139.

Pepe, Michael. 2016. "Eating, Sleeping and Watching Movies in the Shadow of What They Do: Representing Capitalism in Post–2008 Films." *Jump Cut: A Review of Contemporary Media* 57, Fall. Available at: https://www.ejumpcut.org/currentissue/-PepeFinancialCrisis/.

Peters, Mark. 2006. "Getting a Wiggins and Being a Bitca: How Two Items of Slayer Slang Survive on the Television Without Pity Message Boards." *Slayage: The Journal of Whedon Studies* 5.4 (May), n. pag. Available at: http://www.whedonstudies.tv/uploads/2/6/2/8/26288593/peters_slayage_5.4.pdf.

Peterson, Kelsey. 2014. "Competing for Lunch Money: The Food Industry's Presence in American Public Schools." *The Owl: Florida State University's Undergraduate Research Journal* 4, no. 1: 14–29.

Pfohl, Stephen. 2008. "Technologies of the Apocalypse: The *Left Behind* Novels and Flight From the Flesh." In: Kroker, Arthur, and Marilouise Kroker, eds. *Critical Digital Studies: A Reader.* Toronto: University of Toronto Press; 346–367.

Pollack, Andrew. 2015. "Drug Goes from $13.50 a Tablet to $750, Overnight." *New York Times.* September 20. Available at: https://www.nytimes.com/2015/09/21/business/a-huge-overnight-increase-in-a-drugs-price-raises-protests.html?_r=0.

Porter, Heather M., and Sherry Ginn. 2014. "'I Possess the Means to Satisfy My Vagaries': What Motivates the Dollhouse Clients?" In: Ginn, Sherry, Alyson B. Buckman, and Heather Porter, eds. *Joss Whedon's Dollhouse: Confounding Purpose, Confusing Identity.* Lanham, MD: Rowman & Littlefield; 97–110.

Preker, Simon. 2016. "*Star Trek's* Utopia: Dilemmas of the Early 21st and Late 24th Century." *PopMatters.* November 14. Available at: http://www.popmatters.com/feature/star-treks-utopia-defending-utopia-dilemmas-of-the-early-21st-an/.

Purtell, Kelly M., and Elizabeth T. Gershoff. 2014. "Fast Food Consumption and Academic Growth in Late Childhood." *Clinical Pediatrics* 54, no. 9: 871–77.

Q, Shatley. 2012. "Interview with Jane Espenson." In: Money, Mary Alice, ed. *Joss Whedon: The Complete Collection, The TV Series, the Movies, the Comic Books, and More.* London: Titan Books; 134–139.

Q, Shatley. 2015. "Deployment Patterns: How Joss Whedon Leverages Transmedia to Force a Rethink of Old Media." In: Frankel, Valerie, ed. *After the Avengers: From Joss Whedon's Hottest, Newest Franchises to the Future of the Whedonverse.* Chicago: PopMatters Media.

Rennebohm, Kate. 2011. "'The Mind Doesn't

Matter, It's the Body We Want': Identity and the Body in *Dollhouse*." In: Espenson, Jane, ed. *Inside Joss' Dollhouse: From Alpha to Rossum*. Dallas: Ben Bella Books; 5–19.

"Research and Development in the Pharmaceutical Industry." 2006. US Congressional Budget Office. October: 1–55. Available at: https://www.cbo.gov/sites/default/files/cbofiles/ftpdocs/76xx/doc7615/10-02-drugr-d.pdf.

Restaurant Opportunities Centers United. 2016. *The High Cost of Getting Paid: How Payroll Cards Cost Darden Employees*. New York: ROC United.

Rice, Lynnette. 2001. "Slayer It Ain't So." *Entertainment Weekly*. March 23. Available at: http://www.ew.com/ew/article/0,280397,00.html.

Risen J. 2008. "Despite Alert, Flawed Wiring Still Kills G.I.'s." *New York Times*. May 4. Available at: http://www.nytimes.com/2008/05/04/world/middleeast/04electrocute.html?hp.

Rivlin, Gary. 2010. *Broke USA: From Pawnshops to Poverty Inc.—How the Working Poor Became Big Business*. New York: HarperCollins.

Roberts, Dan. 2014. "US Jury Convicts Blackwater Guards in 2007 Killing of Iraqi Civilians: Security Guards for Private US Contractor Guilty of Manslaughter for Notorious 2007 Incident That Left 17 Dead in Baghdad." *The Guardian*. October 23. Available at: https://www.theguardian.com/us-news/2014/oct/22/us-jury-convicts-blackwater-security-guards-iraq.

Robinson, Tasha. 2001. "Interview: Joss Whedon." *AV Club*. September 5. Available at: http://www.avclub.com/article/joss-whedon-13730.

Rochlin, Margy. 1997. "Slay Belle." *TV Guide*. August 2: 17–21.

Rogers, Adam. 2012. "With the Avengers, Joss Whedon Masters the Marvel Universe." *Wired*. April 30. Available at: https://www.wired.com/2012/04/ff-whedon/.

Rollman, Hans. 2016. "Was Your iPhone Produced by Slaves? Has It Made You One, As Well?" *PopMatters*. November 30. Available at: http://www.popmatters.com/column/was-your-iphone-produced-by-slaves-has-it-made-you-one-as-well/.

Romano, Aja. 2015. "Marvel's Toy Line Just Erased Black Widow from Her Own Scene in 'Age of Ultron.'" *The Daily Dot*. May 11. Available at: http://www.dailydot.com/parsec/black-widow-toy-ultron-motorcycle-replaced-captain-america/.

Ross, Tracy. 2016. "Roseanne Barr on Trump 'Playing the Heel for Hilary,' Pot and Being a Farmer." *The Hollywood Reporter*. June 7. Available at: http://www.hollywoodreporter.com/news/roseanne-barr-us-would-be-900413.

Ryan, Maureen. 2009. "Sex, Secrets, and 'Dollhouse': Joss Whedon Talks About the End of His Fox Show." *Chicago Tribune*. December 3. Available at: http://featuresblogs.chicagotribune.com/entertainment_tv/2009/12/dollhouse-fox-joss-whedon.html.

Saulsberry, Rejena. 2016. "An Inevitable Tragedy: The Troubled Life of Charles Gunn as an Allegory for General Strain Theory." In: Iatropoulos, Mary Ellen, and Lowery A. Woodall III, eds. *Joss Whedon and Race: Critical Essays*. Jefferson, NC: McFarland; 150–165.

Schlosser, Eric. 2000. *Fast Food Nation: The Dark Side of the All-American Meal*. Boston: Mariner Books.

Schuppe, Jon. 2016. "Senate Panel Opens Probe of EpiPen Price Hike." NBC News. September 7. Available at: http://www.nbcnews.com/news/us-news/senate-panel-opens-probe-epipen-price-hike-n644241.

Selznick, Barbara. 2009. "Branding the Future: Syfy in the Post-Network Era." *Science Fiction Film and Television* 2.2: 177–203.

Shales, Tom. 2009. "'Dollhouse': On Fox, a Strange New Toy." *Washington Post*. February 13. Available at: http://www.washingtonpost.com/wp-dyn/content/article/2009/02/12/AR2009021203994.html.

Shipler, David K. 2005. *The Working Poor: Invisible in America*. New York: Random House; 2005.

Signh, Siddharth. 2015. "How Long Will Fossil Fuels Last? It Is Argued That Oil Will Run Out in 53 Years, Natural Gas in 54, and Coal in 110. How Likely Is It?" *Business Standard*. September 23. Available at: http://www.business-standard.com/article/punditry/how-long-will-fossil-fuels-last-115092201397_1.html.

Soffen, Kim and Denise Lu. 2017. "What Trump Cut in His Budget." *Washington Post*. March 16. Available at: https://www.washingtonpost.com/graphics/politics/trump-presidential-budget-2018-proposal/?utm_term=.cb12f4ddaf59.

South, James. 2001. "'All Torment, Trouble,

Wonder, and Amazement Inhabits Here': The Viccissitudes of Technology in *Buffy the Vampire Slayer.*" *Journal of American and Comparative Cultures* 24, no. 1–2, Spring/Summer: 93–102.

South, James B., and William Irwin. 2003. *Buffy the Vampire Slayer and Philosophy: Fear and Trembling in Sunnydale.* Chicago: Open Court Press.

Souza, Christopher. 2011. "Boyd Langton and the Fantasy of Trust." In: Espenson, Jane, ed. *Inside Joss' Dollhouse: From Alpha to Rossum.* Dallas: Ben Bella Books; 205–217.

Stafford, Nikki. 2004. *Once Bitten: The Unofficial Guide to the World of* Angel. Toronto: ECW Press.

Stanley, Alessandra. 2009. "Directions: Brainwash, Rinse, Repeat." *New York Times.* February 12. Available at: http://www.nytimes.com/2009/02/13/arts/television/13doll.html?_r=1&.

Stelter, Brian. 2009. "Fox TV's Gamble: Fewer Ads in a Break, but Costing More." *New York Times.* February 12. Available at: http://www.nytimes.com/2009/02/13/business/media/13adco.html.

Sternako, Jim. 2013. "Jim Sternako on 'Agents of SHIELD': Smoother, But Too Unfocused to Be Satisfying." *Hollywood Reporter.* October 2. Available at: http://www.hollywoodreporter.com/heat-vision/jim-sternako-agents-shield-smoother-641579.

Stevenson, Richard W. 1990. McDonnell Douglas Plans Wide Layoffs and Cost Cuts." *New York Times.* June 21. Available at: http://www.nytimes.com/1990/06/21/business/mcdonnell-douglas-plans-wide-layoffs-and-cost-cuts.html.

Stockman, Farah. 2008. "Top Iraq Contractor Skirts US Taxes Offshore: Shell Companies in Cayman Islands Allow KBR to Avoid Medicare, Social Security Deductions." *Boston Globe.* March 6. Available at: http://www.boston.com/news/world/articles/2008/03/06/top_iraq_contractor_skirts_us_taxes_offshore/.

Stout, Martha. 2006. *The Sociopath Next Door.* Danvers, MA: Harmony Books.

Subers, Ray. 2012. "Friday Report: 'Hunger Games' Beats 'Stooges,' 'Cabin.'" Box Office Mojo. April 14. Available at: http://www.boxofficemojo.com/news/?id=3419&p=s.htm.

Sutherland, Sharon and Sarah Swan. 2005. "The Rule of Prophecy: Source of Law in the City of *Angel.* In: Abbott, Stacey, ed. *Reading* Angel: *The TV Spin-off with a Soul.* London: I.B. Tauris; 132–145.

Symonds, Gwyn. 2007. "The Superhero vs. the Troubled Teen: Parenting Connor, and the Fragility of 'Family' in *Angel.* In: Haslem, Wendy, Angela Ndalianis, C. J. Mackie, eds. *Super/heroes: From Hercules to Superman.* Washington, D.C.: New Academia Publishing; 155–165.

Thompson, Derek. 2016. "Who Are Trump's Supporters, Really? Four Theories to Explain the Front-Runner's Rise to the Top of the Polls." *The Atlantic.* March 16. Available at: https://www.theatlantic.com/politics/archive/2016/03/who-are-donald-trumps-supporters-really/471714/.

Tobias, Scott. 2009. "Interview: Eliza Dushku." *AV Club.* February 27. Available at: http://www.avclub.com/article/eliza-dushku/24418/.

Todreas, Timothy. 1999. *Value Creation and Branding in Television's Digital Age.* Westport, CT: Quorum Books.

Tresca, Don. 2012. "'Fantasy Is Their Business, But It Is Not Their Purpose': The Metaphor of *Dollhouse.* In: Money, Mary Alice, ed. *Joss Whedon: The Complete Collection, The TV Series, the Movies, the Comic Books, and More.* London: Titan Books; 411–425.

"The Tuskegee Timeline." 2016. Centers for Disease Control and Prevention. December 8. Available at: https://www.cdc.gov/tuskegee/timeline.htm Web.

"2008–2009 Primetime Wrap." 2009. ABC Medianet. May 25. Available at: http://abcmedianet.com/web/dnr/dispDNR.aspx?id=051909-05.

Upstone, Sara. 2005. "'LA's Got It All': Hybridity and Otherness in *Angel*'s Postmodern City." In: Abbott, Stacey, ed. *Reading Angel: The TV Spin-Off With a Soul.* London: I.B. Tauris; 101–113.

Valentine, Evan. 2014. "Marvel's Agents of S.H.I.E.L.D.: The H.I.G.H.S. and L.O.W.S. of the ABC Series' Freshman Season." Collider. May 31. Available at: http://collider.com/marvels-agents-of-shield-season-1-review.

Vary, Adam B. 2008. "'Dr. Horrible': An Oral History." *Entertainment Weekly.* July 25. Available at: http://www.ew.com/article/2008/07/25/dr-horrible-oral-history/.

Verrier, Richard. 2007. "Writers Guild Votes Overwhelmingly to Authorize a Strike." *Los Angeles Times.* October 20.

Vogel, Chris. 2009. "KBR in Iraq—Come for

the Nation-Building, Stay for the Brothels." *Houston Press.* July 14. Available at: http://blogs.houstonpress.com/hairballs/2009/07/kbr_sexual_abuse_and_brothels.php.

Waxman, Sharon. 2007. "Marvel Wants to Flex Its Own Heroic Muscles as a Moviemaker." *New York Times.* June 18. Available at: http://www.nytimes.com/2007/06/18/business/media/18marvel.html?_r=0.

Weissman, Robert. 2017. "Trump's Corporate Cabinet." *Huffington Post.* January 10. Available at: http://www.huffingtonpost.com/robert-weissman/trumps-corporate-cabinet_b_14087282.html.

Wemple, Erik. 2016. "Study: Clinton-Trump Coverage Was a Feast of False Equivalency." *Washington Post.* December 7. Available at: https://www.washingtonpost.com/blogs/erik-wemple/wp/2016/12/07/study-clinton-trump-coverage-was-a-feast-of-false-equivalency/?utm_term=.4cdffdcfb98f.

Wharton, Ken. 2007. "The Alliance's War on Science." In: Espenson, Jane, and Leah Wilson, eds. *Serenity Found: More Unauthorized Essays on Joss Whedon's Firefly Universe.* Dallas: Ben Bella Books; 141–150.

Whedon, Joss. 2002. "Joss at the Bronze. March 24, 2000." Official Quotes on the Willow/Tara Storyline. Buffyguide.com. June 30. Available at: http://www.buffyguide.com/extras/josswt.shtml.

Whedon, Joss, and Matthew B. 2005. *Those Left Behind: Issues 1–3.* Dark Horse Comics; July 20–September 9.

Whedon, Joss. 2007. "From the Front Lines." Whedonesque.com. November 6. Available at: http://whedonesque.com/comments/14639#195462.

Whedon, Joss and Drew Goddard. 2012. The Cabin in the Woods: *The Official Visual Companion.* London: Titan Books.

Wilcox, Rhonda. 2005. *Why Buffy Matters: The Art of* Buffy the Vampire Slayer. London: I.B. Tauris.

Wilcox, Rhonda. 2010. "Echoes of Complicity: Reflexivity and Identity in Joss Whedon's Dollhouse. *Slayage: The Journal of Whedon Studies* 8.2 and 8.3 (Summer/Fall), n. pag. Available at: http://www.whedonstudies.tv/uploads/2/6/2/8/26288593/wilcox_slayage_8.2-3.pdf.

Williams, Amy. 2014. "'All the Cash, All the Fame, and Social Change!' Teaching Dr. Horrible's Sing-along Blog as a Social Message Film." *Slayage: The Journal of Whedon Studies* 11.2/12.1 (38–39), Special Issue: *"Joss in June: Selected Essays."* Eds. K. Dale Coontz and Ensley Guffey. Available at: http://www.whedonstudies.tv/uploads/2/6/2/8/26288593/williams.pdf.

Williams, Raymond. 2003. *Television: Technology and Cultural Form.* London: Routledge.

Willingham, Emily. 2016. "Why Did Mylan Hike Epi-Pen Prices 400%? Because They Could." *Forbes.* August 21. Available at: https://www.forbes.com/sites/emilywillingham/2016/08/21/why-did-mylan-hike-epipen-prices-400-because-they-could/#74ecbf7c280c.

Wright, Julia M. 2008. "Latchkey Hero: Masculinity, Class and the Gothic in Eric Kripke's Supernatural." *Genders Online Journal* 47, n. pag. Available at: https://www.atria.nl/ezines/IAV_606661/IAV_606661_2011_53/genders/g47_wright.html.

Yeoman B. 2003. "Soldiers of Good Fortune." *Mother Jones.* May/June. Available at: http://motherjones.com/politics/2003/05/soldiers-good-fortune.

Zeller, Tom Jr. 2011. "Experts Had Long Criticized Potential Weakness in Design of Stricken Reactor." *New York Times.* March 15: A14. Available at: http://www.nytimes.com/2011/03/16/world/asia/16contain.html?_r=1&scp=2&sq=general%20electric&st=cse.

Zhang, Angela. 2012. "'Buffy' and 'Dollhouse': Visions of Female Empowerment and Disempowerment." In: Money, Mary Alice, ed. *Joss Whedon: The Complete Collection, The TV Series, the Movies, the Comic Books, and More.* London: Titan Books; 401–406.

Zuckerman, Esther. 2017. "Buffy's James Marsters on the Hardest Day of Professional Life." *AV Club.* March 9. Available at: http://www.avclub.com/article/buffys-james-marsters-hardest-day-his-professional-251544.

# Television and Filmography

"Afterboom." *Gilmore Girls: The Complete Fourth Season*. Writ. Sheila R. Lawrence. Dir. Michael Zinberg. Warner Home Video, 2006. DVD.

"Aftershocks." *Agents of S.H.I.E.L.D.: The Complete Second Season*. Writs. Jed Whedon and Maurissa Tancharoen. Dir. Billy Gierhart. ABC Studios, 2015. DVD.

"The Age of Steel." *Doctor Who: The Complete Second Series*. Writ. Tom MacRae. Dir. Graeme Harper. BBC Home Entertainment, 2007. DVD.

"Amends." *Buffy the Vampire Slayer: The Complete Third Season*. Writ. and dir. Joss Whedon. Twentieth Century Fox Home Entertainment, 2002. DVD.

"Anne." *Buffy the Vampire Slayer: The Complete Third Season*. Writ. and dir. Joss Whedon. Twentieth Century Fox Home Entertainment, 2003. DVD.

"Another Mouth to Shut Up." *Roseanne: Season 8*. Writs. Eric Gilliland, Janet Leahy, and Richard Kaplan. Dir. Mark K. Samuels. Anchor Bay Entertainment, 2007. DVD.

"Apocalypse Now-ish." *Angel: Season Four*. Writ. Steven S. DeKnight. Dir. Vern Gillum. Twentieth Century Fox Home Entertainment, 2004. DVD.

"April Fool's Day." *Roseanne: Season 2*. Writ. Stephen Paymer. Dir. John Pasquin. Anchor Bay Entertainment, 2005. DVD.

"Ariel." *Firefly: The Complete Series*. Writ. Jose Molina. Dir. Allan Kroeker. Twentieth Century Fox Home Entertainment, 2003. DVD.

"Ascension." *Agents of S.H.I.E.L.D.: The Complete Third Season*. Writ. Jed Whedon. Dir. Kevin Tancharoen. ABC Studios, 2017. Blu-Ray.

"The Attic." *Dollhouse: The Complete Second Season*. Writs. Maurissa Tancharoen and Jed Whedon. Dir. John Cassaday. Twentieth Century Fox Home Entertainment, 2010. DVD.

*The Avengers*. Writ. and dir. Joss Whedon. Walt Disney Video, 2012. DVD.

*The Avengers: Age of Ultron*. Writ. and dir. Joss Whedon. Walt Disney Studios Home Entertainment, 2015. DVD.

"Baby." *Supernatural: The Complete Eleventh Season*. Writ. Robbie Thompson. Dir. Thomas J. Wright. Warner Home Video, 2016. DVD.

"Bargaining (Part 1)." *Buffy the Vampire Slayer: The Complete Sixth Season*. Writ. Marti Noxon. Dir. David Grossman. Twentieth Century Fox Home Entertainment, 2004. DVD.

"Bargaining (Part 2)." *Buffy the Vampire Slayer: The Complete Sixth Season*. Writ. David Fury. Dir. David Grossman. Twentieth Century Fox Home Entertainment, 2004. DVD.

"Becoming (Part 1)." *Buffy the Vampire Slayer: The Complete Second Season*. Writ. and dir. Joss Whedon. Twentieth Century Fox Home Entertainment, 2002. DVD.

"Becoming (Part 2)." *Buffy the Vampire Slayer: The Complete Second Season*. Writ. and dir. Joss Whedon. Twentieth Century Fox Home Entertainment, 2002. DVD.

"Beginning of the End." *Agents of S.H.I.E.L.D.: The Complete First Season*. Writs. Jed Whedon and Maurissa Tancharoen. Dir. David Straiton. ABC Studios, 2014. DVD.

"Belle Chose." *Dollhouse: The Complete Second Season*. Writ. Tim Minear. Dir. David Solomon. Twentieth Century Fox Home Entertainment, 2010. DVD.

"Belonging." *Angel: Season Two.* Writ. Shawn Ryan. Dir. Turi Meyer. Twentieth Century Fox Home Entertainment, 2003. DVD.

"Belonging." *Dollhouse: The Complete Second Season.* Writs. Maurissa Tanchareon and Jed Whedon. Dir. Jonathan Frakes. Dollhouse. Twentieth Century Fox Home Entertainment, 2010. DVD.

"Beneath You." *Buffy the Vampire Slayer: The Complete Seventh Season.* Writ. Douglas Petrie. Dir. Nick Marck. Twentieth Century Fox Home Entertainment, 2004. DVD.

"Billy." *Angel: Season Three.* Writs. Tim Minear and Jeffrey Bell. Dir. David Grossman. Twentieth Century Fox Home Entertainment, 2004. DVD.

"Blind Date." *Angel: Season 1.* Writ. Jeannine Renshaw. Dir. Thomas J. Wright. Twentieth Century Fox Home Entertainment, 2003. DVD.

"Blood Money." *Angel: Season Two.* Writs. Shawn Ryan and Mere Smith. Dir. R. D. Price. Twentieth Century Fox Home Entertainment, 2003. DVD.

"The Body." *Buffy the Vampire Slayer: The Complete Fifth Season.* Writ. and dir. Joss Whedon. Twentieth Century Fox Home Entertainment, 2003. DVD.

"BOOM." *Agents of S.H.I.E.L.D.: Season 4.* Writs. Nora Zuckerman and Lilla Zuckerman. Dir. Billy Gierhart. ABC Studios, 2017. TV.

"Briar Rose." *Dollhouse: Season 1.* Writ. Jane Espenson. Dir. Dwight Little. Twentieth Century Fox Home Entertainment, 2009. DVD.

"Buckwhacked." *Firefly: The Complete Series.* Writ. and dir. Tim Minear. Twentieth Century Fox Home Entertainment, 2003. DVD.

"Buffy vs. Dracula." *Buffy the Vampire Slayer: The Complete Fifth Season.* Writ. Marti Noxon. Dir. David Solomon. Twentieth Century Fox Home Entertainment, 2003. DVD.

*The Cabin in the Woods.* Writ. Joss Whedon. Dir. Drew Goddard. Lionsgate, 2012. DVD.

"Calvary." *Angel: Season Four.* Writs. Jeffrey Bell, Steven S. DeKnight, and Mere Smith. Dir. Bill L. Norton. Twentieth Century Fox Home Entertainment, 2004. DVD.

*Captain America: Civil War.* Writs. Christopher Markus and Stephen McFeely. Dirs. Anthony and Joe Russo. Walt Disney Studios Home Entertainment, 2016. DVD.

*Captain America: The Winter Soldier.* Writs. Christopher Markus and Stephen McFeely. Dirs. Anthony and Joe Russo. Walt Disney Studios Home Entertainment, 2014. DVD.

"Changing Channels." *Supernatural: The Complete Fifth Season.* Writ. Jeremy Carver. Dir. Charles Beeson. Warner Home Video, 2010. DVD.

"Checkpoint." *Buffy the Vampire Slayer: The Complete Fifth Season.* Writs. Douglas Petrie and Jane Espenson. Dir. Nick Marck. Twentieth Century Fox Home Entertainment, 2003. DVD.

"Chicken Hearts." *Roseanne: Season 2.* Writ. Joss Whedon. Dir. John Pasquin. Anchor Bay Entertainment, 2005. DVD.

"Chosen." *Buffy the Vampire Slayer: The Complete Seventh Season.* Writ. and dir. Joss Whedon. Twentieth Century Fox Home Entertainment, 2004. DVD.

"City of." *Angel: Season 1.* Writs. Joss Whedon and David Greenwalt. Dir. Joss Whedon. Twentieth Century Fox Home Entertainment, 2003. DVD.

"Conviction." *Angel: Season Five.* Writ. and dir. Joss Whedon. Twentieth Century Fox Home Entertainment, 2005. DVD.

"Crime and Punishment." *Roseanne: Season 5.* Writ. Bruce Rasmussen. Dir. Andrew D. Weyman. Anchor Bay Entertainment, 2006. DVD.

"The Dark Ages." *Roseanne: Season 5.* Writs. Eric Gilliland and Mike Gandolfi. Dir. Andrew D. Weyman. Anchor Bay Entertainment, 2006. DVD.

"Dead End." *Angel: Season Two.* Writ. David Greenwalt. Dir. James A. Contner. Twentieth Century Fox Home Entertainment, 2002. DVD.

"Deep Down." *Angel: Season Four.* Writ. Steven S. DeKnight. Dir. Terrence O'Hara. Twentieth Century Fox Home Entertainment, 2004. DVD.

"Defining Moments: A Retrospective with Joss Whedon" [DVD Extra]. *Dollhouse: The Complete Section Season.* DVD Extra. Twentieth Century Fox Home Entertainment, 2010. DVD.

*Democracy on Deadline: The Global Struggle for an Independent Press.* 2006. Dir. Cal Skaggs. First Run Features. DVD.

*Demolition Man.* Writs. Daniel Waters, Robert Reneau, and Peter M. Lenkov. Dir. Marco Brambilla. Warner Home Video, 1997. DVD.

"Destiny." *Angel: Season Five.* Writs. David Fury and Steven S. DeKnight. Dir. Skip Schoolnik. Twentieth Century Fox Home Entertainment, 2005. DVD.

"Dirty Girls." *Buffy the Vampire Slayer: The Complete Seventh Season.* Writ. Drew Goddard. Dir. Michael Gershman. Twentieth Century Fox Home Entertainment, 2004. DVD.

"The Dirty Half Dozen." *Agents of S.H.I.E.L.D.: The Complete Second Season.* Writs. Brent Fletcher and Drew Z. Greenberg. Dir. Kevin Tancharoen. ABC Studios, 2015. DVD.

"Disharmony." *Angel: Season Two.* Writ. David Fury. Dir. Fred Keller. Twentieth Century Fox Home Entertainment, 2003. DVD.

"Disney World War II." *Roseanne: Season 8.* Writ. Allan Stephen Blasband, dir. Gail Mancuso. Anchor Bay Entertainment, 2007. DVD.

*Dr. Horrible's Sing-Along Blog.* Writs. Joss Whedon, Zack Whedon, Maurissa Tancharoen, Jed Whedon. Dir. Joss Whedon. Mutant Enemy Inc, 2008. DVD.

"Double or Nothing." *Angel: Season Three.* Writ. David H. Goodman. Dir. David Grossman. Twentieth Century Fox Home Entertainment, 2003. DVD.

"Doublemeat Palace." *Buffy the Vampire Slayer: The Complete Sixth Season.* Writ. Jane Espenson. Dir. Nick Marck. Twentieth Century Fox Home Entertainment, 2004. DVD.

"Echo." *Dollhouse: Season 1.* Writ. and dir. Joss Whedon. Twentieth Century Fox Home Entertainment, 2009. DVD.

"Echoes." *Dollhouse: Season 1.* Writs. Elizabeth Craft and Sarah Fain. Dir. James Contner. Twentieth Century Fox Home Entertainment, 2009. DVD.

"Elizabeth Warren: January 24, 2012." *The Daily Show with Jon Stewart: Season 17.* Writs. Rory Albanese and Kevin Bleyer. Dir. Chuck O'Neil. Comedy Partners, 2012. TV.

"Empty Places." *Buffy the Vampire Slayer: The Complete Seventh Season.* Writ. Drew Z. Greenberg. Dir. James A. Contner. Twentieth Century Fox Home Entertainment, 2004. DVD.

"End of Days." *Buffy the Vampire Slayer: The Complete Seventh Season.* Writs. Douglas Petrie and Jane Espenson. Dir. Marita Grabiak. Twentieth Century Fox Home Entertainment, 2004. DVD.

"Epiphany." *Angel: Season Two.* Writ. Tim Minear. Dir. Thomas J. Wright. Twentieth Century Fox Home Entertainment, 2003. DVD.

"Epitaph One." *Dollhouse: Season 1.* Writs. Maurissa Tancharoen and Jed Whedon. Dir. David Solomon. Twentieth Century Fox Home Entertainment, 2009. DVD.

"Epitaph Two: Return." *Dollhouse: The Complete Second Season.* Writs. Maurissa Tancharoen, Jed Whedon, and Andrew Chambliss. Dir. David Solomon. Twentieth Century Fox Home Entertainment, 2010. DVD.

"Expecting." *Angel: Season 1.* Writ. Howard Gordon. Dir. David Semel. Twentieth Century Fox Home Entertainment, 2003. DVD.

"Failed Experiments." *Agents of S.H.I.E.L.D.: The Complete Third Season.* Writ. Brent Fletcher. Dir. Wendey Stanzler. ABC Studios, 2017. Blu-Ray.

"Family." *Buffy the Vampire Slayer: The Complete Fifth Season.* Writ. and dir. Joss Whedon. Twentieth Century Fox Home Entertainment, 2003. DVD.

"Fan Fiction." *Supernatural: The Complete Tenth Season.* Writ. Robbie Thompson. Dir. Phil Sgriccia. Warner Home Video, 2015. DVD.

"Finding Echo." *Dollhouse: Season 1.* DVD Extra. Twentieth Century Fox Home Entertainment, 2009. DVD.

"First Impressions." *Angel: Season Two.* Writ. Shawn Ryan. Dir. James A. Contner. Twentieth Century Fox Home Entertainment, 2002. DVD.

"Fizz Ed." *Daria: The Complete Animated Series.* Writ. Glenn Eichler. Dir. Karen Disher. MTV/Paramount, 2010.

"Flooded." *Buffy the Vampire Slayer: The Complete Sixth Season.* Writs. Jane Espenson and Douglas Petrie. Dir. Douglas Petrie. Twentieth Century Fox Home Entertainment, 2004. DVD.

"Forever." *Buffy the Vampire Slayer: The Complete Fifth Season.* Writ. and dir. Marti Noxon. Twentieth Century Fox Home Entertainment, 2003. DVD.

"Fredless." *Angel: Season Three.* Writ. Mere Smith. Dir. Marita Grabiak. Twentieth Century Fox Home Entertainment, 2003. DVD.

"The French Mistake." *Supernatural: The Complete Sixth Season.* Writ. Ben Edlund. Dir. Charles Beeson. Warner Home Video, 2011. DVD.

"Get It Done." *Buffy the Vampire Slayer: The Complete Seventh Season.* Writ. and dir. Douglas Petrie. Twentieth Century Fox Home Entertainment, 2004. DVD.

"Getting Closer." *Dollhouse: The Complete Second Season.* Writ. and dir. Tim Minear.

Twentieth Century Fox Home Entertainment, 2010. DVD.

"Ghost." *Dollhouse: Season 1.* Writ. and dir. Joss Whedon. Twentieth Century Fox Home Entertainment, 2009. DVD.

"The Gift." *Buffy the Vampire Slayer: The Complete Fifth Season.* Writ. and dir. Joss Whedon. Twentieth Century Fox Home Entertainment, 2003. DVD.

"Gingerbread." *Buffy the Vampire Slayer: The Complete Third Season.* Writs. Thania St. John and Jane Espenson. Dir. James Whitmore, Jr. Twentieth Century Fox Home Entertainment, 2002. DVD.

"The Girl in Question." *Angel: Season Five.* Writs. Steven S. DeKnight and Drew Goddard. Dir. David Greenwalt. Twentieth Century Fox Home Entertainment, 2005. DVD.

"Graduation Day (Part 1)." *Buffy the Vampire Slayer: The Complete Third Season.* Writ. and dir. Joss Whedon. Twentieth Century Fox Home Entertainment, 2002. DVD.

"Graduation Day (Part 2)." *Buffy the Vampire Slayer: The Complete Third Season.* Writ. and dir. Joss Whedon. Twentieth Century Fox Home Entertainment, 2002. DVD.

"Gray Hour." *Dollhouse: Season 1.* Writs. Sarah Fain and Elizabeth Craft. Dir. Rod Hardy. Twentieth Century Fox Home Entertainment, 2009. DVD.

"Grumpy Old Liv." *iZombie: The Complete Second Season.* Writ. Rob Thomas. Dir. Michael Fields. Warner Home Video, 2016. DVD.

"Guilt by Disassociation." *Roseanne: Season 2.* Writ. Tom Arnold. Dir. John Pasquin. Anchor Bay Entertainment, 2005. DVD.

"Guise Will Be Guise." *Angel: Season Two.* Writ. Jane Espenson. Dir. Krishna Rao. Twentieth Century Fox Home Entertainment, 2003. DVD.

"Habeas Corpses." *Angel: Season Four.* Writ. Jeffrey Bell. Dir. Skip Schoolnik. Twentieth Century Fox Home Entertainment, 2004. DVD.

"The Happiest Show on Earth." *Boy Meets World: The Complete Third Season.* Writs. Mark Blutman and Howard Busgang. Dir. Jeff McCracken. Buena Vista Home Entertainment, 2005. DVD.

"Happy Anniversary." *Angel: Season Two.* Writs. David Greenwalt and Joss Whedon. Dir. Bill L. Norton. Twentieth Century Fox Home Entertainment, 2003. DVD.

"Haunted." *Dollhouse: Season 1.* Writs. Jane Espenson, Maurissa Tancharoen, and Jed Whedon. Dir. Elodie Keene. Twentieth Century Fox Home Entertainment, 2009. DVD.

"Heart of Gold." *Firefly: The Complete Series.* Writ. Brett Matthews. Dir. Thomas J. Wright. Twentieth Century Fox Home Entertainment, 2003. DVD.

"Hellbound." *Angel: Season Five.* Writ. and dir. Steven S. DeKnight. Twentieth Century Fox Home Entertainment, 2005. DVD.

"Hell's Bells." *Buffy the Vampire Slayer: The Complete Sixth Season.* Writ. Rebecca Rand Kirschner. Dir. David Solomon. Twentieth Century Fox Home Entertainment, 2004. DVD.

"A Hen in the Wolf House." *Agents of S.H.I.E.L.D.: The Complete Second Season.* Writ. Brent Fletcher. Dir. Holly Dale. ABC Studios, 2015. DVD.

"Hero." *Angel: Season 1.* Writs. Howard Gordon and Tim Minear. Dir. Tucker Gates. Twentieth Century Fox Home Entertainment, 2003. DVD.

"A Hole in the World." *Angel: Season Five.* Writ. and dir. Joss Whedon. Twentieth Century Fox Home Entertainment, 2005. DVD.

"The Hollow Men." *Dollhouse: The Complete Second Season.* Writs. Michele Fazekas, Tara Butters, and Tracy Bellomo. Dir. Terrence O'Hara. Twentieth Century Fox Home Entertainment, 2010. DVD.

"Hollywood Babylon." *Supernatural: The Complete Second Season.* Writ. Ben Edlund. Dir. Phil Sgriccia. Warner Home Video, 2007. DVD.

"Home." *Angel: Season Four.* Writ. and dir. Tim Minear. Twentieth Century Fox Home Entertainment, 2004. DVD.

"Home-Ec." *Roseanne: Season 3.* Writ. Mark Lloyd Rappaport. Dir. John Whitesell. Anchor Bay Entertainment, 2006. DVD.

"The House Always Wins." *Angel: Season Four.* Writ. David Fury. Dir. Marita Grabiak. Twentieth Century Fox Home Entertainment, 2004. DVD.

"How to Win Friends and Influence Monsters." Writ. Ben Edlund. Dir. Guy Bee. *Supernatural: The Complete Seventh Season.* Warner Home Video, 2012. DVD.

"Hush." *Buffy the Vampire Slayer: The Complete Fourth Season.* Writ. and dir. Joss Whedon. Twentieth Century Fox Home Entertainment, 2003. DVD.

"The I in Team." *Buffy the Vampire Slayer: The*

*Complete Fourth Season.* Writ. David Fury. Dir. James A. Contner. Twentieth Century Fox Home Entertainment, 2003. DVD.

"I Will Remember You." *Angel: Season 1.* Writs. David Greenwalt and Jeannine Renshaw. Dir. David Grossman. Twentieth Century Fox Home Entertainment, 2003. DVD.

*Idiocracy.* Writs. Etan Cohen and Mike Judge. Dir. Mike Judge. Twentieth Century Fox Home Entertainment, 2011. DVD.

"In the Dark." *Angel: Season 1.* Writ. Douglas Petrie. Dir. Bruce Seth Green. Twentieth Century Fox Home Entertainment, 2003. DVD.

"Innocence." *Buffy the Vampire Slayer: The Complete Second Season.* Writ. and dir. Joss Whedon. Twentieth Century Fox Home Entertainment, 2002. DVD.

"Inside Out." *Angel: Season Four.* Writ. and dir. Steven S. DeKnight. Twentieth Century Fox Home Entertainment, 2004. DVD.

"Instinct." *Dollhouse: The Complete Second Season.* Writs. Michele Fazekas and Tara Butters. Dir. Marita Grabiak. Twentieth Century Fox Home Entertainment, 2010. DVD.

"Into That Good Night." *Roseanne: Season 9.* Writs. Jessica Pentland, Roseanne Barr, and Allan Stephen Blasband. Dir. Gary Halvorson. Anchor Bay Entertainment, 2007. DVD.

"Into the Woods." *Buffy the Vampire Slayer: The Complete Fifth Season.* Writ. and dir. Marti Noxon. Twentieth Century Fox Home Entertainment, 2003. DVD.

*Iron Man.* Writs. Mark Fergus, Hawk Ostby, Art Marcum, and Matt Holloway. Dir. Jon Favreau. Paramount, 2008. DVD.

*Iron Man 2.* Writ. Justin Theroux. Dir. Jon Favreau. Paramount, 2010. DVD.

"Jaynestown." *Firefly: The Complete Series.* Writ. Ben Edlund. Dir. Marita Grabiak. Twentieth Century Fox Home Entertainment, 2003. DVD.

"Judgment." *Angel: Season Two.* Writs. Joss Whedon and David Greenwalt. Dir. Michael Lange. Twentieth Century Fox Home Entertainment, 2003. DVD.

"Just Rewards." *Angel: Season Five.* Writs. David Fury and Ben Edlund. Dir. James A. Contner. Twentieth Century Fox Home Entertainment, 2005. DVD.

"Keg! Max!" *Gilmore Girls: The Complete Third Season.* Writ. Daniel Palladino. Dir. Chris Long. Warner Home Video, 2005. DVD.

"Lanford's Elite." *Roseanne: Season 9.* Writs. Allan Stephen Blasband, Richard Whitley, and Bob Rubin. Dir. Gary Halvorson. Anchor Bay Entertainment, 2007. DVD.

"Laws of Inferno Dynamics." *Agents of S.H.I.E.L.D.: Season 4.* Writ. Paul Zbyszewski. Dir. Kevin Tancharoen. ABC Studios, 2016. TV.

"Leave It to Beaver." *Veronica Mars: The Complete First Season.* Writs. Rob Thomas and Diane Ruggiero. Dir. Michael Fields. Warner Home Video, 2005. DVD.

"The Left Hand." *Dollhouse: The Complete Second Season.* Writ. Tracy Bellomo. Dir. Wendy Stanzler. Twentieth Century Fox Home Entertainment, 2010. DVD.

"Let's Call It Quits." *Roseanne: Season 1.* Writs. Daiv McFadzean and Lauren Eve Anderson. Dir. John Sgueglia. Anchor Bay Entertainment, 2005. DVD.

"Life of the Party." *Angel: Season Five.* Writ. Ben Edlund. Dir. Bill L. Norton. Twentieth Century Fox Home Entertainment, 2005. DVD.

"Life Serial." *Buffy the Vampire Slayer: The Complete Sixth Season.* Writs. David Fury and Jane Espenson. Dir. Nick Marck. Twentieth Century Fox Home Entertainment, 2004. DVD.

"Lineage." *Angel: Season Five.* Writ. Drew Goddard. Dir. Jefferson Kibbee. Twentieth Century Fox Home Entertainment, 2005. DVD.

"Little Sister." *Roseanne: Season 2.* Writ. Joss Whedon. Dir. John Pasquin. Anchor Bay Entertainment, 2005. DVD.

"Lonely Hearts." *Angel: Season 1.* Writ. David Fury. Dir. James A. Contner. Twentieth Century Fox Home Entertainment, 2003. DVD.

"Love in the Time of Hydra." *Agents of S.H.I.E.L.D.: The Complete Second Season.* Writ. Brent Fletcher. Dir. Jesse Bochco. ABC Studios, 2015. DVD.

"A Love Supreme." *Dollhouse: The Complete Second Season.* Writ. Jenny DeArmitt. Dir. David Straiton. Twentieth Century Fox Home Entertainment, 2010. DVD.

"Lullaby." *Angel: Season Three.* Writ. and dir. Tim Minear. Twentieth Century Fox Home Entertainment, 2003. DVD.

"The Magic Bullet." *Angel: Season Four.* Writ. and dir. Jeffrey Bell. Twentieth Century Fox Home Entertainment, 2004. DVD.

"The Magical Place." *Agents of S.H.I.E.L.D.: The Complete First Season.* Writs. Paul

Zbyszewski and Brent Fletcher. Dir. Kevin Hooks. ABC Studios, 2014. DVD.

"Mall Story." *Roseanne: Season 1*. Writ. Laurie Gelman. Dir. John Sgueglia. Anchor Bay Entertainment, 2005. DVD.

"Man on the Street." *Dollhouse: Season 1*. Writ. Joss Whedon. Dir. David Straiton. Twentieth Century Fox Home Entertainment, 2009. DVD.

"Many Heads, One Tale." *Agents of S.H.I.E.L.D.: The Complete Third Season*. Writs. Jed Whedon and DJ Doyle. Dir. Garry A Brown. ABC Studios, 2017. Blu-Ray.

"Meet Jane Doe." *Dollhouse: The Complete Second Season*. Writs. Maurissa Tancharoen, Jed Whedon, and Andrew Chambliss. Dir. Wendy Stanzler. Twentieth Century Fox Home Entertainment, 2010. DVD.

"Melinda." *Agents of S.H.I.E.L.D.: The Complete Second Season*. Writ. DJ Doyle. Dir. Garry A Brown. ABC Studios, 2015. DVD.

"Meta Fiction." Writ. Robbie Thompson, dir. Thomas J. Wright. *Supernatural: The Complete Ninth Season*. Warner Home Video, 2014. DVD.

"The Monster at the End of This Book." *Supernatural: The Complete Fourth Season*. Writ. Julie Siege. Dir. Mike Rohl. Warner Home Video, 2009. DVD.

*Much Ado About Nothing* [commentary track]. Writ. William Shakespeare. Dir. Joss Whedon. Lionsgate, 2012. DVD.

"Needs." *Dollhouse: Season 1*. Writ. Tracy Bellomo. Dir. Felix Alcala. Twentieth Century Fox Home Entertainment, 2009. DVD.

"A New World." *Angel: Season Three*. Writ. Jeffrey Bell. Dir. Tim Minear. Twentieth Century Fox Home Entertainment, 2003. DVD.

"No Place Like Home." *Buffy the Vampire Slayer: The Complete Fifth Season*. Writ. Douglas Petrie. Dir. David Solomon. Twentieth Century Fox Home Entertainment, 2003. DVD.

"Not Fade Away." *Angel: Season Five*. Writs. Jeffery Bell and Joss Whedon. Dir. Jeffrey Bell. Twentieth Century Fox Home Entertainment, 2005. DVD.

"Objects in Space." *Firefly: The Complete Series*. Writ. and dir. Joss Whedon. Twentieth Century Fox Home Entertainment, 2003. DVD.

"Omega." *Dollhouse: Season 1*. Writ. and dir. Tim Minear. Twentieth Century Fox Home Entertainment, 2009. DVD.

"Once More With Feeling." *Buffy the Vampire Slayer: The Complete Sixth Season*. Writ.

and dir. Joss Whedon. Twentieth Century Fox Home Entertainment, 2004. DVD.

"The Only Light in the Darkness." *Agents of S.H.I.E.L.D.: The Complete First Season*. Writ. Monica Owusu-Breen. Dir. Vincent Misiano. ABC Studios, 2014. DVD.

"Origin." *Angel: Season Five*. Writ. Drew Goddard. Dir. Terrence O'Hara. Twentieth Century Fox Home Entertainment, 2005. DVD.

"Our Mrs. Reynolds." *Firefly: The Complete Series*. Writ. Joss Whedon. Dir. Vondie Curtis Hall. Twentieth Century Fox Home Entertainment, 2003. DVD.

"Out of Gas." *Firefly: The Complete Series*. Writ. Tim Minear. Dir. David Solomon. Twentieth Century Fox Home Entertainment, 2003. DVD.

"Pangs." *Buffy the Vampire Slayer: The Complete Fourth Season*. Writ. Jane Espenson. Dir. Michael Lange. Twentieth Century Fox Home Entertainment, 2003. DVD.

"Paradise Lost." *Agents of S.H.I.E.L.D.: The Complete Third Season*. Writs. George Kitson and Sharla Oliver. Dir. Wendey Stanzler. ABC Studios, 2017. Blu-Ray.

"Parting Gifts." *Angel: Season 1*. Writs. David Fury and Jeannine Renshaw. Dir. James A. Contner. Twentieth Century Fox Home Entertainment, 2003. DVD.

"Passion." *Buffy the Vampire Slayer: The Complete Second Season*. Writ. Ty King. Dir. Michael Gershman. Twentieth Century Fox Home Entertainment, 2002. DVD.

"Peace Out." *Angel: Season Four*. Writ. David Fury. Dir. Jefferson Kibbee. Twentieth Century Fox Home Entertainment, 2004. DVD.

"Pilot." *Agents of S.H.I.E.L.D.: The Complete First Season*. Writs. Joss Whedon, Jed Whedon, and Maurissa Tancharoen. Dir. Joss Whedon. ABC Studios, 2014. DVD.

"Presenting Lorelai Gilmore." *Gilmore Girls: The Complete Second Season*. Writ. Sheila R. Lawrence. Dir. Chris Long. Warner Home Video, 2004. DVD.

"Primeval." *Buffy the Vampire Slayer: The Complete Fourth Season*. Writ. David Fury. Dir. James A. Contner. Twentieth Century Fox Home Entertainment, 2003. DVD.

"The Prodigal." *Angel: Season 1*. Writ. Tim Minear. Dir. Bruce Seth Green. Twentieth Century Fox Home Entertainment, 2003. DVD.

"The Prom." *Buffy the Vampire Slayer: The Complete Third Season*. Writ. Marti Noxon. Dir. David Soloman. Twentieth Century Fox Home Entertainment, 2003. DVD.

"Prophecy Girl." *Buffy the Vampire Slayer: The Complete First Season*. Writ. and dir. Joss Whedon. Twentieth Century Fox Home Entertainment, 2002. DVD.

"The Public Eye." *Dollhouse: The Complete Second Season*. Writ. Andrew Chambliss. Dir. David Solomon. Twentieth Century Fox Home Entertainment, 2010. DVD.

"Rat Saw God." *Veronica Mars: The Complete Second Season*. Writs. John Enbom and Phil Klemmer. Dir. Kevin Bray. Warner Home Video, 2006. DVD.

"The Real Ghostbusters." *Supernatural: The Complete Fifth Season*. Writ. Eric Kripke. Dir. James L. Conway. Warner Home Video, 2010. DVD.

"Release." *Angel: Season Four*. Writs. Steven S. DeKnight, Elizabeth Craft, and Sarah Fain. Dir. James A. Contner. Twentieth Century Fox Home Entertainment, 2004. DVD.

"The Replacement." *Buffy the Vampire Slayer: The Complete Fifth Season*. Writ. Jane Espenson. Dir. James A. Contner. Twentieth Century Fox Home Entertainment, 2003. DVD.

"Restless." *Buffy the Vampire Slayer: The Complete Fourth Season*. Writ. and dir. Joss Whedon. Twentieth Century Fox Home Entertainment, 2003. DVD.

"Reunion." *Angel: Season Two*. Writs. Tim Minear and Shawn Ryan. Dir. James A. Contner. Twentieth Century Fox Home Entertainment, 2003. DVD.

"Revelations." *Buffy the Vampire Slayer: The Complete Third Season*. Writ. Douglas Petrie. Dir. James A Contner. Twentieth Century Fox Home Entertainment, 2002. DVD.

"Rise of the Cybermen." *Doctor Who: The Complete Second Series*. Writ. Tom MacRae. Dir. Graeme Harper. BBC Home Entertainment, 2007. DVD.

Rossum Corporation Channel. "November Ad." Available at: www.youtube.com/user/RossumCorporation.

"Sacrifice." *Angel: Season Four*. Writ. Ben Edlund. Dir. David Straiton. Twentieth Century Fox Home Entertainment, 2004. DVD.

"Safe." *Firefly: The Complete Series*. Writ. Drew Z. Greenburg. Dir. Michael Grossman. Twentieth Century Fox Home Entertainment, 2003. DVD.

"Salvation Army." *iZombie: The Complete Second Season*. Writs. Rob Thomas, Diane Ruggierio-Wright, and Kit Boss. Dir. Michael Fields. Warner Home Video, 2016. DVD.

"Sanctuary." *Angel: Season 1*. Writs. Tim Minear and Joss Whedon. Dir. Michael Lange. Twentieth Century Fox Home Entertainment, 2003. DVD.

"Save the Day." Available at: http://savetheday.vote/.

"Scars." *Agents of S.H.I.E.L.D.: The Complete Second Season*. Writs. Rafe Judkins and Lauren LeFranc. Dir. Bobby Roth. ABC Studios, 2015. DVD.

"School Hard." *Buffy the Vampire Slayer: The Complete Second Season*. Writ. David Greenwalt and Joss Whedon. Dir. John T. Kretchmer. Twentieth Century Fox Home Entertainment, 2002. DVD.

"School Reunion." *Doctor Who: The Complete Second Series*. Writ. Toby Whithouse. Dir. James Hawes. BBC Home Entertainment, 2009. DVD.

"Seeing Red." *Buffy the Vampire Slayer: The Complete Sixth Season*. Writ. Steven S. DeKnight. Dir. Michael Gershman. Twentieth Century Fox Home Entertainment, 2004. DVD.

"Self Control." *Agents of S.H.I.E.L.D.: Season 4*. Writ. and dir. Jed Whedon. ABC Studios, 2017. TV.

"Serenity" [commentary track]. *Firefly: The Complete Series*. Writ and dir. Joss Whedon. Twentieth Century Fox Home Entertainment, 2003. DVD.

"Serenity." *Firefly: The Complete Series*. Writ and dir. Joss Whedon. Twentieth Century Fox Home Entertainment, 2003. DVD.

*Serenity*. Writ. and dir. Joss Whedon. Universal Pictures, 2005. DVD.

"Shells." *Angel: Season Five*. Writ. and dir. Steven S. DeKnight. Twentieth Century Fox Home Entertainment, 2005. DVD.

"Shindig." *Firefly: The Complete Series*. Writ. Jane Espenson. Dir. Vern Gillum. Twentieth Century Fox Home Entertainment, 2003. DVD.

"Shiny Happy People." *Angel: Season Four*. Writs. Elizabeth Craft and Sarah Fain. Dir. Marita Grabiak. Twentieth Century Fox Home Entertainment, 2004. DVD.

"Sleep Tight." *Angel: Season Three*. Writ. David Greenwalt. Dir. Terrence O'Hara. Twentieth Century Fox Home Entertainment, 2003. DVD.

"Slouching Toward Bethlehem." *Angel: Season Four*. Writ. Jeffrey Bell. Dir. Skip Schoolnik. Twentieth Century Fox Home Entertainment, 2004. DVD.

"Smile Time." *Angel: Season Five*. Writs. Joss

Whedon and Ben Edlund. Dir. Ben Edlund. Twentieth Century Fox Home Entertainment, 2005. DVD.

"S.O.S. Part 2." *Agents of S.H.I.E.L.D.: The Complete Second Season.* Writs. Jed Whedon and Maurissa Tancharoen. Dir. Billy Gierhart. ABC Studios, 2015. DVD.

"Soul Purpose." *Angel: Season Five.* Writ. Brent Fletcher. Dir. David Boreanaz. Twentieth Century Fox Home Entertainment, 2005. DVD.

"Springtime for David." *Roseanne: Season 8.* Writs. Garland Testa and David Forbes. Dir. Mark K. Samuels. Anchor Bay Entertainment, 2007. DVD.

"A Spy in the House of Love." *Dollhouse: Season 1.* Writ. Andrew Chambliss. Dir. David Solomon. Twentieth Century Fox Home Entertainment, 2009. DVD.

"Stage Fright." *Dollhouse: Season 1.* Writs. Maurissa Tancharoen and Jed Whedon. Dir. David Solomon. Twentieth Century Fox Home Entertainment, 2009. DVD.

"Stop-Loss." *Dollhouse: The Complete Second Season.* Writ. Andrew Chambliss. Dir. Felix Alcala. Twentieth Century Fox Home Entertainment, 2010. DVD.

"Supersymmetry." *Angel: Season Four.* Writs. Elizabeth Craft and Sarah Fain. Dir. Bill L. Norton. Twentieth Century Fox Home Entertainment, 2004. DVD.

"Survival of the Fittest." *Supernatural: The Complete Seventh Season.* Writ. Sera Gamble. Dir. Robert Singer. Warner Home Video, 2011. DVD.

"Survival of the Fittest" [commentary]. *Supernatural: The Complete Seventh Season.* Writ. Sera Gamble. Dir. Robert Singer. Warner Home Video, 2011. DVD.

"Tabula Rasa." *Buffy the Vampire Slayer: The Complete Sixth Season.* Writ. Rebecca Rand Kirschner. Dir. David Grossman. Twentieth Century Fox Home Entertainment, 2004. DVD.

"T.A.H.I.T.I." *Agents of S.H.I.E.L.D.: The Complete First Season.* Writ. Jeffrey Bell. Dir. Bobby Roth. ABC Studios, 2014. DVD.

"The Target." *Dollhouse: Season 1.* Writ. and dir. Steven S. DeKnight. Twentieth Century Fox Home Entertainment, 2009. DVD.

"Ted." *Buffy the Vampire Slayer: The Complete Second Season.* Writ. David Greenwalt and Joss Whedon. Dir. Bruce Seth Green. Twentieth Century Fox Home Entertainment, 2002. DVD.

"Terms of Estrangement: Part 1." *Roseanne:*

*Season 5.* Writs. Sy Dukane and Denise Moss. Dir. Andrew D. Weyman. Anchor Bay Entertainment, 2006. DVD.

"Terms of Estrangement: Part 2." *Roseanne: Season 5.* Writ. Rob Ulin. Dir. Andrew D. Weyman. Anchor Bay Entertainment, 2006. DVD.

"That Vision Thing." *Angel: Season Three.* Writ. Jeffrey Bell. Dir. Bill L. Norton. Twentieth Century Fox Home Entertainment, 2003. DVD.

"There Will Be Blood." *Supernatural: The Complete Seventh Season.* Writ. Andrew Dabb and Daniel Loflin, dir. Guy Bee. Warner Home Video, 2012. DVD.

"The Thin Dead Line." *Angel: Season Two.* Writs. Jim Kouf and Shawn Ryan. Dir. Scott McGinnis. Twentieth Century Fox Home Entertainment, 2003. DVD.

"The Things We Bury." *Agents of S.H.I.E.L.D.: The Complete Second Season.* Writ. DJ Doyle. Dir. Milan Cheylov. ABC Studios, 2015. DVD.

"Through the Looking Glass." *Angel: Season Two.* Writ. and dir. Tim Minear. Twentieth Century Fox Home Entertainment, 2003. DVD.

"Time Bomb." *Angel: Season Five.* Writ. Ben Edlund. Dir. Vern Gillum. Twentieth Century Fox Home Entertainment, 2005. DVD.

"To Shanshu in LA." *Angel: Season 1.* Writ. and dir. David Greenwalt. Twentieth Century Fox Home Entertainment, 2003. DVD.

"Tooth or Consequences." *Roseanne: Season 2.* Writ. Leslie Reider. Dir. Gail Mancuso. Anchor Bay Entertainment, 2006. DVD.

"Tough Love." *Buffy the Vampire Slayer: The Complete Fifth Season.* Writ. Rebecca Rand Kirschner. Dir. David Grossman. Twentieth Century Fox Home Entertainment, 2003. DVD.

"T.R.A.C.K.S." *Agents of S.H.I.E.L.D.: The Complete First Season.* Writs. Lauren LeFranc and Rafe Judkins. Dir. Paul Edwards. ABC Studios, 2014. DVD.

"The Train Job." *Firefly: The Complete Series.* Writs. Joss Whedon and Tim Minear. Dir. Joss Whedon. Twentieth Century Fox Home Entertainment, 2003. DVD.

"Trash." *Firefly: The Complete Series.* Writs. Ben Edlund and Jose Molina. Dir. Vern Gillum. Twentieth Century Fox Home Entertainment, 2003. DVD.

"True Believer." *Dollhouse: Season 1.* Writ. Tim Minear. Dir. Allan Kroeker. Twentieth Century Fox Home Entertainment, 2009. DVD.

"Turn, Turn, Turn." *Agents of S.H.I.E.L.D.: The Complete First Season.* Writs. Jed Whedon and Maurissa Tencharoen. Dir. Vincent Misiano. ABC Studios, 2014. DVD.

"Underneath." *Angel: Season Five.* Writs. Elizabeth Craft and Sarah Fain. Dir. Skip Schoolnik. Twentieth Century Fox Home Entertainment, 2005. DVD.

"Unleashed." *Angel: Season Five.* Writs. Sarah Fain and Elizabeth Craft. Dir. Marita Grabiak. Twentieth Century Fox Home Entertainment, 2005. DVD.

"Uprising." *Agents of S.H.I.E.L.D.: Season 4.* Writ. Craig Titley. Dir. Magnus Martens. ABC Studios, 2016. TV.

"Villains." *Buffy the Vampire Slayer: The Complete Sixth Season.* Writ. Marti Noxon. Dir. David Solomon. Twentieth Century Fox Home Entertainment, 2004. DVD.

"Vows." *Dollhouse: The Complete Second Season.* Writ. and dir. Joss Whedon. Twentieth Century Fox Home Entertainment, 2010. DVD.

"Waiting in the Wings." *Angel: Season Three.* Writ. and dir. Joss Whedon. Twentieth Century Fox Home Entertainment, 2004. DVD.

"A Wanted (In)Human." *Agents of S.H.I.E.L.D.: The Complete Third Season.* Writ. Monica Owusu-Breen. Dir. Garry A. Brown. ABC Studios, 2017. Blu-Ray.

"War Stories." *Firefly: The Complete Series.* Writ. Cheryl Cain. Dir. James Contner. Twentieth Century Fox Home Entertainment, 2003. DVD.

"War Zone." *Angel: Season 1.* Writ. Gary Campbell. Dir. David Straiton. Twentieth Century Fox Home Entertainment, 2003. DVD.

"We're Going to Disney World." *Roseanne: Season 8.* Writ. Matt Berry. Dir. Gail Mancuso. Anchor Bay Entertainment, 2007. DVD.

"We're Going to Disney World (Part 1)." *Family Matters: The Complete Sixth Season.* Writ. Jim Geoghan. Dir. Richard Correll. Warner Archive Collection, 2016. DVD.

"We're Going to Disney World (Part 1)." *Step by Step: Season Five.* Writs. Brian Bird and John Wierick. Dir. Richard Correll.

"We're Going to Disney World (Part 2)." *Family Matters: The Complete Sixth Season.* Writ. Fred Fox, Jr. Dir. Richard Correll. Warner Archive Collection, 2016. DVD.

"We're Going to Disney World (Part 2)." *Step by Step: Season Five.* Writ. Casey Maxwell Clair. Dir. Richard Correll.

"What If...." *Agents of S.H.I.E.L.D.: Season 4.* Writ. and dir. Jed Whedon. ABC Studios, 2017. TV.

"What's My Line, Part Two." *Buffy the Vampire Slayer: The Complete Second Season.* Writ. Marti Noxon. Dir. David Semel. Twentieth Century Fox Home Entertainment, 2002. DVD.

"The White Sheep of the Family." *Roseanne: Season 8.* Writ. David Raether. Dir. Gail Mancuso. Anchor Bay Entertainment, 2007. DVD.

"Who Are You." *Buffy the Vampire Slayer: The Complete Fourth Season.* Writ. and dir. Joss Whedon. Twentieth Century Fox Home Entertainment, 2003. DVD.

"Why We Fight." *Angel: Season Five.* Writs. Drew Goddard and Steven S. DeKnight. Dir. Terrence O'Hara. Twentieth Century Fox Home Entertainment, 2005. DVD.

"The Wish." *Buffy the Vampire Slayer: The Complete Third Season.* Writ. Marti Noxon. Dir. David Greenwalt. Twentieth Century Fox Home Entertainment, 2003. DVD.

"Yes Men." *Agents of S.H.I.E.L.D.: The Complete First Season.* Writ. Shalisha Francis. Dir. John Terlesky. ABC Studios, 2014. DVD.

"The Yoko Factor." *Buffy the Vampire Slayer: The Complete Fourth Season.* Writ. Douglas Petrie. Dir. David Grossman. Twentieth Century Fox Home Entertainment, 2003. DVD.

# Index

Abbott, Stacey  2, 11, 15, 28–29, 33, 62, 75, 76–77, 78, 99, 101
ABC Network  9, 18, 29n183, 49, 63–64, 76
Acker, Amy  24, 123, 176
Actives  33, 41, 43, 73, 88, 91–93, 95–97, 101, 103–107, 111, 115–117, 119–121, 123–125, 128, 135–139, 140, 143–149, 151–152, 154–155, 158, 164, 166, 167–173
Adalain, Josef  85
Adam (character, Buffy)  119, 124, 125, 163–164
Advanced Threat Containment Unit  *see* ATCU
Afghanistan  80, 143–144, 170
*Agent Carter* (television series)  61
*Agents of S.H.I.E.L.D.* (television series)  11, 18, 19, 61–62, 66, 67–68, 71, 72–79, 87, 106, 110, 121–122, 122n184, 125, 153, 157, 160–161, 164, 176, 180; "Aftershocks" 161; "Ascension" 78, 162; "Beginning of the End" 73; "BOOM" 75; "The Dirty Half Dozen" 78; "Failed Experiments" 162; "Laws of Inferno Dynamics" 74; "Love in the Time of Hydra" 111; "The Magical Place" 75, 111; "Melinda" 122; "The Only Light in the Darkness" 75; "Paradise Lost" 74; "Pilot" 75, 77, Xn183; "Scars" 78, 161–162; "Self-Control" 122; "S.O.S. Part 2" 161; "T.A.H.I.T.I." 111; "The Things We Bury" 161 "T.R.A.C.K.S." 73; "Turn, Turn, Turn" 72, 161; "Uprising" 72; "A Wanted (In)Human" 161; "What If…" 72, 122; A Wolf in the Hen House" 72
Aida (character)  74–75, 121–122
The Alliance  14, 38–43, 73, 104, 108, 110, 178, 180
Alliance government  *see* The Alliance
Alliance of Motion Picture and Television Producers  *see* AMPTP
Alpha (character)  123, 140, 167, 168, 170n185
Amazon.com  5, 9, 63, 97, 120
Ambrose, Clive (character)  134, 145, 145n185, 147, 158, 171, 175
AMPTP  81, 82

Anderson, Devon  118
Anderson, Tami  116
Anderson-Connor, Crystal (character)  49
Angel (character)  10, 18, 22–23, 24–37, 27n183, 67, 104, 106, 107, 110, 124, 150, 151, 159–160, 162–163, 179, n183
*Angel* (television series)  1–2, 11, 14, 16, 17, 18, 18n183, 22–44, 27n183, 60, 61, 67, 73, 75, 85n184, 93, 99, 101, 103, 104, 105, 106, 107, 109, 110, 111, 124, 143, 150, 151, 157, 158, 159n185, 159–160, 161, 162–163, 166, 169, 173, 176, 178, 179, 180; "Apocalypse Nowish" 35; "Belonging" 25, 159; "Billy" 34; Blind Date" 29, 30; "Blood Money" 30; "Calvary" 36; "City of" 28, 159n185; "Conviction" 27, 32, 43, 151; "Dead End" 36; "Deep Down" 36, 37; "Destiny" 28; "Disharmony" 29; "Double or Nothing" 26; "Epiphany" 23, 179; "Expecting" 160; "First Impressions" 25, 26; "Fredless" 159; "The Girl in Question" 160; "Guise Will Be Guise" 29; "Habeas Corpses" 36; "Happy Anniversary" 110; "Hellbound" 151, 163; "Hero" 24; "A Hole in the World" 33, 143, 163; "Home" 31, 36, 160, 162; "The House Always Wins" 29; "I Will Remember You" 10; "In the Dark" 26, 32; "Inside Out" 31, 36, 162; "Judgment" 24, 27; "Just Rewards" 32; "Life of the Party" 37; "Lineage" 25, 159; "Lonely Hearts" 25; "Lullaby" 25, 160; "The Magic Bullet" 27, 162; "A New World" 25; "Not Fade Away" 23, 36, 163, 179; "Origin" 33; "Parting Gifts" 24, 25, 160; "Peace Out" 162; "The Prodigal" 159; "Release" 27n183; "Reunion" 22; "Sacrifice" 140, 162; "Sanctuary" 10, 25; "Shells" 33, 143, 159; "Shiny Happy People" 162; "Sleep Tight" 29, 33, 35, 162; "Slouching Toward Bethlehem" 35, 73; "Smile Time" 33, 37, 67, 107; "Soul Purpose" 37; "Supersymmetry" 25, 37; "That Vision Thing" 34, 73; "The Thin Dead Line" 33; "Through the Looking Glass" 159; "Time Bomb" 35, 151, 163; "To Shan-

shu in LA" 23, 30; "Underneath" 33; "Unleashed" 33; "Waiting in the Wings" 162; "War Zone" 24, 25, 26, 32, 159
Angel Investigations 25, 26, 32, 33, 34, 35–36, 37, 73, 109
Anne (character) 30, 179
Anti-depressants (Paxil/Prozac) 42, 113, 143
Armstrong, Karen 147–148
Arvidsson, Adam 71
Astra-Zeneca 133, 145n185
ATCU 72
The Attic 120, 125, 137, 143, 155n185, 171, 175
The Avengers (film) 11, 18, 19, 38, 61, 62, 67–68, 68–71, 72, 75, 76–77, 78, 88, 164, 165, 176, 177
The Avengers: Age of Ultron (film) 11, 18, 19, 61, 62, 68–71, 74, 76–77, 78, 164, 165

Bakan, Joel 17, 30, 33, 93, 113, 115, 116, 124, 133–134, 136, 141, 157, 174
Ballard, Paul (character) 94, 103, 117–118, 120, 121, 123, 130, 142, 155, 167, 168, 170–171
Barr, Roseanne 14, 45, 48, 49, 59
Barton, Cliff/Hawkeye (character) 165
Basinger, Jeanine 12
Battis, Jes 109
Bedell, Sally 9, 64
Beeler, Stan 27, 37
Bellwether Pictures (studio) 18n183, 177
Bennett, Eve 2, 3, 92, 97, 107, 114–115, 117, 141, 163
Benson, Amber 70, 105
Berman, Gail 10, 12
Bianculli, David 98
Billson, Anne 12
Billy/Dr. Horrible (character) 80, 83–87, 105, 106, 110, 180
Black Widow (character) 62, 70–71, 165
Blackwater Security Consulting 140, 142, 176
Blowback 42–43, 112
Blue Sun Corporation 1, 14–15, 18, 22–24, 37–43, 46, 106, 108, 110, 151, 166, 177, 179, 180
Book, Derriel (character) 23, 38, 104
Boreanaz, David 10, 22
Boston Diva Productions 82, 87, 100
Boulware, Taylor 97, 122, 127–128
Brand ambassador 69, 77–78, 87, 180
Branding/branded/brand equity 23, 39, 41, 45, 61–68, 66n184, 70–72, 75–79, 80, 86–87, 100, 102–103, 146, 153–154, 179
Brian (character/"Chicken Hearts") 50–52, 133
Brink, Topher (character) 20, 93, 107, 108, 116, 117, 119–125, 126, 135, 136, 137, 138, 141, 143, 146–147, 167, 168–175
British Petroleum (BP) 93, 133–134, 171
Brown and Root *see* Halliburton

Buchanan, Ginger 85
Buckman, Alyson 40–41, 84–85, 97n184
*Buffy the Vampire Slayer* (film) 10, 61–62
*Buffy the Vampire Slayer/Buffy* (television series) 1, 3, 10, 12–14, 17, 18n183, 19, 22, 24–25, 28–29, 31, 33, 43, 45–60, 59n184, 61–62, 70, 72–73, 75–76, 85, 99, 103–107, 109, 110, 119, 124, 125, 143, 150–151, 153, 157–159, 163–164, 169, 173, 177, 179; "Amends" 105, 159; "Anne" 56, 57; "Bargaining, Parts 1 and 2" 55; "Becoming, Part 1" 54, 151; Becoming, Part 2" 24, 54, 55; "Beneath You" 33; "The Body" 55, 164; "Buffy Vs. Dracula" 164; "Checkpoint" 12; "Chosen" 13, 43; "Dirty Girls" 12; "Doublemeat Palace" 19, 56, 57–59, 150, 151; "Empty Places" 150; "End of Days" 12; "Family" 158–159; "Flooded" 13, 55; "Forever" 159; "Get It Done" 12, 43; "The Gift" 54–55, 173; Gingerbread" 151, 159; Graduation Day, Part 1" 54–55, 151; "Graduation Day, Part 2" 55; "Hell's Bells" 159; "Hush" 158; "The I in Team" 72; "Innocence" 24; "Into the Woods" 55; "Life Serial" 56; "No Place Like Home" 55, 159; "Once More with Feeling" 107; "Pangs" 10; "Passion" 105; "Primeval" 54, 110; "The Prom" 159; "Prophesy Girl" 54, 56; "The Replacement" 159; "Restless" 55, 159, 164; "Revelations" 13; "Seeing Red" 105; "School Hard" 150; "Tabula Rasa" 164; "Ted" 150; "Tough Love" 55; "Villains" 164; "What's My Line, Part 2" 13; "Who Are You" 10; "The Wish" 56; "The Yoko Factor" 54, 164
Burgess, Rance (character) 44
Burkle, Fred (character) 24, 25, 31, 32, 33, 34, 35–37, 44, 67, 143, 159, 160, 162, 163
Bush, George W. *see* Bush administration
Bush administration 59, 129, 132, 139, 151, 153
Bussolini, Jeffrey 42–43, 112, 119, 163–164

*The Cabin in the Woods* (film) 16, 17, 19, 79, 80–81, 87–91, 92, 93–94, 106, 112, 176, 178, 180
Cal (character) 161–162
Caldwell, John 66
Calvert, Bronwen 77–78
Cameron, Dr. Ewan 131–132, 148, 149–150
Canavan, Gerry 42
Captain America (character) 69, 165
*Captain America: Civil War* (film) 78–79
*Captain America: The Winter Soldier* (film) 68, 72, 78
Captain Hammer (character) 83–84, 85, 86–87, 105
Capitalism, socially responsible 30, 68, 133
Carbado, Devon W 33
Cargill, Matt (character) 140, 173
CBS Network 9, 64

# Index

Ceccoli, Anthony (character)  43, 88, 122, 138, 143–144, 147, 151, 168–170, 170n185, 172–173
Central Intelligence Agency  see CIA
Chandler, Holly  12
Chase, Cordelia  24, 25, 28, 29, 31, 34, 36, 159–160
Chilcoat, Laura  42
Chow, Lesley  111, 120
Christianity (legalistic/evangelical/reconstructionalist)  44, 128, 146–148, 154
Churchill, Ward (activist)  42
CIA  148, 149
Citizens United  2, 6, 8, 20, 108, 128, 154
Clifton, Jacob  178–179
Clinton, Bill  see Clinton administration
Clinton, Hillary  5–6, 128
Clinton administration  59, 139
Cobb, Jayne (character)  15, 38, 40–41
Connor (character)  25, 27n183, 31, 37, 160
Connor, Becky (character)  50, 51
Connor, Dan (character)  49, 51–52, 53, 55
Connor, Darlene (character)  48, 53
Connor, Roseanne (character)  18, 47–53, 54, 55, 57, 188
Cook, Tim (Apple CEO)  133
Coontz, Stephanie  48
Cooper, L. Andrew  89–90
Corporate media/media conglomerates  6, 19, 31, 48, 63, 66, 66n184, 79, 80–81, 82–83, 86, 92, 94, 98, 115, 138, 141, 149, 175, 177, 178, 181
Corporatism (definition)  5
Corporatocracy (definition)  5, 129
Cost-benefit analysis  32
Costly, Madeleine  103, 119, 121, 136, 142–144, 155, 167–168, 170, 171
Coulson, Phil (character)  75, 78, 122, 161, 165, 170
Created/chosen family  20, 109, 157–175
Croft, Carl William (character)  see Alpha
Curt (character)  90–91
Curtin, Michael  9, 65
CW (television channel)  63, 98

Dana (character)  90–91
Darden Corporation  50
Daredevil (television series)  61, 63, 64, 79
Daria (television series)  39n183
Dark Horse Comics  18n183
The Darkhold (fictional mystical text)  74, 121
Darla (character)  23, 27, 30–31
Day, Deanna  89
DC Comics/DC Vertigo (television)  63
Deepwater Horizon spill  see British Petroleum
Democracy on Deadline (film)  5
Demolition Man (film)  14, 41, 45
Demon Research Initiative  see The Initiative

Denisof, Alexis  24, 104, 176
DeWitt, Adelle (character)  96, 102, 106–107, 112, 116–121, 125, 129–131, 135, 137, 142, 145–147, 149, 152–154, 158, 167–173, 174
Diamond, Reed  130, 176
Digital Video Recorder (DVR)  99–100
Direct-to-consumer (DTC) advertising  114
Disney (studio)  11, 29n183, 46, 49, 62, 67, 105
Dobson, Lawrence (character)  23, 38
Dr. Horrible's Sing-along Blog (web series)  10–11, 18, 19, 34, 77, 79, 80–87, 94, 99, 104, 106, 110
Doctor Who (television series)  6–7, 142n184; "Age of Steel" 7; "Rise of the Cybermen" 7; "School Reunion" 142n184
Dollhouse (television series)  2, 10–11, 14–18, 22, 33, 37, 40, 41, 43, 44, 50, 60, 61, 73, 75, 77, 79, 80, 81, 86, 87–94, 96–175, 176, 177, 179, 180, 185; "The Attic" 125, 141, 154, 169, 155n185; "Belle Chose" 77, 92, 102, 124, 130, 140, 173–174; "Belonging" 24, 102, 103n184, 111, 116, 125, 137, 167, 169–170; "Briar Rose" 102, 111, 116, 118, 120, 135, 167; "Echo" 88, 100, 102, 121, 158; "Echoes" 17, 92, 102, 130, 134–135, 140, 157–158, 166, 167, 170, 173; "Epitaph One" 17, 92, 101, 102, 119–120, 125, 139, 144, 146–147, 169; "Epitaph 2: Return" 96, 119, 139, 144–147, 155–156, 166, 168–169, 170n185; "Getting Closer" 8, 96, 103, 136, 166, 169, 170; "Ghost" 92, 102, 119, 124, 140, 148, 155, 158, 167, 170n185, 173; "Grey Hour" 102, 106, 124, 167; "Haunted" 103, 118, 125, 155; "The Hollow Men" 17, 96, 121, 147, 148, 155, 170–171, 173–175; "Instinct" 16, 102, 120, 137, 170; "The Left Hand" 138, 148, 152; "A Love Supreme" 102, 104, 140–141, 148, 166, 167, 173, 175; "Man on the Street" 101, 102, 103–104, 111–112, 117–118, 132, 140, 148–149, 155, 167, 169, 173; "Meet Jane Doe" 155, 167, 172, 173; "Needs" 124, 136, 170; "Omega" 80, 92, 111, 123–124, 142, 147, 148, 168; "The Public Eye" 116, 127, 138, 142, 144, 152, 173; "A Spy in the House of Love" 102, 103, 130, 135, 154; "Stage Fright" 102, 105, 120, 167, 169; "Stop-Loss" 80, 106, 111, 120, 142–143, 155, 170, 172; "The Target" 92, 102, 148, 166; "True Believer" 103, 124, 130, 135; "Vows" 102, 107, 112, 123, 127, 135
Dolls  see Actives
Dominic, Laurence  130–131, 154
Donaton, Scott  99
Doublemeat Palace (franchise)  see "Doublemeat Palace" (episode)
Downey, Robert, Jr.  18, 43, 177
Doyle, Francis Allan (character)  24, 25
Drutman, Lee  129
Du Clark, Vaughn (character)  7
Durand, Michael  12–13

# Index

Dushku, Eliza 82, 87, 88, 96, 99–100, 101, 102, 153, 162
DVD format 2, 64, 66, 77, 81, 83, 86, 88, 98–99, 100, 115, 143

Echo (character) *see* Farrell, Caroline (character)
ECT 131, 149
Ehrenreich, Barbara 60
Electroconvulsive therapy *see* ECT
Eliot, T.S. 155, 171
Enron Corporation 2, 138, 154
*Epitaphs* (graphic novels) 146, 169
Erickson, Gregory 43
Evil League of Evil (fictional organization) 80, 83, 84, 87
Externalities/externalized consequences 33, 46, 89, 92, 136, 139

The Facility 16, 17, 19, 81, 89–91, 92, 93, 180
Fahrenthold, David 28–29
Fang Gang 158, 162–163
Farrell, Caroline 43, 88, 91–93, 96, 101, 103–104, 103n184, 106, 118, 121–126, 128–129, 134–136, 139–140, 146–147, 147n185, 152–156, 157–158, 161, 166–175, 170n185
Fienberg, Daniel 86, 100
*The Fifth Element* (film) 14, 41
Fillion, Nathan 15, 38, 104, 176
Fillmore Graves (fictional corporation) 6–7
Finn, Riley (character) 55, 72, 153
*Firefly* (television series) 1, 2, 10, 13n183, 14–16, 17, 18, 18n183, 22–44, 60, 61, 68, 73, 75, 79, 85–86, 88, 99, 100–101, 104, 106, 108, 110, 111, 112, 131, 143, 150, 151, 157, 158, 160, 162, 165, 169, 173, 176, 179–180; "Ariel" 14, 38, 39–41; "Bushwhacked" 38; "Heart of Gold" 38, 44; "Jaynestown" 15, 43; Objects in Space" 41; "Our Mrs. Reynolds" 38; "Out of Gas" 38; "Safe" 160; "Serenity" 14, 16, 23, 38, 39, 40, 44, 104; "Shindig" 23, 38, 40; "The Train Job" 15, 38, 39, 44; "Trash" 15, 38; "War Stories" 43, 44, 131
Fitz, Leo (character) 75, 161
Foucault, Michel 120
The Framework (alternate reality) 74–75, 121–122, 126
Framkin, Gregor (character) 67
Frankenstein as metaphor 110, 118
"Friday Night Death Slot" 85–86, 100
Friedman, Milton 20, 73, 89, 92–93, 128, 131–133, 137–139, 151, 171
Fries, Corbin (character) 32
Frutkin, Alan James 86, 100
Frye, Kaylee 23, 160
Fury, Nick (character) 61, 72, 78, 165

Garrett, John (character) 73, 161
Giannini, Erin 5, 14, 23, 39, 41, 48, 87, 89, 92, 108, 166

Gibson, William 39
Giles, Rupert (character) 54, 56, 159, 164, 167, 170, 173, 151n185
*Gilmore Girls* (television series) 1, 97, 107n184, 181; "Afterboom" 181; "Introducing Lorelai Gilmore" 181; "Keg! Max" 181
Ginn, Sherry 145
Giroux, Henry 97
Glass, Ron 23, 75
Glorificus (character) *see* Glory (character)
Glory (character) 55
Goldman-Sachs 128, 154
Goldsmith, P. Gardner 68
Grainge, Paul 63, 65–66
Great Recession (2008) 10, 40, 69, 71, 154
"Green" energy initiatives 68–69, 93, 133, 151, 171
Gregg, Clark 122, 176
Grossman, Jacob 124
Guffey, Ensley 176
Gunn, Alonna (character) 26, 31, 32
Gunn, Charles (character) 24, 25–27, 29, 31, 32–35, 37, 44, 67, 143, 159, 160, 162, 163, 179

Hadas, Leora 76–77
Hadley (character) 89, 90, 92
Hadyk-Delodder 42
Hahn, Kelsie 34
Hainsley, Magnus (character) 32
Hallett, Andy 24, 27n183
Halliburton 140, 142, 144
Halverson, Bennett (character) 94, 103, 166, 175
Handler(s) 104, 138, 148, 152, 166–168, 171
Harding, Matthew (character) 137, 145, 145n185, 172–173
Harris, Jackie (character) 49, 49n183, 54
Harris, Xander (character) 54, 56, 58, 164
Harrison, Jeannine 2, 32, 35–36
Head, Anthony Stewart 54, 142n184
"Heart, Broken" (song) 77, 86, 153
Herman, David 25, 26
Hibberd, James 100
Hilmes, Michelle 5, 9
Hive (character) *see* Ward, Grant (character)
Holden (character) 90–91
Holtz (character) 27, 170
Howard, K. Shannon 32
Hulu 5, 9, 47, 97
Hydra (fictional organization) 67–68, 70, 71, 72–76, 122, 161

Ian Quinn (character) 73–74
Iatropoulos, Mary Ellen 76, 181
*Idiocracy* (film) 45
Illyria (character) 35, 36
*In Your Eyes* (film) 11, 18n183, 177
The Initiative 72, 124, 150, 163–164
Interrante, Scott 75

# Index

Iraq  59, 132, 139, 140, 143, 144
*Iron Fist* (television series)  61, 63
Iron Man (character)  *see* Stark, Tony
*Iron Man* (film)  69, 70
*Iron Man 2* (film)  68
Ivy (character)  116, 135
*iZombie* (television series)  6, 7, 63, 85; "Grumpy Old Liv" 6; "Salvation Army" 7

Jaramillio, Deborah  66n184
Jarvis, Christine  38, 39, 148, 171
Jasmine (character)  31, 36, 39, 178
Jenkins, Anya (character)  5, 151n184, 159
*Jessica Jones* (television series)  61, 63, 76
Jiaying (character)  161–162
Johnson, Catherine  63, 65, 66
Johnson, Daisy (character)  73, 75, 161, 162
Jones, Adam Zimmerman  119, 121
Jowett, Lorna  75, 77
Jules (character)  90–91

Kahm, Howard  15, 40
Kane Industries  6, 181
Karrens, Terry (character)  130, 173–174
Kennedy, Anthony  *see* Citizens United
Kessel, Mark  113–114
Keyes, Rob  61, 70, 79
King, Stephen  6, 7, 117
Kinnard, Nolan (character)  137, 152, 170
Klein, Naomi  41, 73, 93, 106, 128, 131–133, 138–140, 144, 148–149, 155–156
Koenig brothers (characters)  75
Kompare, Derek  64, 98
Koontz, K. Dale  96n184
Kranz, Fran  10, 20, 90, 93, 176
Kuzui, Fran, and Kaz  10, 61, 62

Lachman, Dichen  88, 161
LaMorte, Robia  105
Lanford (fictional Illinois town)  54
Langton, Boyd (character)  93, 103n184, 104, 112, 118, 121, 142, 145–148, 151, 154, 158, 161, 166–168, 170–175, 180
Lapote, Philip  9, 181
Lasn, Kalle  24, 41
Lavery, David  2, 10, 11–12, 18
Lear, Norman  47, 47n183, 59n184
*Left Behind* (novel series)  146
Lehane, Faith  153
Lehne, Frederic  44
Lenk, Leah  153
Leo (character, *Dollhouse*)  134, 175
Leonato (character)  176–177
Life Model Decoy  *see* LMD
Little, Tracy  56
Littleton, Cynthia  47, 70
LMD (Life Model Decoy)  74, 125
Longworth, James  26
Lorne (character)  24, 25, 27, 34–35, 37, 159, 160, 162, 163

Los Angeles  24, 27, 34, 56, 80, 91, 96, 103, 107, 111, 146, 151
Lotz, Amanda  9, 65, 114
Lowry, Brian  99, 102, 109
*Luke Cage* (television series)  61, 63
Lury, Celia  62–63
Lynch, Denise  153

Mace, Jeffrey  74
Mack (character)  161
MacKenzie, Alphonse (character)  *see* Mack
Maclay, Tara (character)  70, 105, 158–159
Maher, Sean  23, 176
Malick, Gideon (character)  72, 74
Manners, Holland (character)  22, 29
Marsters, James  27, 105
Marty (character)  90–91
Marvel Cinematic Universe  *see* MCU
Marvel Studios  2, 11, 18n183, 19, 43, 61–79, 87, 106, 153, 157, 161, 177, 180
Massan, Cynthea  77, 174
The Master (character)  56–57, 150
Max Rager  *see* Vaughn Du Clark
Maximoff twins  70
May, Melinda (character)  75, 122, 161
McChesney, Robert  5, 8–9, 48, 138, 149
McDonald, Lindsey (character)  29–30
McDonalds Corporation/McDonaldization  14, 46, 56–57, 59, 180
MCU (Marvel Cinematic Universe)  61–63, 65–66, 69–71, 74, 77–79, 83
Megacorporation  14, 39, 73, 151
Mellie (character)  *see* Costly, Madeleine
Merrill Lynch  69, 71, 154
Miranda (fictional planet)  42, 73, 110, 178
*Mr. Robot* (television series)  7, 8–9
Mr. Universe (character)  73, 178–179
Moore, Robert  12
Morgan, Lilah (character)  29–30, 34, 35–36
Morris, Wesley  47–48
Morse, Bobbi (character)  75
*Much Ado About Nothing* (2012 film)  11, 18n183, 176–177
Muntersbjorn, Madeleine  106, 158
Murray, Simone  63
Mutant Enemy Productions  41, 61–79, 72n184, 87, 142, n184
Mynor, Joel (character)  103, 117–118, 140, 173

Nabbit, David (character)  25–26
Nadkarni, Samira  13n183, 68–69, 73, 160, 172
National Security Agency  *see* NSA
NBC/Universal Network  8, 9, 64, 115
Netflix  5, 9, 47, 63–64, 66, 76, 79, 97
*New York Times* (newspaper)  9, 47, 82
Nielsen (TV audience ratings system)  49, 81, 101
9/11  73, 132, 140, 145, 148

Noone, Kristin 96n184
November Ad (*Dollhouse* paratext) 41, 120, 142
November (character) *see* Costly, Madeleine
NSA 130–131, 140

Old Ones (fictional monsters) 17, 89, 91–94
Oswalt, Patton 75, 117

Pateman, Matthew 61
Pax (fictional drug) 42, 85
Pearl, J. Levitt 123–124
Penny (character) 34, 83–85, 87, 105, 110
Pepe, Michael 9–10, 11–18
Perrin, Cindy 138, 152
Perrin, Daniel (character) 17, 93, 104, 108, 112, 127, 129, 137–139, 144, 149, 151–155
Pfohl, Stephen 146
Pharmaceuticals/pharmaceutical corporations 16, 19–20, 38–39, 41–43, 112–116, 113n184, 128–129, 132, 141, 143, 145n185, 163, 178
Porter, Heather 145
Post-traumatic stress disorder 69, 142–143, 170
Power-That-Was *see* Jasmine
Powers-That-Be 23, 34
Preker, Simon 14
Profit motive 69, 114, 133, 134, 163
Pylea 25, 31

Q, Shatley 59, 72, 76

Radcliffe, Holden (character) 74, 121
Randolph, Clyde (character) 121, 171, 175, 180
The Rapture 146–147, 154
Reavers (characters) 38, 41–43, 104, 143, 178
Reilly, Kevin 86, 101
Remote-Free TV 100, 100n184
Rennebohm, Kate 97, 122, 146, 168
Reynolds, Malcolm 15–16, 23, 38, 39, 43, 104, 160, 178
Richard Roman Enterprises (fictional corporation) 6, 7
Richards, J. August 24, 75
Rivlin, Gary 50
Robinson, Tasha 85, 149
Rogers, Adam 71
Rogers, Steve (character) *see* Captain America (character)
Romanoff, Natasha (character) *see* Black Widow (character)
Romanov, Stephanie 29
*Roseanne* (television series) 2, 10, 11, 18–19, 45–60, 59n184, 133, 177, 180, 181; "Another Mouth to Shut Up" 53; "April Fool's Day" 52; "Crime and Punishment" 54; "Chicken Hearts" 19, 45, 47, 50–52, 57, 133; "The Dark Ages" 52; "Disney World War II" 49; "Guilt by Disassociation" 49; "Home-Ec" 48; "Into That Good Night" 50; "Lanford's Elite" 53; "Let's Call It Quits" 49; "Little Sister" 49, 49n193; "Mall Story" 52; "Springtime for David" 50; "Terms of Estrangment Parts 1 and 2" 52; "Tooth or Consequences" 52; "We're Going to Disney World" 49; "The White Sheep of the Family" 53
Rosenberg, Willow (character) 54, 70, 105, 158–159, 164
Rossum Corporation 2, 16, 19, 20, 41, 43, 81, 88, 92–94, 96–175, 155n185, 177, 180
*RUR* (play) 96n184
Ryan, Maureen 88, 100

Sam (character, *Dollhouse*) 134–135, 170
Saulsberry, Rejena 33–34
Saunders, Dr. Claire (character) 93, 123, 169
Scarlet Witch/Quicksilver *see* Maximoff twins
Schlosser, Eric 39, 45, 46, 58
Scytheon (fictional private military contractor) 40, 106, 139–144, 155
Selznick, Barbara 63
Senior Partners 16, 37, 151, 163
September 11, 2001 73, 132, 140, 145, 148
*Serenity* (film) 5, 10, 14n183, 15, 22, 23, 41–43, 73, 104, 108, 112, 143, 160, 177–178, 179–180
Serenity (Firefly class ship) 14, 14n183, 15, 22, 38, 40, 104, 109, 158, 160, 166, 178
Shipler, David K 52–53, 60
"Shock" economics/"shock" doctrine 20, 131–139, 148
Shuttac, Jane 9, 65
Sidell, Professor Oliver (character) 25, 37
Sierra (character) *see* Tsetsang, Priya (character)
Simmons, Jemma (character) 75, 161
Sitterson (character) 89, 90, 91, 92
Skreli, Martin 112–113
Skye (character) *see* Johnson, Daisy (character)
*Slayage: The Online Journal of Whedon Studies* 1, 10, n184
Slayer (character) *see* Lehane, Faith; Summers, Buffy
Slayers (characters) 13, 25, 43, 150
Sociopaths/sociopathy 124, 152, 161, 173–175
South, James 2, 56–57, 181
Souza, Christopher 97, 104, 170, 175
Spike (character) 27–28, 33, 37, 54, 75, 105, 124
Stafford, Nikki 26
*Star Trek* (film and television series) 14
Stark, Tony 18, 43, 61, 64, 68–71, 74, 165, 180
Stark Industries 18, 67, 68–71
Stearns, Lee 11, 12

# Index

Summers, Buffy (character) 11–14, 18, 24, 43, 47, 54–59, 72–73, 75, 106, 107, 150–151, 153, 159, 164, 167, 173, 180
Summers, Dawn (character) 55, 57, 159, 164, 173
Summers, Joyce (character) 54, 55, 159, 164
Sunnydale (fictional California city) 24, 29, 53–54, 55, 56, 150, 158
*Supernatural* (television series) 6, 7, 48, 63, 107n184; "Baby" 107n184; "Changing Channels" 107n184; "Fan Fiction" 107n184; "The French Mistake" 107n184; "Hollywood Babylon" 107n184; "How to Win Friends and Influence Monsters" 7; "Meta Fiction" 107n184; "The Monster at the End of This Book" 107n184; "The Real Ghostbusters" 107n184; "Survival of the Fittest" 7–8; "There Will Be Blood" 7
Sutherland, Sharon 16, 44
Swan, Sarah 16, 44
Sweeps period 81, 102

Tam, River (character) 18, 22, 23, 33, 38, 39–43, 44, 73, 106, 160, 166, 178
Tam, Simon (character) 23, 38, 160, 178
Tancharoen, Maurissa 62, 77, 84, 72n184
Telecommunications Act of 1996 5, 138
Thirkell, Robert 177
Thompson, Fred Dalton 49
*Those Left Behind* (comic book) 14n183, 40
Thought-pocalypse 121, 138–139, 144, 154
Tina (character) 28
Tobias, Scott 88, 99, 101
Todreas, Timothy 62
Torres, Gina 15, 38
"Transgressive mothers" 73, 172
The Trio (characters Warren Meers, Andrew Wells, Jonathan Levinson) 56
Trump, Donald 5–6, 28, 47–48, 68, 148
Tsetsang, Priya (character) 43, 88, 91, 104, 136–138, 143, 152, 154, 167, 168–171, 170n185, 172, 173, 175
Tudyk, Alan 34, 123
20th Century Fox Fox Network 61, 63, 69, 79, 85–86, 88, 96, 98, 99–101, 100n184, 114, 115, 141, 142, 163
*24* (television series) 8, 9, 97
2016 Election 5, 128, 177

Ultron (character) 69–70, 74
The Upfronts 9, 65
UPN (television channel) 9, 98
Upstone, Sara 26, 34

*Veronica Mars* (television series) 6, 85, 181; "Leave It to Beaver" 181;"Rat Saw God" 181
Victor (character) *see* Anthony Ceccoli (character)

Wal-Mart Corporation 169, 181
Walsh, Maggie (character) 72–73, 163–164
War on Terror *see* Iraq, Afghanistan
Ward, Grant (character) 73, 75, 153, 161, 162
Wash (character) *see* Washburne, Hoban (character)
Washburne, Hoban (character) 34, 38, 104, 160
Washburne, Zoe (character) 15–16, 160
*Watcher Junior* 1
Watchers/Watchers Council (characters) 12–13, 24, 25, 54, 150, 151n184, 159
WB Network/Warner Brothers 9, 10, 85, 101, 107n184, 163
Wellman Plastics (fictional factory) 49, 53
Wes (character) *see* Wyndham Pryce, Wesley
WGA (Writers Guild of America) 81–82, 83, 85
Wharton, Ken 40
Whedon, Jed 11, 62, 72n184, 77, 84, 86, n184
Whedon, Tom 11–12
Whiskey (character) *see* Saunders, Dr. Claire (character)
Wilcox, Rhonda 57–59, 99, 104, 106, 114–115, 150
Williams, Amy 83, 84, 86
Williams, Matt 51, 59
Williams, Raymond 114
Winchester, Sam, and Dean (characters) 8, 107n184
Winters, Russell (character) 28–29
Wolfram and Hart (fictional corporation) 16, 18, 22, 23, 24, 28–30, 32–37, 43, 46, 67, 73, 104, 151, 162–163, 177, 179
Working poor/working class 47–49, 52, 53, 54, 128, 47n183, 59n184
WorldCom Corporation 2, 138
Wright, Julia 48
Writers Guild of America *see* WGA
Writer's strike (2007–2008) 81–83, 88, 99, 100, 162
Wyndham-Pryce, Roger 25
Wyndham-Pryce, Wesley (character) 24, 25, 29, 35, 36, 37, 159–160, 162, 163

Zhang, Angela 137–138, 150–151
Zone (character) 147n185, 168

www.ingramcontent.com/pod-product-compliance
Ingram Content Group UK Ltd.
Pitfield, Milton Keynes, MK11 3LW, UK
UKHW041957140426
5217IPUK00015B/835